THE UNLIKELY
FATHER OF
MODERN
PENTECOSTALISM

CHARLES FOX
PARHAM

LARRY MARTIN

w
WHITAKER
HOUSE

Note: In quoted material, the original spelling, punctuation, and capitalization have been retained. For clarity, "[*sic*]" has been added after misspelled words and incorrect punctuation where there might be a question about how they appeared in the original.

Unless otherwise indicated, all Scripture quotations are taken from the King James Version of the Holy Bible. Scripture quotation marked (NIV) is taken from the *Holy Bible, New International Version*®, NIV®, © 1973, 1978, 1984, 2011 by Biblica, Inc.® Used by permission. All rights reserved worldwide. The "NIV" and "New International Version" are trademarks registered in the United States Patent and Trademark Office by Biblica, Inc.®

CHARLES FOX PARHAM:
The Unlikely Father of Modern Pentecostalism

Dr. Larry Martin
P.O. Box 5, Duncan OK 73534
mail@drlarrymartin.org
drlarrymartin.org

ISBN: 978-1-64123-801-4
eBook ISBN: 978-1-64123-802-1
Printed in the United States of America
© 2022 by Larry Martin

Whitaker House
1030 Hunt Valley Circle
New Kensington, PA 15068
www.whitakerhouse.com

Library of Congress Control Number: 2022931232

1 2 3 4 5 6 7 8 9 10 11 **WH** 29 28 27 26 25 24 23 22

CONTENTS

PREFACE

As I have studied the life of Charles Fox Parham, I have often thought of "He Chose Me," a gospel song penned by prolific hymn writer Mosie Lister. Lister wrote, "There were so many others that He might have chosen."

The question that keeps coming to me is, why did God choose Charles Parham as the unlikely founder of a great spiritual movement? As you read this book, you may ask the same question. Parham was a very flawed man. Surely, there were others God might have chosen. But, in His sovereignty, He chose Parham.

A Baptist friend of mine frequently defined sovereignty as "God is God, and you ain't." Maybe that says everything that needs to be said. God, who knows everything, selected a marred vessel. That should remind us that we are all marred in some way. The glorious gospel of Jesus Christ is entrusted to vessels made of clay. If that is the greatest lesson of this book, so be it.

For over twenty-five years, I have collected materials for this biography. There were times when I was not sure if I would write it. There were other times when I was quite sure I *wouldn't*. I have self-published a number of books, but I did not want to publish this one myself. If I was going to put the necessary time and energy into this project, I wanted it to have wider distribution.

Besides, telling a story like this one has risks. There are Pentecostals who will not like this book because of the disturbing truths it brings to light. Some will not like me because I wrote it. Too many people would rather look the other way, afraid to confront the weaknesses of our spiritual fathers. Yet we celebrate the Word of God because it lays bare the failures of some of our greatest biblical heroes. Hopefully, we won't repeat the same mistakes, and we will learn from our past. I pray that we will do so.

On the other hand, some Pentecostal antagonists will welcome this book. They will use Parham's life as a brush to paint a broad swath against all Pentecostals. Such attacks would be unfair. Pentecostals have never condoned Parham's failures and never will.

I am a lifelong Pentecostal. With tongue in cheek, I refer to myself as a "hard-shell holy roller." I will always feel a debt to Charles Parham for restoring the power of Pentecost to the church. It pains me to give ammunition to his critics; yet, as uncomfortable as the truth may be, the ugly parts of the story are still the truth.

In early 2021, I received a message from Dale Gentry, a friend and a true prophet. Dale said, "Larry, I hear the Spirit saying you need to finish what you started." I bathed the word in prayer. I am sorry to admit that I have way too many unfinished tasks. My mind, however, kept coming back to this Parham biography. Perhaps God wanted me to finish it. I knew that someday the unseemly truth would be told. It could be told by someone intent on disparaging all Pentecostals and charismatics. I felt that, as a Pentecostal, I could tell the story with sympathy toward Parham and the movement as a whole while presenting the unvarnished truth.

A while back, I had written one chapter for the book and then put it on the shelf. However, I sent that chapter to evangelist Tim Enloe, another lover of Pentecostal history. Tim liked the chapter and encouraged me to finish the book. He contacted Don Milam at Whitaker House, and Don contacted me. After going through a review process, the book was accepted by Whitaker. I am deeply grateful.

This book would not have been possible if I hadn't had help from dozens of denominational, governmental, and educational archives and libraries. I cannot list everyone who helped with my research, but please know my appreciation runs deep. Glenn Gohr at the Flower Pentecostal Heritage

Center, Gary W. Garrett at the Apostolic Archives, Daniel Isgrigg at the Holy Spirit Research Center, Esther Park at Fuller Theological Seminary, and Karen Oakes at the Apostolic Faith Bible College were particularly helpful in providing access to their collections of material on Parham's life and ministry.

I am especially thankful for my wife, Lynda, who encouraged me while she endured the process.

May God be with you as you journey through the life of Charles Fox Parham, the very unlikely father of modern Pentecostalism.

ABBREVIATIONS FOR PERIODICALS AND COLLECTIONS CITED IN THE NOTES

AFBC   Parham Collection, Apostolic Faith Bible College, Baxter Springs, Kansas

BB   *The Baldwin Bee* (Kansas)

CDJ   *The Coffeyville Daily Journal* (Kansas)

CFSOP   Center for the Study of Oneness Pentecostalism, Florissant, Missouri

CS   *The Cheney Sentinel* (Kansas)

GDN   *Galveston Daily News*

GET   *Galena Evening Times* (Kansas)

FPHC   *Flower Pentecostal Heritage Center*

HSRC   Pauline Parham Collection, Holy Spirit Research Center, Oral Roberts University, Tulsa, Oklahoma

HLFTS   David Allan Hubbard Library, Fuller Theological Seminary

JG   *The Joplin Globe* (Missouri)

KCJ   *Kansas City Journal*

KCT   *The Kansas City Times*

KHS   Kansas Historical Society

KWC   *The Kansas Weekly Capital*

LAH   *Los Angeles Herald*

LCI   *Lake County Independent* (Illinois)

LDJ   *Lawrence Daily Journal*

LDW   *Lawrence Daily World* (Kansas)

LWW   *Lawrence Weekly World* (Kansas)

MB   *Kansas Farmer and Mail and Breeze* (Topeka)

MDJ	*Muscatine Daily Journal*
MNT	*Muscatine News-Tribune*
MWK	*The Muscatine Weekly Journal*
NC	*The News-Courant* (Cottonwood Falls, Kansas)
OT	*The Ottawa Weekly* (Kansas)
SAE	*The San Antonio Daily Express*
SAG	*San Antonio Gazette*
SAL	*San Antonio Light*
SC	Southwestern College archives, Winfield, Kansas
SNC	*Saginaw News Courier* (Michigan)
TAF	*The Apostolic Faith* (Charles Parham)
TAFGC	*The Apostolic Faith* (Goose Creek, Texas)
TAFLA	*The Apostolic Faith* (Los Angeles)
TBM	*The Bridegroom's Messenger*
TC	*The Topeka Daily Capital*
TEG	*The Everlasting Gospel*
TGK	*The Gospel of the Kingdom*
THP	*The Houston Post*
TJG	*The Jeffersonian Gazette* (Lawrence, Kansas)
TM	*The Tonganoxie Mirror* (Kansas)
TPE	*The Pentecostal Evangel*
TPH	*The Pentecostal Herald*
TSJ	*The Topeka State Journal*
TWE	*The Weekly Evangel*
WAW	*Word and Witness*
WM	*Western Methodist*
WNS	*Waukegan News-Sun* (Illinois)
ZCH	*Zion City Herald*

Charles Fox Parham. Courtesy of *The Apostolic Faith Report*

1

THE FATHER OF MODERN PENTECOSTALISM

Charles Fox Parham is indisputably the founder of the modern Pentecostal and charismatic movements. I begin with this bold assertion because his role has come into question in the last few decades. It is important to examine the actual records to uncover the truth about Parham, honestly acknowledging both his contributions and his shortcomings. However awkward the facts may be, discovering and embracing the historical narrative can give us a deeper appreciation for God's will, His ways, and His works. This may be especially true when He chooses and uses broken vessels.

Parham was the unlikely father of the spiritual wave that has swept the world over the past one hundred and twenty years. He was a very flawed, even disgraced, minister. He espoused radical and unorthodox doctrines. He had a particularly peculiar personality. He was antiestablishment and had an intemperate distaste for organization. Before white privilege was a popular talking point, Parham codified it in his tenets of faith and practiced it in his daily life. If all this were not enough to disqualify him as a spiritual father, Parham was repeatedly accused of the worst of moral transgressions in a movement that placed a hyper-emphasis on sanctification and personal holiness.

In the earliest days of the movement, Pentecostal adherents were frequently called "Parhamites." Yet the half-million-plus people who claim the Pentecostal experience today certainly do not consider themselves followers of Parham. Millions wouldn't even know his name, let alone his contribution to the movement. There are no Parhamites among contemporary Pentecostals.

Nonetheless, it is undeniable that Parham founded the movement. There is no unbiased, intelligent argument against it. The importance of his role may be questioned. But, after the questioning, there is only one answer: Charles F. Parham started the Pentecostal revival.

This unlikely founder of Pentecostalism was not the first person to preach a baptism in the Holy Spirit in modern times. As the nineteenth century closed, there was a climate for Pentecost. The prayer revival of 1858–59 had produced a number of firebrands who called the world to a closer walk with God. Terms like "baptism in the Holy Spirit," "baptism in fire," and "deeper life" were common.

Driven by an eschatology that predicted the second coming of Christ at the end of the century, biblically conservative believers fervently sought a fresh awakening. Conferences, conventions, and camps were popular places to seek a deeper experience with God.

Many of the more conservative Holiness congregations, alienated by the trend toward a social gospel,[1] split from the Methodist Church. New denominations like the Pentecostal Church of the Nazarene, Pentecostal Holiness, Free Methodists, and Fire Baptized Holiness Church sought a crisis experience beyond conversion.

When D. L. Moody passed in 1899, his protégé R. A. Torrey credited Moody's great success as an evangelist to a baptism in the Holy Spirit. Moody believed he had experienced an enduement of power separate from his salvation experience.

---

1. "Social gospel," as defined by this author, refers to the church moving away from preaching strictly biblical themes, such as salvation, sanctification, and so forth, and replacing this emphasis with a primary focus on remedying social ills, such as poverty, labor issues, and social and economic inequality, which became more prevalent in American urban life after the Civil War.

Benjamin Irwin, Frank Sanford, and many others were promoting a distinct experience in the baptism in the Holy Ghost. Irwin went so far as to claim multiple baptisms, including baptisms in "fire," "dynamite," and "lucite."

Many people before Parham had taught, preached, and even experienced a baptism in the Holy Spirit. But Parham's teaching was unique: from a study of Acts, he concluded that a biblical baptism was always evidenced by speaking in an unknown language. This revelation was so radical that it birthed a spiritual revolution.

Parham was also not the first person to advocate speaking in tongues, and he was certainly not the first person to speak in tongues in this period of church history. In fact, several of Parham's adherents in Topeka, Kansas, spoke in tongues before he did. Thus, the unlikely founder of Pentecostalism wasn't even the first to demonstrate the theology he defined.

Throughout church history, there have been sporadic episodes involving manifestations of spiritual gifts like those recorded in the New Testament. One of the better-known outpourings of the Holy Spirit was led by Edward Irving, a Scottish minister. In the early nineteenth century, he established the Catholic Apostolic Church, a charismatic group that exhibited many of the spiritual gifts, including speaking in other tongues.

As the 1800s drew to a close, the appearance—or perhaps documentation—of these manifestations became more frequent in meetings across the United States and even around the world. For example, a Holiness group near Graham, Texas, experienced tongues speaking. There were examples in the meetings of healing evangelist Maria Woodworth-Etter. The founding of the Church of God in 1896 was accompanied by tongues speaking. In Russia, the family of Full Gospel Business Men's Fellowship International founder Demos Shakarian had spoken in tongues. There are certainly many, many more examples.

Writing for the *Bridegroom's Messenger*, J. T. Reed compiled a list of more than forty examples of tongues speaking before Parham. Relying on several sources, he traced the phenomenon from late in the first century through the twentieth century. Although Reed's claim that notables like Charles Finney and D. L. Moody spoke with tongues may be questionable, the article provides multiple examples with verifiable documentation.[2] It seems clear that many of these people had a Pentecostal experience, but their experience was not the Pentecostal movement.

Although undoubtedly genuine, none of these outpourings was universal, and none was continuing. The experience was often confined to a small geographical area and a relatively small group of people. The manifestations were also short-lived. At times, they lasted no longer than a single revival meeting. In other cases, like the revival led by Edward Irving, the experiences died with the gifted leader.

More important, none of these people tied the manifestation of speaking with other languages to the biblical experience of a Holy Spirit baptism. To these believers, glossolalia was just another manifestation of the Spirit akin to shaking, trembling, or falling. Many such phenomena were present in the emotionally charged atmosphere of revival.

However, as I mentioned previously, Parham found biblical grounds in the book of Acts to unite Holy Spirit baptism with speaking in tongues. He was the first to claim a biblical reason to marry the two spiritual experiences. As Parham saw it, everyone in the early church received the Spirit baptism, and all who did spoke in tongues; thus, tongues speaking was the biblical evidence of Spirit baptism.

The connection sets Parham's movement apart from all previous awakenings. This theological difference is what makes the Topeka experience, which we will discuss in chapter 3, more than just one of several stepping-stones in the origins of the movement. This was the *genesis* of the movement. And this is what makes Parham the father of Pentecostalism.

Parham may not have been the first person to connect the dots, but he was certainly the first person to establish the connection as a church doctrine and the cornerstone of a movement. Unlike the previous tongues-speaking episodes, the movement defined, designed, and launched by Parham has been both universal and continuing. For more than a century, on every continent of the globe, hundreds of millions of believers have received the

---

2. J. T. Reed, comp., "History of Tongues, Part 1," *The Bridegroom's Messenger,* January 1968, 3–4 (hereafter cited as *TBM*); "History of Tongues, Part 2," *TBM*, February 1968, 3–4; "History of Tongues, Part 3," *TBM*, March 1968, 3–4, ifphc.org.

baptism in the Holy Spirit in the same manner that Parham first presented it to the world in Topeka, Kansas.

Parham regularly referred to himself as the "Founder of the Apostolic Faith."[3] The subtitle of Sarah Parham's biography of her husband is "Founder of the Apostolic Faith Movement." There is no doubt that Parham and his wife identified him as the father of Pentecostalism. Some would dismiss this claim as egotism on their part. However, the Parhams were there from the beginning and could trace the birth and expansion of the fledgling movement. Moreover, they were far from alone in their assessment of Charles Parham's role. Respected historians and many of Parham's contemporaries confirmed the same.

In the first and best study to date of the life and influence of Parham, James R. Goff Jr. concluded, "It was Parham who first formulated the theological definition of Pentecostalism by linking tongues with the Holy Spirit baptism.... As the initial evidence, glossolalia becomes the *sine qua non* of the experience and its importance is hard to overestimate."[4]

Pentecostal historian John Thomas Nichol also gave credit to Parham's founding and leadership:

> It was he who coined the distinctive name that was widely used by early Pentecostals—the Apostolic Faith. It was he who published the first Pentecostal periodical, *The Apostolic Faith*; it was he who organized the first large gatherings of Pentecostal believers on an interstate level; and it was he who first issued ministerial credentials to those who allied themselves with him.[5]

---

3. *The Apostolic Faith* (Alvin, TX), September 1907, 2. Note: *Apostolic Faith* editions followed either by locations in parentheses or extended abbreviations (such as *TAFGC*) were published by groups other than Charles Parham's organization. Please refer to the source abbreviation guide found directly before chapter 1 of this book. *TAF*, by itself, always refers to the *Apostolic Faith* periodical published by Parham. The paper was first published in Topeka, Kansas, but Parham published the paper from various cities where he lived, including Melrose, Kansas, and Houston, Texas. After May 1906, the paper was published in Baxter Springs, Kansas. In 1953, the name of the periodical was changed to *The Apostolic Faith Report*.

4. James R. Goff Jr., *Fields White Unto Harvest: Charles F. Parham and the Missionary Origins of Pentecostalism* (Fayetteville, AR: University of Arkansas Press, 1988), 11.

5. John Thomas Nichol, *The Pentecostals* (Plainfield, NJ: Logos International, 1966), 81.

It could be added that the first Pentecostal church building in the world was constructed in Keelville, Kansas, after Parham's meetings there. Parham wrote the first Pentecostal book, *Kol Kare Bomidbar: A Voice Crying in the Wilderness*. He led the first Pentecostal Bible school and formulated the first Pentecostal curriculum. He held the first Pentecostal meetings.

Nevertheless, many people remain ambivalent or even antagonistic about his unparalleled role in the formation of modern Pentecostalism. Some simply don't like Parham. It is easier to ignore him than to explain him. To many, he is an embarrassment. As the movement has grown and gained credibility in Christendom, it is inconvenient to acknowledge a flawed founder.

To borrow a word from today's culture, the father of Pentecostalism is often "canceled." As early as 1914, in his thesis on the history of the gift of tongues, Charles W. Shumway noted the pretermission of Parham. Shumway observed that "Parham's work receives but scant recognition," but, based on his studies, he concluded that "the movement would not have been possible without his labors."[6]

Many Pentecostals prefer a romantic, almost mystical, view of the founding of Pentecostalism. The movement, they argue, had no founder but the Holy Spirit. Grant Wacker dealt with this fanciful view in his book *Heaven Below: Early Pentecostals and American Culture*:

> When saints looked at their own beginnings they were pleased to discover that they had no founders—no Martin Luther, no John Wesley, and certainly no Joseph Smith. Just like the Bible itself, the pentecostal revival had come directly from the divine hand, in all essential points already fully formed. One Azusa pioneer made the point with memorable simplicity: "The source is from the skies."[7]

6. Charles W. Shumway, "A Critical Study of 'The Gift of Tongues'" (A. B. thesis, University of Southern California, 1914), 164. Shumway was a Methodist minister and educator. He held five academic degrees, culminating with the PhD. He also taught in at least five institutes of higher education, including Evansville College, Boston University, and Oklahoma City University. He was the author of several books, including a book on Pentecostalism and a textbook on American history. Shumway was personally acquainted with Parham and "almost all of the persons and places concerned."
7. Grant Wacker, *Heaven Below: Early Pentecostals and American Culture* (Cambridge, MA: Harvard University Press, 2003), 142.

It isn't true, but it feels good to think that way. Pentecostalism is an emotional, feel-good faith. Pentecostals, even Pentecostal historians, have been known to compromise inconvenient facts for comfortable feelings.

Some historians were apparently embarrassed by Parham's obvious flaws and missteps. When Assemblies of God editor Stanley H. Frodsham published a history of the Pentecostal movement in 1946, he totally ignored Parham's influence. In the second chapter of his book, Frodsham tells the story of the Bethel Bible College, the Topeka outpouring, and Agnes Ozman's Spirit baptism without mentioning Parham.

In an inexcusable omission, Frodsham quotes Ozman in this way:

On watchnight we had a blessed service, praying that God's blessing might rest upon us as the new year came in. During the first day of 1901 the presence of the Lord was with us in a marked way, stilling our hearts to wait upon Him for greater things. A spirit of prayer was upon us in the evening. It was nearly eleven o'clock on this first of January that it came into my heart to ask that hands be laid upon me that I might receive the gift of the Holy Ghost. As hands were laid upon my head the Holy Spirit fell upon me, and I began to speak in tongues, glorifying God.[8]

The original testimony reads:

On watch night we had a blessed service, praying that God's blessing might rest upon us as the New Year came in. During the first day of 1901 the presence of the Lord was with us in a marked way, stilling our hearts to wait upon Him for greater things. The spirit of prayer was upon us in the evening. It was nearly seven o'clock on the first of January that it came into my heart to ask Bro. Parham to lay his hands upon me that I might receive the Holy Spirit. It was as his hands were laid upon my head the Holy Spirit fell upon me, and I began to speak in tongues, glorifying God.[9]

---

8. Stanley H. Frodsham, *With Signs Following* (Springfield, MO: Gospel Publishing House, 1946), 20.
9. Sarah E. Parham, *The Life of Charles F. Parham: Founder of the Apostolic Faith Movement* (Birmingham, AL: Commercial Printing Company, 1930), 66.

Other people have a definite bias against acknowledging Parham's role. While condemning Parham for his racist views, they end up dismissing him because of his race. In the past fifty years, it has become popular to favor William J. Seymour as the founder of Pentecostalism. It is much more palatable for Black Pentecostals to identify Seymour, a Black man, the son of slaves, as the originator of the Pentecostal movement than a white supremacist. This is easy to understand. Even Pentecostals who know it isn't true wish that it was. Some pretend it is true.

The notion is prevalent enough that in *From Aldersgate to Azusa Street*, Pentecostal seminarian Steven J. Land called Seymour "the father of the Holiness-Pentecostal Movement" without further explanation.[10] It is as if no other interpretation is possible and no evidence is necessary. History has been rewritten. The unpopular truth is falling prey to the newly adopted myth. This is especially oxymoronic since, in the previous essay in the very same book, Leslie Callahan presented clear and convincing evidence that Parham preceded Seymour as the movement's founder.

Rufus G. W. Sanders, a Black Seymour biographer, titled his book *William Joseph Seymour: Black Father of the Twentieth Century Pentecostal/ Charismatic Movement*. Yet, on the very first page, Sanders acknowledges that Seymour was "initiated in the doctrines of Pentecostalism in Houston, Texas, by Charles Fox Parham." Sanders says, "Parham planted the seed, but Seymour gave birth…to the experience of Pentecostalism." The statement is demonstratively erroneous. Sanders's entire work rests on the faulty premise that "American racism disallowed the honor of 'Father' of the Pentecostal movement to be bestowed on William J. Seymour."

Sanders is so adamant that Seymour should be the father of the movement that he seemingly allows his feelings to blind him to historical facts. He recounts the incidents at Topeka, Kansas, that clearly started the worldwide Pentecostal revival but then denies their significance, saying that "Parham may have been one of the first twentieth century religious leaders to *experiment* [emphasis added] with tongues." Experiment? Parham developed the doctrine, published it, and advanced it throughout much of America.

---

10. Steven J. Land, "William J. Seymour: The Father of the Holiness-Pentecostal Movement," in *From Aldersgate to Azusa: Wesleyan, Holiness, and Pentecostal Visions of the New Creation*, ed. Henry H. Knight III (Eugene, OR: Pickwick Publications, 2010), 218.

Sanders irresponsibly misidentifies Seymour's father as a Louisiana judge murdered by white men. That never happened. Sanders also fictionalized other parts of Seymour's early life, creating sympathy for the man of God.[11] No rewriting of history or panegyrizing of Seymour can change the facts. Charles Parham was the founder of the Pentecostal movement.

Similarly, a popular African-American journalist, Simeon Booker, stated that Pentecostalism was "founded by a Black man." Building on this invalid statement, he went further, claiming that "Pentecostalism flourished so quickly in the South that White leaders, in order to appeal to their massive White audiences, laundered the birth of the faith and the presence of its Black founder."[12] Telling the truth about the origins of the movement is not "laundering."

Is there racism in America? Yes. Does it find its way into church history? Yes. Does that change the fact that Parham was the founder of Pentecostalism? No.

Anyone could see why Black Pentecostals would rather celebrate Seymour. He is a hero, a respected figure in a culture that needs role models deserving of such celebration. It is also no wonder that the Black community would fail to acknowledge Parham as a spiritual father. At best, he was patronizing of Blacks. At worst, he was bigoted and hateful. Seymour himself recognized this reality when he and Parham parted ways.

It is even easy to understand why white Pentecostals would prefer to celebrate Seymour. If the facts of history allowed it, and if given the choice, a vast majority would pick Seymour over Parham. Seymour was the kind of man Parham was not: Seymour was humble and morally pure. In every way known to us, it seems he was a better man.

This author is a great fan of Seymour. He is my foremost hero of the faith. Twenty years ago, I wrote and published the first fully documented Seymour biography. I discovered things about his life and family that had not previously been known. I hold William Joseph Seymour in the highest regard. He was a great preacher, a great Christian, and a great man.

11. Rufus G. W. Sanders, *William Joseph Seymour: Black Father of the Twentieth Century Pentecostal/Charismatic Movement* (Sandusky, OH: Alexandria Publications, 2001), 1, 5–7, 35.
12. Simeon Booker, "Untold Story of Black Founder of Pentecostal Church Body Rocked by Sex Scandal of Whites," *Jet*, May 18, 1987, 12.

Seymour became a notable leader against the greatest of odds. His parents were slaves on a plantation, and he was born in the slave quarters where they lived. When Seymour was a youth, his father died from an illness he contracted while serving in the Union Army during the Civil War. Seymour was reared in abject poverty. A government affidavit once estimated the family's entire net worth as less than one dollar. He was a Black man in the South during Reconstruction. He was hated for his race. His young life was immersed in cruelty and fear. Smallpox left him scarred and blind in one eye for life. Few men overcame so much to accomplish as much. William Seymour was a remarkable person. He was a more likely candidate for the father of Pentecostalism.

It feels better to call Seymour the father of the movement. From the beginning, some Pentecostals have earned a reputation for preferring feelings to facts. In a faith where emotion is a welcome part of worship, there is always a tension between the heart and the head. Seymour is a wonderful heart choice, yet Parham is the only honest head choice. Unfortunately, even seminarians and historians are not exempt from the temptation to lean toward the heart. None of that, however, can change the facts of history, which demonstrate that Parham founded modern Pentecostalism.

As I stated previously, early Pentecostals were often called "Parhamites" or the "sect of Parhamites." This was the case both before and after Seymour led the revival at Azusa Street. The term "Parhamites" can be found in hundreds of newspapers in at least forty states. Parham was universally accepted as the founder and leader of the movement. Searching the historical records has not produced even one instance in which Pentecostals were called "Seymourites." They never were.

As important as Seymour was to the spread of Pentecostalism from Los Angeles in 1906 and a few years following, he did not start the movement, and he never led it. The fact is, Seymour didn't even start the Azusa Street mission. After arriving in Los Angeles, he joined himself with a small congregation already meeting on Bonnie Brae Street at the Richard and Ruth Asberry residence. The Holy Spirit fell on that group on April 9, 1906, and the next week, they moved to the abandoned church building on Azusa Street.

Seymour himself never claimed to be the founder of Pentecostalism. He recognized Parham as the legitimate father of the movement. The Azusa Street pastor discovered no doctrine on glossolalia and Spirit baptism. He neither defined nor developed Pentecostal theology. His teaching was what he learned from Parham. He attended Parham's Bible school in Houston. Seymour was the student; Parham was the teacher. Seymour and Parham preached together in Houston, but Parham opened the doors for Seymour. Seymour was a disciple of Parham. Parham commissioned Seymour and gave him ministerial credentials. It was Parham who contributed finances toward buying Seymour's ticket to California.

Bishop Seymour recognized that his mission in Los Angeles was not a movement but was part of a movement. He acknowledged Parham as his spiritual father. He borrowed the name "Apostolic Faith" from Parham. The earliest official letterhead from the Azusa Street Apostolic Faith Mission lists Seymour as pastor and Parham as "Projector" of the movement. Parham claimed the title for himself. He was the self-proclaimed "Projector" of the Apostolic Faith. Seymour agreed. Trying to explain Parham's choice of this title, Callahan refers to the *Oxford English Dictionary*. The dictionary defines this meaning of *projector* as "one who forms a project, who plans or designs some undertaking; a founder."[13] Charles Parham saw himself as the founder of the Apostolic Faith movement. Seymour gave his assent and legitimized it in his publication.

Seymour also spoke affectionately of Parham as his father. The congregants at Azusa Street waited with excitement and anticipation for Parham's first visit to Los Angeles. They wanted to meet the Black man's white "father." Parham's visit was a disaster; after this, Seymour and his adherents no longer submitted to Parham's leadership. Yet the breach between them does not change the fact that Parham was Seymour's spiritual father.

How could Seymour be the father of the Pentecostal movement if he recognized Parham as his spiritual father? For those who hold to a literal interpretation of Holy Scripture, all humans trace their genealogy to Noah. All other people were destroyed in the great flood. All the members

---

13. Leslie D. Callahan, "Charles Parham: Progenitor of Pentecostalism," in *From Aldersgate to Azusa: Wesleyan, Holiness and Pentecostal Visions of the New Creation*, ed. Henry H. Knight III (Eugene, OR: Pickwick Publications, 2010), 213.

of humankind are the sons and daughters of Noah. So, is Noah the father of the human race? Absolutely not. Noah had a father, and his father had a father. Among Bible believers, Adam is universally accepted as the father of humanity. A man with a father cannot be the founder of a race. Similarly, a man with a spiritual father who established the doctrines and practice of a movement cannot be the founder of that same movement.

On the first page of the first edition of Azusa Street's *Apostolic Faith*, Parham is called "God's leader in the Apostolic Faith Movement." The same issue of the newspaper gives a brief history of the movement that clearly identifies Parham as the founder and head of the Apostolic Faith:

> This work began about five years ago last January, when a company of people under the leadership of Chas. Parham, who were studying God's word, tarried for Pentecost in Topeka, Kan. After searching through the country everywhere, they had been unable to find any Christians that had the true Pentecostal power. So they laid aside all commentaries and notes and waited on the Lord, studying His word, and what they did not understand they got down before the bench and asked God to have wrought out in their hearts by the Holy Ghost. They had a prayer tower from which prayers were ascending night and day to God. After three months, a sister who had been teaching sanctification for the baptism with the Holy Ghost, one who had a sweet, loving experience and all the carnality taken out of her heart, felt the Lord lead her to have hands laid on her to receive the Pentecost. So when they prayed, the Holy Ghost came in great power, and she continued speaking in an unknown tongue. This made all the Bible school hungry, and three nights afterward, twelve students received the Holy Ghost, and prophesied, and cloven tongues could be seen upon their heads. They then had an experience that measured up with the second chapter of Acts, and could understand the first chapter of Ephesians.
>
> Now after five years something like 13,000 people have received this gospel. It is spreading everywhere...."[14]

---

14. "Pentecost Has Come," *TAF* (Los Angeles), September 1906, 1 (hereafter cited as *TAFLA*).

In the second issue of the *Apostolic Faith*, the newspaper said Parham was the man "whom the Lord raised up five years ago to spread this truth." The West Coast Pentecostals were anxiously awaiting Parham's imminent visit to their mission.[15]

Seymour called his periodical the *Apostolic Faith*, another name borrowed from Parham, whose newspaper had the same title. The paper itself was not published by Seymour but by workers in his mission. Other people transcribed Seymour's sermons and printed them in the paper. When the publishers of the newspaper moved from Los Angeles to Portland, Oregon, the *Apostolic Faith* went with them. Additionally, the only book Seymour ever wrote was a church discipline published in 1915. Ninety-five percent of the book or more was taken from existing Methodist disciplines. Seymour traveled east and established a handful of small churches, but his expansion looks nothing like a movement and cannot be compared to the vast number of congregations established by Parham and his lieutenants.

Seymour is often lauded for the interracial makeup of the Azusa Street mission, and rightly so. Frank Bartleman famously said that the blood of Jesus washed away the color line. However, even that result at Azusa was short-lived. As the heated passion of revival cooled, so did the experiment with total integration. Later in the life of the mission, Seymour's church bylaws allowed only people of color to serve in leadership.

Again, Seymour was a great man. Perhaps he was one of the greatest men in the history of the church. Nevertheless, nothing he did qualifies him to be called the father of Pentecostalism. To argue otherwise simply ignores or denies the facts.

Howard N. Kenyon is typical of those who dismiss or downplay Parham's role. In *Ethics in the Age of the Spirit*, Kenyon emphatically states,

> The birth of the Pentecostal movement is properly understood as happening in 1906. What occurred in Topeka was certainly a critical stage in the gestation of the movement which had begun well before 1901. However, Pentecostalism prior to Azusa Street was little more than a white-led, white-membered, and white-oriented regional phenomenon.[16]

15. "The Pentecostal Baptism Restored," *TAFLA*, October 1906, 3.
16. Howard M. Kenyon, *Ethics in the Age of the Spirit: Race, Women, War, and the Assemblies of God* (Eugene, OR: Pickwick Publications, 2019), 51.

The weakness of this argument can be illustrated by similar events in the history of religious movements. When Joseph Smith, the founder of Mormonism, was killed in 1844, the Mormon membership was about twenty-five thousand. The Church of Jesus Christ of Latter-day Saints was a "white-led, white-membered, and white-oriented regional phenomenon." When Smith's successor, Brigham Young, died three decades later, the cult had more than quadrupled in size, expanded its geography, and extended its influence. Yet what serious historian would credit Young and not Smith with founding the LDS? The answer is obvious—no one.

How about John Wesley? Was he the founder of the Methodist Church? There were certainly clergymen who preached holiness before Wesley. A decade after Wesley released the general rules for his "united societies" that became the Methodist Discipline, the fledgling organization was "little more than a white-led, white-membered, and white-oriented regional phenomenon." Wesley sent Thomas Coke to establish the Methodist Church in America. Today, Methodists in the United States number nine million, dwarfing the mother church in England, which has no more than two hundred thousand active members. Following Kenyon's logic, shouldn't Coke be recognized as the founder of Methodism? Again, no one would or should make such a senseless argument.

Let's consider one other example, from American history. In 1789, when the United States Constitution was established, America consisted of only thirteen states that occupied a small region of the present country. The country existed before 1789. The land had been settled more than a century earlier, and its people had declared independence thirteen years earlier. The country was white-led and, in regard to citizenship, largely white-membered and white-oriented. Yet when George Washington was elected the first president, he gained the title "Father of Our Country." Does the fact that the country has expanded geographically and in population and is more racially diverse change the indisputable fact that Washington was the first president? Could we contend that Dwight D. Eisenhower was the first president because the states of Alaska and Hawaii were added during his administration? Of course not. To argue that Washington's tenure was merely a critical stage in the gestation of a nation that had begun well before his election would be laughable.

THE FATHER OF MODERN PENTECOSTALISM 25

Common-sense historical comparisons like these three examples are almost without number. They illustrate the absurdity of diminishing or dismissing Parham's role. Without further redundancy, surely this point has been made to anyone who is willing to examine the historical evidence without prejudice: Parham, and Parham alone, was the founder of the Pentecostal movement.

Not only did Parham start the movement, but he was also its undisputed leader for at least the first six years. In fact, he was the only leader. Under his guiding hand, the movement had tremendous success. Before there was an Azusa Street, the Apostolic Faith had spread through several states, from Kansas to Texas, and had gathered thousands of adherents. When the Los Angeles work was barely two weeks old, the *Houston Post* reported that Parham had "hundreds" of followers in Texas alone. He had "half a hundred workers," including a number of evangelists.[17]

In the first decade, workers who were never influenced by the California revival were sent forth as Apostolic missionaries. Marie Burgess and Jessie Brown from Zion City, Illinois, took the revival to New York City. Cyrus B. Fockler took the movement to Milwaukee. Howard Goss and an associate were sent to South Texas and told to "stop anywhere we could find a place to preach." John G. Lake took the message to Africa.[18] There are hundreds of other such examples. Gospel heralds with no connection to or affiliation with Azusa Street were spreading Pentecost throughout the nation and beyond.

Early Pentecostal leaders recognized Parham as the founder and leader of the movement. Goss, a Pentecostal and one of the organizers of the Assemblies of God, stated that in the summer of 1906, Parham "had been the only general leader."[19] This was at a time when Goss and others

17. "A Farewell Sermon," *The Houston Post*, April 20, 1906, 11 (hereafter cited as *THP*), newspapers.com.
18. Zelma Argue, "Chosen of God: The Story of Mrs. Robert A. Brown," Christ's Ambassadors Herald, August 1940, 6, ifphc.org; Ethel E. Goss, *The Winds of God* (Hazelwood, MO: Word Aflame, 1958), 76; Gordon P. Gardiner, *Out of Zion into All the World* (Shippensburg, PA: Companion Press, 1990), 12, 20–21.
19. H. A. Goss, "Article VIII: Reminiscences of an Eyewitness," in "Apostolic Faith Restored: A History of the Present Latter Rain Outpouring of the Holy Spirit Known as the Apostolic or Pentecostal Movement," ed. B. H. Lawrence, *The Weekly Evangel*, March 4, 1916, 4 (hereafter cited as *TWE*), ifphc.org. *The Weekly Evangel* was subsequently renamed *The Pentecostal Evangel*.

were chosen to serve with Parham in leading the movement. Goss made these observations more than a decade after the beginning of the revival in Los Angeles and after that revival had largely waned. There was never a question as to who was at the helm.

W. F. Carothers, another Parham lieutenant, wrote, "Later in the winter of 1906, or after nine months of unity with the original movement the work in Los Angeles separated from us...." Carothers used words like "original" and "older" to describe the work that had been started by Parham. Rather than suggest that Pentecostalism started in Los Angeles, he said the Azusa split caused "great damage" to the movement. He wrote as if the original work and the California faction were two streams of the same river, saying, "From Zion City and the older Movement on the one hand and from Azusa Street, Los Angeles, on the other, by the word of mouth, and by letter, by the Spirit and by the Word, over all lands and across the seas, the tidings have been carried until they have circled the globe."[20]

It should be noted that although both men rightly recognized Charles Parham as the founder and leader of the movement, neither Carothers nor Goss was a great supporter of Parham. In fact, both men worked to disfellowship him from the organization he had created. Parham's many flaws did not change the facts of his foundational contribution to the work.

J. G. Campbell, a Pentecostal editor from Alvin, Texas, called Parham "the man through whom God in these last days has introduced the baptism of the Holy Ghost evidenced by speaking in tongues."[21] In another edition, Campbell said emphatically that it was Parham who introduced the baptism in the Holy Ghost "to the world." He railed against those who teach and believe "the Pentecostal Movement, [was] started on the Pacific-Coast, by a negro (Seymour)." He said those who propagate this teaching are "publishing...false-hoods, (in some cases ignorantly)." Since the Bible says the devil is a liar and the father of it, Campbell cannot help but conclude that "Satan is at the bottom of it."[22] Further distinguishing Parham's work

20. W. F. Carothers, "Article VII: Houston, Texas and W. J. Seymour," in "Apostolic Faith Restored: A History of the Present Latter Rain Outpouring of the Holy Spirit Known as the Apostolic or Pentecostal Movement," ed. B. H. Lawrence, *TWE*, February 19, 1916, 4–5, ifphc.org.

21. J. G. Campbell, "Explanation to 'Costumes of the Holy-Land,'" *The Gospel of the Kingdom*, April 1909, 1 (hereafter cited as *TGK*), ifphc.org.

22. J. G. Campbell, "Pentecostal Papers," *TGK*, April 1910, 2, ifphc.org.

from Azusa Street, Campbell wrote, "There is one true Apostolic Faith Movement and all other movements claiming the name are usurpers."[23] In 1913, when Campbell seemed to have fallen out with Parham over some of his doctrine, he continued to insist that the movement was "founded by Chas. F Parham."[24]

On the fiftieth anniversary of the Topeka outpouring, Assemblies of God General Secretary J. Roswell Flower wrote an article for the *Pentecostal Evangel* entitled "Birth of the Pentecostal Movement." Flower told the story of Parham and his Bible school in Topeka and said that Parham's students "had deduced from God's Word that in apostolic times, the speaking in tongues was considered to be the initial physical evidence of a person's having received the Baptism in the Holy Spirit." Flower further stated, "It was this decision which has made the Pentecostal Movement of the Twentieth Century." He concluded, "The Pentecostal Movement was indeed fairly launched in January, 1901."[25]

Flower was just as specific when he was interviewed by *Christian Life* the following year. Here is part of that interview:

Question: Is there any precise event, Dr. Flower, which you believe gave birth to the Pentecostal movement?

Flower: The nearest thing we can identify as a specific event happened at a small Bible school in Topeka, Kansas. Coming from a Methodist background, one minister, the Reverend Charles F. Parham, taught his students at the Bethel Bible College the necessity for holiness of life and experience. Students, having been encouraged to study the Book of Acts, came to believe that when the Holy Spirit is outpoured on the believers there should be a physical manifestation. Therefore, they determined to seek the Lord until they should receive an experience similar to that recounted in Acts.[26]

---

23. J. G. Campbell, "The Original Apostolic Faith Movement," *TGK*, August 1910, 1, ifphc. org.

24. J. G. Campbell, "Take Notice," *TGK*, March–July 1913, 1, ifphc.org.

25. J. Roswell Flower, "Birth of the Pentecostal Movement," *The Pentecostal Evangel*, November 26, 1950, 3, 13 (hereafter cited as *TPE*), ifphc.org.

26. "Fifty Years of Signs and Wonders," *TPE*, October 7, 1951, 5, reprinted from *Christian Life*, ifphc.org.

A few years later, Flower addressed the World Pentecostal Conference in Stockholm, Sweden. He shared the established view on the beginning of the movement with delegates from around the world. On this occasion, he clarified the connection between Topeka and Los Angeles:

> The outpouring of the Holy Spirit in Los Angeles, and the revival at the Azusa Street mission (which many mistakenly have thought was the birthplace of the Pentecostal Movement) was in fact one link in the chain and one effect of chain reaction. William J. Seymour, a colored Holiness preacher, came under the influence of the Apostolic Faith Movement (as the Pentecostal Movement was first known) in Houston, Texas, and although admonished by the brethren in Houston not to go to Los Angeles until he had received the Pentecostal baptism, nevertheless felt impelled to accept the invitation which had been given to him. The result of his going to Los Angeles is well known, for in Los Angeles, Calif. on the 9th day of April, 1906, when the first persons in that city received the Holy Spirit according to the pattern, another spiritual atom was exploded, which scattered the Pentecostal message to the ends of the earth.
>
> The brilliance of that Pentecostal explosion (if we may use that term) was so great, that many were unaware of the links in the chain. It can be traced back to Houston, Texas, where a great Pentecostal revival was still in progress, and still farther back to the Bethel Bible College in Topeka, Kans., which had been closed soon after that initial outpouring of the Spirit. The Apostolic Faith Movement which was centered in Houston, Texas, was steadily growing in spiritual power and influence. It has been estimated that at that time there were approximately one thousand persons in the Midwest who had received the Pentecostal Baptism, and sixty or more recognized Pentecostal ministers.[27]

There are many more examples of the earliest Pentecostals affirming that Parham was the founder of the movement. These are men whose lives were contemporaneous with the beginning of Pentecostalism. They were

---

27. Roswell J. Flower, "The Genesis of the Pentecostal Movement," *TPE*, January 29, 1956, 6–7, ifphc.org.

aware of what happened before, during, and after Azusa Street, yet they did not for a moment see the Los Angeles revival as launching a movement that had already existed for more than five years.

Many of Parham's converts were quality men and women with considerable influence. Would John G. Lake, converted by Parham in Zion, have spread Pentecost to South Africa if there had been no Azusa Street? There is no satisfactory reason why he wouldn't have. Would Gordon Lindsay, another Parham convert, have established Christ For The Nations if there had been no Azusa? Why not?

Would great Pentecostal denominations like the Assemblies of God have been formed if there had been no Azusa? Of course, to say either way is speculative, but as many of the founders of the Assemblies of God traced their spiritual lineage to Topeka as they did to Los Angeles.

These are the kinds of questions that many people today are unwilling to explore because such inquiries are inconvenient.

Parham's work was not done in a corner and cannot be so easily dismissed as an unspectacular regional movement. Its expansion was exponential. Thomas Atteberry, an early adherent, wrote, "Before Pentecost came to Los Angeles there were persons in almost every state in the Union who had received the baptism of the Holy Spirit, witnessed by speaking in tongues, while in the Southwestern states alone there were several thousand who had received this Pentecostal blessing."[28]

By the end of the first decade of the Apostolic Faith, the *Brownwood News* claimed the movement had two hundred thousand adherents, with twenty thousand in Texas alone. Parham's meeting in Baxter Springs, Kansas, in late 1910 had attendees from twenty-four states.[29]

As important as Azusa Street was, with Parham's successes in Texas and Illinois, it can easily be argued that the movement would have continued to spread around the world absent the Los Angeles revival. If William J. Seymour had never met Charles F. Parham in Houston, there would still have been a worldwide Pentecostal revival. Would it have grown as rapidly? Perhaps not, but it almost certainly would have continued to grow.

---

28. Thomas G. Atteberry, "A Bit of History," *The Pentecostal Witness*, December 1908, 10.
29. "From Brownwood, Texas," *TGK*, n.d., 3 (document 1 of non-dated issues), ifphc.org.

We can therefore reasonably conclude that Charles Parham is the indisputable founder of the Pentecostal movement. Considering the significance of his role in the formulation and propagation of one of the world's largest Christian bodies, it is important to know who he was and why he is despised by so many people. Why is Charles Parham such an unlikely founder? Only a history of the man, his shortcomings, and his times can answer these questions.

2

THE MAKING OF
THE MAN

Charles Fox Parham was born in Muscatine, Iowa, on June 4, 1873. He was named after Charles Fox, the husband of his mother's sister.

Muscatine was first settled in the 1830s. Its distinctive name was derived from the Mascoutin Indians, who had previously settled the area. Located on the mighty Mississippi, by the time of Parham's birth, Muscatine had become a regular stop for riverboats and had a growing lumber industry. From 1870 to 1877, the town's population grew from under seven thousand to nearly eleven thousand.[30]

Both sides of Parham's family migrated to Muscatine from Pennsylvania in the mid-1800s. His grandparents were Joseph and Deborah Parham and Levi and Catherine (Cressman) Eckel. They were all people of influence in the community.

Joseph and Deborah moved to Muscatine in 1858, just before the Civil War. Joseph was a plasterer by trade, but, "having means sufficient for support," he was "chiefly occupied with looking after his investments." For a time, he struggled with alcohol addiction but successfully overcame it and

---

30. muscatinecountyiowa.gov; Jennifer Howell, email message to author, February 17, 2021. Jennifer Howell is the Local History Librarian at the Musser Public Library in Muscatine, Iowa.

became a "zealous member and accomplished secretary" in the local temperance movement. In 1867, Joseph would enter into a partnership with Levi Eckel to build a lumberyard in Muscatine.[31]

Levi and Catherine moved to Muscatine in 1863. Levi's great-grandfather Henry Eckel had been a colonial settler, arriving in Pennsylvania in 1765. Before leaving Pennsylvania, Levi was an expert tanner. In Iowa, he was involved in the cattle business, owning the Hawkeye Cattle Company. In the lumber business, he and Joseph sold shingles, pickets, doors, and other wood products. Levi's Methodist pastor called him a man of "ideal character."[32]

Catherine was a lifelong member of the Methodist Church and was "steadfast" in her duties and service to the church. She was a "constant attendant at divine services."[33]

Charles Parham's parents were William M. and Anna M. (Eckel) Parham. William worked as a farmer, painter, and laborer, but his chief occupation was harness maker. In the days of horse and wagon travel, a harness maker was an essential vocation. William was a Methodist and a man of deep religious convictions. He often spoke of "the love of the Master and how sweet his love was to him." Those who knew him said his life mirrored these words of Solomon: "The path of the just shineth more and more until that perfect day."[34]

Charles was the middle child among the five sons born to William and Anna. Harry Clayton and Edgar Levi were born before him. Frank Elmore and Arthur M. were born afterward.

---

31. "New Establishment in Projection," *Muscatine Weekly Journal*, March 2, 1867 (hereafter cited as *MWK*), newspapers.com; "Lumber," *Muscatine Daily Journal*, May 29, 1867, 1 (hereafter cited as *MDJ*), newspapers.com; "The Blue Ribbon," *MWK*, June 14, 1878, 4, newspapers.com; "Death of Joseph C. Parham," *MDJ*, June 8, 1878, 1, newspapers.com; "A Pioneer Gone," *Muscatine News Tribune*, January 22, 1893, 2 (hereafter cited as *MNT*), newspapers.com.

32. ancestry.com; findagrave.com; "Levi Eckel: Lumber Bearer," *MDJ*, April 1, 1883, 2, newspapers.com; "Personal Points," *San Antonio Light*, October 2, 1884, 1 (hereafter cited as *SAL*), newspapers.com; "A Pioneer Dies," *MDJ*, March 13, 1905, 4, newspapers.com; "News of the Northwest," *The Independent* (Hawarden, Iowa), June 28, 1890, 2, newspapers.com; "The Last Sad Services Held," *MNT*, March 17, 1905, 4, newspapers.com.

33. "Mrs. Levi Eckel Has Succumbed," *MDJ*, March 29, 1910, 8, newspapers.com; "Mrs. Levi Eckel Died Last Eve," *MNT*, March 25, 1910, 5, newspapers.com.

34. "William Parham Was One of Cheney's Pioneers," *The Cheney Sentinel* (Kansas), December 13, 1923, 7 (hereafter cited as *CS*), newspapers.com. The words quoted from Solomon come from Proverbs 4:18.

Throughout his childhood, Parham battled a number of serious illnesses. He described his maladies in this way:

At six months of age I was taken with a fever that left me an invalid. For five years I suffered with dreadful spasms, and enlargement of the head, until my forehead became abnormally large. At nine years of age I was stricken with the first case of inflammatory rheumatism, virtually tied up in a knot, with other complication I suffered much. Until, when the affliction left I could count the bones in my hand by holding it up to the light. About this time I took medicine of various kinds to destroy a tape worm. One concoction was of such a nature that it destroyed the lining of my stomach and so dwarfed me so that I did not grow any for three years.[35]

In addition to these problems, Parham's mind "was almost wrecked."[36] In childhood, he was described as "neurotic, eccentric, and dull in all things except Bible reading and memorizing."[37] He personally confirmed that, throughout his youth, he did not have the "full use of his mind" from the time he was five.[38] His eyes were so bad that he had to wear powerful glasses. He also claimed to have "sick headaches" and "an abscess" on his liver. He said he almost died from heart failure four times. No wonder he lamented that he was a "wreck on the shores of despair."[39]

When Parham was only five years of age, his family packed all their belongings into a covered wagon and moved to Illinois, Kansas, a small township just outside of Wichita. The overland journey of more than five hundred miles must have been grueling for a sick child.

The Parham family members were among the first settlers to the area. They lived on a farm, and William opened a harness shop in neighboring Cheney.[40]

---

35. Charles F. Parham, "The Personal Testimony of Chas. F. Parham, Editor, to Divine Healing," *TAF*, December 1926, 15, original apostolifaith.org.
36. C. Parham, "Personal Testimony."
37. Charles W. Shumway, "A Critical History of Glossolalia" (Ph.D. diss., Boston University, 1919), 47.
38. Shumway, "A Critical Study of 'The Gift of Tongues,'" 164.
39. Charles Parham, "My Testimony," *TAF*, March 30, 1899, 6, Kansas Historical Society (hereafter cited as KHS).
40. S. Parham, *Life of Charles F. Parham*, 1.

On November 17, 1885, Anna Parham died, surrounded by her loving family. The nature of her illness is not known, but it may have been from complications following the birth of her last child exactly one week before she passed. Charles was at school when heralds beckoned him to return home to see his mother for the last time. She looked at twelve-year-old Charles and said, "Charlie, be good." A grieving son promised his mother he would meet her in heaven.[41] The loss of a mother is always difficult, but it would have been especially so for a child with Parham's infirmities and need for special care.

According to his own testimony, Parham never had a day free from pain until he was eighteen.[42] Because he was sick most of his childhood, he helped around the farm as best he could. One of his tasks was to pluck the geese for the evening meal; when he had the strength, he would help herd the cattle. His brother Arthur was an infant when their mother passed, so Parham's chief task was babysitting while the others did the more taxing chores.[43]

William Parham married Harriet Elizabeth Cook on September 18, 1886, less than a year after Anna's death. Harriet was a lifelong member of the Methodist Church. Her father was an early Methodist circuit-riding preacher in Northern Indiana. She was a "very devout Christian and loved the power of the old time religion with all her heart."[44]

Harriet had previously been married to William Oliver Miller in Indiana. The couple had two children, James and Ida, both grown at the time of her marriage to Parham. Records show Harriet was divorced from her first husband in 1885.[45]

---

41. S. Parham, 1. The death of Parham's mother is somewhat mysterious. There were no notices about it in any of the local newspapers. The notice in the Muscatine newspaper adds to the enigma: "Mrs. Levi Eckel with Miss Irene was called to Cheney, KS., last evening by news of the death of her daughter, Mrs. Anna Parham." This was a full month after Anna's death. See "Advertisements," *MDJ*, December 18, 1885, 2, newspapers.com.
42. C. Parham, "Personal Testimony."
43. S. Parham, *Life of Charles F. Parham*, 2; Charles F. Parham, *Kol Kare Bomidbar: A Voice Crying in the Wilderness*, 3rd ed. (Baxter Springs, KS: Apostolic Faith, n.d.), 12.
44. "Mrs. Harriet Parham Was a Wife and Mother of Devotion," *CS*, February 9, 1922, 4, newspapers.com; "Old Settler Is Dead," *The Wichita Eagle* (Kansas), February 4, 1922, 8, newspapers.com.
45. ancestry.com.

By all accounts, Harriet was a wonderful mother to the Parham children. When she passed in 1922, Charles spoke at her funeral, saying that even though she was his stepmother, he only spoke of her as "Mother." Parham eloquently expressed these sentiments:

> For the sacrifice she made, for the mother love she bestowed upon a worthless brood of motherless children, for the wifely devotion and sweet heart love she gave my father for over thirty years, had I the power today, I'd place a royal diadem of stars upon her head, enthrone majestic sweetness upon her brow, wreath her face in triumphant smile, encircle her throat in a neckless [sic] of pearl, robe her body in bridal lace, and place jeweled slippers upon her feet, and lead her into the throne room to the bridegroom of her soul, her Lord, the king of glory.[46]

According to Parham, there was not a lot of religion in the family home. He said he "scarcely" knew anything of church or Sunday school. Preachers, he said, were as rare as "hen's teeth." Parham only recalled hearing one or two preachers up to the time he was thirteen. This seems like an odd claim considering his maternal grandparents and his parents were deeply committed church members.

Parham said he first felt a call to preach when he was nine years old.[47] He had not yet surrendered his life to Jesus Christ, but he apparently sensed the same urgency as the apostle Paul, who said, "Woe is unto me, if I preach not the gospel!"[48] The family had only a handful of books, but, fortunately, a Bible was among them. The Scriptures were young Charles's "constant companion." He would gather the cattle on a hill and preach to them about the joys of heaven and the torments of hell. Parham would later joke that he had supreme patience with those in his audiences who did not give him their complete attention because he had gotten his ministerial training preaching to bovine that "indifferently munched away" as he enthusiastically warned them about eternity.[49]

---

46. "Mrs. Harriet Parham Was a Wife and Mother of Devotion."
47. C. Parham, *Kol Kare Bomidbar*, 18.
48. First Corinthians 9:16 (KJV).
49. C. Parham, *Kol Kare Bomidbar*, 18.

At the age of thirteen, Parham was converted during a revival meeting conducted by J. H. Lippard, a Congregational minister. Lippard was widely known throughout the Central United States for his citywide ecumenical revival meetings.[50] The revivalist was holding his meetings in a schoolhouse, apparently with no success. He announced on Thursday that unless someone made a decision for Christ, he would close the meetings on Sunday.

Parham knew he would become a Christian some day but didn't see himself being converted in the immediate future. However, he was enjoying the meetings and hated to see them end. So, on Friday night, he stood, claimed Christ, and was counted as a convert. At this meeting, little effort was expended to help him in making his salvation sure. But that night, on the way home, he felt a strong conviction of the Holy Spirit and began to sing William McDonald's hymn "I Am Coming to the Cross." As Parham sang the third stanza, he lifted his face to heaven, and something life-changing happened.

> Here, I give my all to Thee,
> Friends and time and earthly store,
> Soul and body Thine to be;
> Wholly Thine forever more.

At the word "wholly," the young man saw a bright light like the sun. It "penetrated, thrilling every tissue and fiber" of his being.[51] Parham had a "Damascus Road" conversion.[52] Two years later, when he was fifteen, Parham began teaching Sunday school and preaching at some public meetings. In Parham's view, the services had "marked results."[53] He also became a teacher at the only school in his village. He tried to stay ahead of his pupils but struggled to keep up in arithmetic. He admitted he would often

---

50. C. Parham, 13; "Revival Services of Rev. Lippard Create Much Interest," *The Daily Northwesterner* (Oshkosh, WI), April 11, 1893, 1, newspaperarchive.com.

51. C. Parham, *Kol Kare Bomidbar*, 13–15. Again, it seems somewhat odd that Parham, who claimed to have never attended church, would be so familiar with a hymn.

52. See Acts 9:1–20.

53. C. Parham, *Kol Kare Bomidbar*, 25. One report says Parham's early evangelistic work was associated with the Gospel Union. See "Parham–Thistlethwaite," *The Tonganoxie Mirror* (Kansas), December 31, 1896, 8 (hereafter cited as *TM*), newspapers.com.

take a math problem home, let one of his brothers solve it, and then teach it to the students.[54]

At the age of sixteen, Parham enrolled in Southwest Kansas Conference College in Winfield. The college was founded by the Methodists in 1885 and began classes in 1886, so it was almost new when Parham attended. Discipline at the school was quite severe. The college catalog noted, "A wholesome religious atmosphere pervades the school. No one will be permitted to remain in the school whose connection with it is injurious to others or unprofitable to himself." Smoking was "strictly forbidden" and dancing was "not tolerated." One female student was asked to withdraw from the school simply because she continued to dress in a manner the other girls could not afford.[55]

Parham was enrolled only in the academy in precollege courses. The young preacher confessed he was more interested in ministry than in education and that his grades suffered from neglect. In actuality, most of his grades were average, but he made an A in history and failing grades in mathematics.[56]

The burdens associated with a future life in the ministry began to weigh heavily on the struggling student. At his conversion, he had promised God he would become a missionary to Africa. That vow now "tormented" him.[57]

Parham was also troubled by his knowledge that many preachers suffered from financial lack; the prospect of having to constantly pull for money disgusted him. In contrast, medical doctors always seemed to have more than enough money to support themselves. The appeal of becoming a doctor grew until Parham decided to change the trajectory of his life. He would study medicine and serve the hurting as a physician rather than as a clergyman, enjoying "a nice home and some ease and comfort in this world."[58] The fact that he had suffered illness for much of his life provided a fitting justification for his change in direction. He could help others while he helped himself.

---

54. "Kansas City Times," *TAF*, n.d., 8, Flower Pentecostal Heritage Center (hereafter cited as FPHC); "This Is the Third in a Series of Sermons by Charles F. Parham," *TAF*, April 1925, 10, FPHC.
55. Unpublished manuscript, Southwestern College archives (hereafter cited as SC).
56. Transcripts, SC.
57. S. Parham, *Life of Charles F. Parham*, 6.
58. C. Parham, *Kol Kare Bomidbar*, 16.

Like Jonah in the Bible, however, stepping out of God's will did not bode well for him. By his own admission, he totally "backslid." He was guilty of sins of omission and commission. His own associates no longer recognized him as a Christian.

Along with the darkness in his soul came physical torment. One day, he collapsed on the campus and had to be carried home on a stretcher. According to Parham, he had contracted rheumatic fever and was "given up by all physicians and friends."[59] On May 16, 1892, Parham was placed on a train to return to his home in Cheney. While lying on the floor of the depot in Wichita, he wrote to his friends at Southwest, informing them he had arrived safely but was "suffering considerably from pain."[60]

For months, he suffered "the torments of hell."[61] Nothing could describe his misery at this time better than his own words:

> Every joint being so locked that I had to be fed and lifted about even turned over in bed. I was attended by noted Doctors and Scientists. They all finally agreed that nothing could be done. My joints were ossifying, every organ of the body became diseased, consumption upon my lungs, eyesight nearly gone, and mind almost wrecked from suffering. From far and wide came people to see the boy who was ossifying. Then came many physicians who under guise of desiring to help me, used me as a clinic, doping me with all manner of stuff that they had tried on dogs, cats and monkeys, desiring not my healing but that they might see what effect their medicine would have upon a human, thinking perhaps I would die anyway.[62]

The long period of suffering and an apparent morphine addiction had left Parham totally emaciated. A physician told his friends he had only a short time to live. In fact, suffering from agony of both soul and body, Parham wished to die.

In this unbearable condition, he was visited by a "poor, lazy, sissified" preacher. When the dying teen asked for healing prayer, the preacher told

---

59. C. Parham, 16.
60. *Winfield Daily Courier* (Kansas), May 16, 1892, 5, newspapers.com.
61. C. Parham, *Kol Kare Bomidbar*, 16–17.
62. C. Parham, "Personal Testimony."

him that the gift of healing had ended with the apostles, and he would have to wait for heaven to receive his healing.[63]

Not satisfied with this answer, Parham began to reflect on Jesus's power to heal. If Jesus had healed people during His time on earth, as recorded in the Gospels, why could He not heal today? Parham repented of all his sins and made a complete consecration of his life to God, promising to reenter the ministry. If his call were to the slums, to Africa, or to any other place, he was willing to pay whatever price Christ demanded.

A sweet sense of sanctification filled Parham's soul, and his body received a healing touch. His testimony was that the "disease was killed."[64]

After his reconsecration and healing, Parham returned to Southwest College. One affliction, however, remained in his body. His ankles had been weakened by the extended period of sickness. When he stood, his feet would flip outward. This may be hard to imagine, but he said he hobbled around the campus trying to walk on the sides of his feet. One night, under an oak tree on the campus, Parham pleaded with God for deliverance. Like the man at the Beautiful gate of the temple in Jerusalem,[65] his ankle bones received strength, and he was healed.

Parham left the college without finishing a degree or even beginning theological studies. He was licensed as a local preacher by the Kansas District of the Methodist Episcopal Church in 1893.[66]

A Methodist Episcopal church in Eudora, Kansas, had been pastored by Dr. W. R. Davis, the founder of Baker University in Baldwin City, Kansas. After Baker fell ill and died, Parham was appointed as a supply pastor for the church in March 1894.[67]

For a nineteen-year-old pastor in his first church, Parham did quite well. The membership of the church doubled in a year, and Parham reported 126 conversions. Additionally, at nearby Linwood, Kansas, Parham had

---

63. "Personal Testimony."
64. C. Parham, *Kol Kare Bomidbar*, 18.
65. See Acts 3:1–10.
66. Records are scarce, but Parham's name does not appear until the 1894 minutes. *Kansas Annual Conference of the Methodist Episcopal Church, Official Minutes* (Edwin Locke, publ., 1894), 25, FPHC; Sara DeCaro, email to author, March 4, 2021. Sara DeCaro was the Kansas Area Archivist for the Great Plains Conference of the United Methodist Church.
67. "Kansas Methodists," *Leroy Reporter* (Kansas), March 23, 1894, 4, newspapers.com.

organized a new congregation with seventy-five members and was making plans to construct a building.[68]

Unfortunately, things did not go as Parham had planned. He did not fit well in the Methodist system. He described his congregation as "a lot of theater-going, card-playing, wine drinking fashionable, unconverted Methodists."[69] Apparently, they didn't think any better of him. He caused "quite a commotion" in the church when he announced he did not believe in the doctrine of endless punishment.[70]

In September 1895, he was "permitted to withdraw from the M.E. under charges." No records of the charges against him exist. A defender of Parham said the preacher's character was being "blackened" because he was a "young man of independent thought and action" who had no use for "policy religion."[71] Parham reported that the Methodist leaders said, "We have nothing against his character, but we intend to stop his mouth."[72]

The final straw, according to Parham, was an ordination address given by his presiding bishop. The Methodist bishop told the new class of ministers that they should preach prepared sermons to their congregations. Parham was "horror struck" that the candidates for ministry were not free to preach by "direct inspiration." Parham claimed he never once prepared a sermon or preached from notes but that every message he delivered in his entire ministry was extemporaneous and Holy Spirit led.[73]

Parham explained the fracture as follows:

Finding the confines of a pastorate, and feeling the narrowness of sectarian churchism, we were often in conflict with the higher authorities, which eventually resulted in a rupture; and we left denominationalism forever, though suffering bitter persecution at

---

68. W. H. Zimmerman, "Kansas Methodism," *Western Methodist*, April 12, 1894, 2 (hereafter cited as *WM*), April 12, 1894, 2, newspapers.com.
69. "Address," *TAF*, January 1914, 2, originalapostolicfaith.org.
70. O. G. Richards, "Hell for the Wicked," *The Eudora News* (Kansas), March 7, 1895, 3, newspapers.com.
71. "Preachers as Character Assassins," *The Jeffersonian Gazette* (Lawrence, Kansas), September 12, 1895, 3 (hereafter cited as *TJG*), September 12, 1895, 3, newspapers.com.
72. "Aug. 10th, '07, Tonganoxie, Kas.," *TGK*, n.d., n.p., ifphc.org.
73. Shumway, "A Critical Study of 'The Gift of Tongues,'" 164.

the hands of the church, who seemed determined if possible, our soul should never find rest in this world or the world to come.[74]

Parham's parents were very disappointed when he broke from the Methodists. Both being faithful members of the church, they had hoped he would do a "great work" as a Methodist pastor. Parham would joke about it and tell people that they had tried to cut him out for a Methodist preacher but found there wasn't sufficient material, so they threw him in the "scrap" pile.[75]

Separating from the Methodists, Parham entered the "open field" and began preaching revival meetings wherever the doors would open. The Tuttle family in Lawrence, Kansas, opened their home to him and treated him "like their own son." He spent five years on the evangelistic field and reported that "hundreds were converted, scores sanctified, and a few healed."[76]

The young evangelist wrote to the *Eudora Weekly News* to boast that he had "passed the lines of persecution by vile men and [was] marching on.... The crops are very good in this part of the State." Parham also claimed to have preached to nine thousand people on the previous Sunday. Perhaps he did, but it is hard to picture where that crowd would have gathered in the small Kansas towns where Parham most often ministered.[77]

Some of Parham's early meetings must have been quite rowdy as Holiness and Free Methodist groups united to support his campaigns. It was reported that the "yelling of the fanatics could be heard a mile away."[78] Later in his ministry, Parham stressed a much tamer, unemotional response to the gospel message.

A chaplain's position came available at the state penitentiary in 1896, and Parham vigorously pursued the job.[79] He had an eye toward marriage

---

74. C. Parham, *Kol Kare Bomidbar*, 19.
75. S. Parham, *Life of Charles F. Parham*, 25.
76. S. Parham, 25; C. Parham, *Kol Kare Bomidbar*, 19.
77. "From Rev. C. F. Parham," *EN*, July 4, 1895, 3, newspapers.com.
78. "Parham Formerly of Kansas," *The Coffeyville Daily Journal* (Kansas), September 20, 1907, 1 (hereafter cited as *CDJ*), newspapers.com.
79. "Local Laconics," *TM*, December 10, 1896, 8, newspapers.com; *EN*, December 10, 1906, 3, newspapers.com; "City News," *Lawrence Daily World* (Kansas), December 4, 1896, 3 (hereafter cited as *LDW*), newspapers.com.

and a family, and a more settled and secure job would certainly have had its appeal. Although Parham did not get the government job, he still moved forward with his other plans.

On December 31, 1896, Charles married Sarah Eleanor B. Thistlethwaite in a simple Quaker ceremony in Tonganoxie, Kansas. Sarah first learned about Parham while attending school in Kansas City, Missouri. Her parents had written to her about a young evangelist who was holding an extended revival at the Pleasant Valley School House near Lawrence. When the school term ended, Sarah returned home in time to meet Parham and hear him preach at an all-day meeting celebrating his nineteenth birthday.

Sarah had been reared as a Quaker. She knew God but had never heard preaching like Parham's. When she attended his meeting, she felt as if his sermon was being directed right at her. She said it struck her like a "thunderbolt." A sense of conviction overwhelmed her, and she consecrated "her whole life" to the Master.[80]

Sarah's maternal grandfather, David Baker, had been a "birthright Quaker" in England before immigrating to America.[81] He was deeply committed to God and a serious student of the Bible. Parham enjoyed spending hours searching the Scriptures with the elderly gentleman. Baker influenced Parham to adopt one of his most controversial doctrinal positions: the annihilation of the wicked.[82]

After the wedding, Charles and Sarah honeymooned for a few days in Linwood; Kansas City, Missouri; and Wellsville. They took a pleasurable ride by sleigh to Baldwin City.[83] Their vacation was short-lived, and less than two weeks into their marriage, the newlyweds started a revival meeting at the Baptist church in Strong City, Kansas.[84] Parham preached in schoolhouses,

---

80. S. Parham, *Life of Charles F. Parham*, 16–17.
81. Before the mid-twentieth century, all children born to Quaker families were automatically received into membership by right of birth.
82. C. Parham, *Kol Kare Bomidbar*, 14.
83. S. Parham, *Life of Charles F. Parham*, 29; "Wellsville" *The Ottawa Daily Republic* (Kansas), January 8, 1897, 2, newspapers.com; "County News Summary: Wellsville," *The Evening Herald* (Ottawa, Kansas), January 7, 1897, 2, newspapers.com. In *Life of Charles F. Parham*, Sarah says they visited "Wellington" on the way to Strong City. It is more likely it was Wellsville, as reported in the newspapers.
84. "Kaught on the Fly," *The News-Courant* (Cottonwood Falls, Kansas), January 7, 1897, 3 (hereafter cited as *NC*), newspapers.com.

as well as in Baptist, Presbyterian, and Congregational churches.[85] He preached alone and in cooperation with G. S. Anderson, a Salvation Army officer.[86] The couple's schedule was hectic, to say the least. At times, Sarah stayed in a home between Tonganoxie and Eudora while Parham traveled.[87]

Quite quickly after their marriage, Sarah became pregnant with their first child.[88] The pressures of life were mounting for the young evangelist. In March, Parham solicited funds for a "large tent" for his summer campaigns. He had raised fifty dollars but needed another one hundred.[89]

Parham secured the tent and held meetings through the late spring and early summer. In May and June, he hosted an "international" camp meeting at Merchant's Grove, west of Wellsville and south of Baldwin City.[90] These events were true camp meetings in every sense of the word. Interested parties would set up small tents and live on the grounds. Unfortunately, one evening, vandals broke into the Parhams' tent and stole all their provisions. The theft created considerable sympathy for Charles and Sarah, whom the paper said were "working for nothing but their living." Charles W. Ingle, a Free Methodist brother, invited the hungry couple to his farm for dinner. A reporter quipped, "The thought of a square meal tickled the little preacher so much he could be heard to laugh for half a mile."[91]

Shortly thereafter, Parham became quite ill with what Sarah called "the worst form" of heart disease. He collapsed in the pulpit while preaching and was carried to his tent. According to Parham, he "was overcome by heat and nervous prostration…causing angina pectoris or heart stroke." Physicians warned him that he would die if he continued to preach, but Parham would not abandon his "life's work." He announced he would be forced to cancel all

85. *Strong City Derrick* (Kansas), February 5, 1897, 3, newspapers.com; *Chase County Ledger* (Cottonwood Falls, Kansas), March 11, 1897, 5, newspapers.com; *TN*, March 11, 1897, 3, newspapers.com.
86. *Chase County Ledger* (Cottonwood Falls, Kansas), March 11, 1897, 5, newspapers.com.
87. "Local Laconics," *TM*, July 15, 1897, 8, newspapers.com.
88. Sarah gave birth on September 22, eight months and 21 days, or 264 days, after their wedding. A normal pregnancy is 260–280 days. The baby was small and may have come early. A baby born before 259 days is considered premature. The author prefers to give the Parhams the benefit of the doubt. The reader can draw their own conclusion.
89. "Kindly Notice," *NC*, March 11, 1897, 3, newspapers.com.
90. "Local Laconics," *TM*, July 15, 1897, 8, newspapers.com; "Country News," *Lawrence Daily Journal* (Kansas), July 6, 1897, 4 (hereafter cited as *LDJ*), newspapers.com; "Country News," *LDJ*, May 18, 1897, 4; *BB*, June 17, 1897, 5, newspapers.com.
91. "Charles Wesley Ingle," *The Baldwin Ledger* (Kansas), June 18, 1909, 1, newspapers.com; *BB*, June 3, 1897, 5, newspapers.com.

of his meetings for the summer of 1897 and perhaps longer. Parham felt this was part of God's plan and wanted to spend his time writing.[92]

Charles and Sarah moved to the town of Media, near Baldwin City, Kansas.[93] Their house was next door to Media's motel. The Media area was familiar to the couple because Parham had held a revival at the Presbyterian church there in May 1896.[94] They settled into their first home. Sarah described their furnishings as "second-hand" or "home-made" but said the couple was "content."[95] Struggling to support a growing family, Parham applied to be a notary public and was commissioned in this position.[96] Despite the commission, Parham continued to preach whenever doors opened for him to do so.[97]

In August, Parham was invited to accept the pastorate of the Presbyterian church in Media. The church was small, with only thirty-five members, but the congregation welcomed its new pastor. Members of the community showered the Parhams with "beautiful gifts of love and usefulness." Oliver Burton, a local businessman and politician, presented the couple with offerings valued at about twelve dollars.[98]

During the pastorate at Media, the Parhams' first child, Claude Wallace, was born on September 22.[99] Little Claude weighed only five pounds and

---

92. *TJG*, July 15, 1897, 3, newspapers.com; "From Rev. Parham," *NC*, July 15, 1897, 3, newspapers.com; S. Parham, *Life of Charles F. Parham*, 31.

93. S. Parham, *Life of Charles F. Parham*, 31. Media is a ghost town today. Parts of the city were incorporated into present-day Baldwin City.

94. *TJG*, May 11, 1896, 2, newspapers.com.

95. S. Parham, *Life of Charles F. Parham*, 31.

96. "Media Items," *The Baldwin Bee* (Kansas), August 5, 1897, 5 (hereafter cited as *BB*), newspapers.com; "Notaries Receive Commissions," *The Topeka Daily Capital*, August 3, 1897, 8 (hereafter cited as *TC*), newspapers.com.

97. For example, he preached at both the Presbyterian church and the Methodist mission in Media in July. See *BB*, July 15, 1897, 8, newspapers.com.

98. "Donation Party a Success," *BB*, September 2, 1897, 8, newspapers.com; "Local News," *The Wellsville Globe* (Kansas), September 9, 1897, 3, newspapers.com; *BB*, August 19, 1897, 1, newspapers.com. The papers never say that the church Parham pastored was the Presbyterian church. However, there were only two churches in Media: one Catholic and the other Presbyterian. The Methodists had a mission that met in an empty store building and was a preaching station for nearby students at Baker University. The Presbyterian church eventually closed and was purchased and donated to the Methodists. The building is now Ives Chapel United Methodist Church in Baldwin City. See *TJG*, May 20, 1897, 2, newspapers.com. Twelve dollars in 1897 would be worth more than $400 today. See https://www.in2013dollars.com/us/inflation/1897?amount=12 (May 6, 2022).

99. "Media Matters," *BB*, September 30, 1897, 6.

appeared to have inherited his father's illnesses. Doctors offered the couple no remedies, and "for weeks," Sarah said, "the little life seemed hopeless."[100]

One day, the young preacher was called on to pray for a seriously ill gentleman named Jones. While he knelt in prayer, a voice spoke to him, "You need to get healed yourself." The biblical text of Luke 4:23 came to him: "Physician, heal thyself." Parham's faith increased, and he prayed earnestly for himself. So intense was the prayer that he "sank down upon a chair." After fifteen minutes, he felt, as it were, electricity from the crown of his head to the tips of his fingers. He was "made every whit whole," with every organ of his body "tingling with health and strength." Next, he prayed for Claude, who was also healed. The Parhams never again put their faith in the medical community.[101]

Parham did not stay long in Media. Sarah described it as "short time." Indeed it was. By the late fall, the evangelist (though still pastoring) was back on the road, preaching a revival in Ottawa, Kansas. In December, he was assisting with a protracted meeting in Paola. By March, he had relocated to Ottawa and was making plans to start a mission work in the city.[102]

Before leaving the church in Media, Parham conducted a joint revival with Rev. Thomas H. Gourley. It is not clear if the two had met previously, but Gourley must have had a great impact on Parham's life. A former Kansas City police officer, Gourley was an extremely controversial figure who was often called a "hypnotist" preacher. Members of his audience would frequently go into a cataleptic state and lie in trances for hours. More importantly, Gourley was a huge proponent of divine healing and prayed for the sick in his meetings.[103]

---

100. "In Loving Remembrance," *TAF*, February 1929, 2, originalapostolicfaith.org.
101. "In Loving Remembrance," 2; S. Parham, *Life of Charles F. Parham*, 32; "The Sources of Disease," *TAF*, August 1912, 3. Each account is slightly different from the others. Sarah's accounts leave the impression that Parham did not actually pray for Mr. Jones. In any event, we do not know if Jones received a similar healing.
102. S. Parham, *Life of Charles F. Parham*, 31–33; "Media Matters," *BB*, November 4, 1897, 8, newspapers.com; *BB*, November 25, 1897, 5, newspapers.com; *The Ottawa Weekly* (Kansas), March 17, 1898, 3 (hereafter cited as *OT*), newspapers.com; *The Paola Times* (Kansas) December 23, 1897, 8, newspapers.com.
103. *Lawrence Weekly World* (Kansas), January 27, 1898, 5, newspapers.com; "Was He Hypnotized?" *TM*, September 30, 1897, 1, newspapers.com; *LDJ*, July 31, 1897, 4, newspapers.com; *The Okaloosa Times* (Kansas), January 21, 1898, 4, newspapers.com; *TJG*, February 17, 1898, 3, newspapers.com; "Coucluded [sic] to Leave," *OT*, June 3, 1898, 4, newspapers.com.

Sarah said that Parham first publicly prayed for the sick while they were in Ottawa. Before then, he had offered private prayers for healing but had never prayed for people in his meetings.[104] There is little doubt that he would have been influenced by Gourley. Gourley believed that a Christian could reach a state of perfect health in which disease could not harm them.[105] Parham also embraced this extreme view.[106] Later, Gourley joined Parham at his healing home in Topeka.[107]

By May 1898, the nomadic parson had moved from Ottawa to Topeka. After holding services in the capital city, he launched a more permanent ministry.[108] For several months, his fledgling congregation met in the parlors of his adherents' homes.

Parham complained that he had the support of only one local pastor, Elisha Palmer of the North Congregational Church. There were, however, nine Christian workers whom he endorsed. The group consisted of men and women who were gifted as teachers, elders, deaconesses, and evangelists.[109]

In January of the following year, Parham was able to rent a building on the corner of Fourth and Jackson in downtown Topeka. Parham called his ministry Bethel Divine Healing Home and Mission. Initially, the name was hyphenated "Beth-el." The new building was dedicated on February 5, 1899.[110] This large brick structure had ample room for a chapel that seated 200, a reading room, a print shop where tracts and leaflets were produced, and living quarters for Parham's family. There were fourteen rooms on the

---

104. S. Parham, *Life of Charles F. Parham*, 33. Sarah also said that when Charles began praying for people, "he did not personally know any one else who was preaching divine healing" (S. Parham, 33). That may be the way she remembered it, but it was obviously not the case. He had preached a joint meeting with Gourley a few months earlier.
105. The best work on Gourley is by James Goff Jr., although Goff was unaware of this early connection between Parham and Gourley. See James R. Goff Jr., "Thomas Hampton Gourley: Defining the Boundaries," in *Portraits of a Generation: Early Pentecostal Leaders*, ed. James R. Goff Jr. and Grant Wacker (Fayetteville, AR: University of Arkansas Press, 2002).
106. C. Parham, *Kol Kare Bomidbar*, 51–52.
107. *TAF*, May 17, 1899, 3, newspapers.com.
108. *The Topeka State Journal*, May 21, 1898, 7 (hereafter cited as *TSJ*), newspapers. com; *OEH*, June, 8 1898, 2, newspapers.com; "City News Briefs," *OEH*, May 9, 1898, 3, newspapers.com.
109. *TAF*, March 22, 1899, 3, 8, newspapers.com.
110. "Sunday at the Churches," *TSJ*, February 4, 1899, 7, newspapers.com; *TAF*, March 22, 1899, 8, newspapers.com.

second floor that served as classrooms and dormitories. The sick and diseased were welcomed to the home for rest, convalescence, and prayer.[111]

One of the guests at the home described her experience in this way:

> Surely it is none other than the House of God. Everything moves in love and harmony. On entering the rooms one is impressed with the divine influence shed abroad there. Here is a place where the sin-sick soul may come and be taught the way of salvation and a higher life; also where those who are sick may be taught that it is "God who healeth all our diseases and redeemeth our life from destruction. Psalm 103:3–4."[112]

On November 29, 1898, Sarah and Charles Parham had their second child and only daughter, Esther May. The children were affectionately called the "babes of Bethel."[113]

A weekly newspaper called the *Apostolic Faith* was first published by the ministry in March 1899. Apparently, the ministry press was not adequate, and the paper was printed by the *Kansas Farmer*. It contained sermons and articles by Parham and other prominent preachers. A key feature was testimonies of answers to prayer.

The original publisher was James A. Staples, a United Brethren pastor in Topeka. Staples, also a stenographer for the railroad, a printer, and a real-estate developer, preached in Baptist and Methodist churches in the area. Parham and Staples were both listed as editors of the publication. In May, after what may have been a conflict over changing the frequency of the newspaper, Parham became both publisher and editor.[114]

Parham held services several times a week and preached on various topics, including holiness, healing, Armageddon, and rescue work. Like

111. "The Work Here, *TAF*, March 30, 1899, 4, newspapers.com.

112. S. Parham, *Life of Charles F. Parham*, 42.

113. S. Parham, 44.

114. S. Parham, 39; *TAF*, March 22, 1899, 2, KHS; *TAF*, May 3, 1899, 2, KHS; "Queen Victoria's Descent from Adam," *TAF*, April 6, 1899, 6, newspapers.com; "In Society," *TSJ*, December 20, 1900, 5, newspapers.com; "Passing of Another Pioneer," *The Osage County Chronicle* (Kansas), October 28, 1915, 1, newspapers.com; "East Side," *TSJ*, January 6, 1907, 4, newspapers.com; "Local News," *The Oakdale Blade* (Kansas), December 13, 1907, 4, newspapers.com.

most congregations, Bethel had baptismal services and basket dinners. Parham also added programs for the poor and unemployed.[115]

On New Year's Eve 1899, Parham hosted a free dinner for the poor citizens of Topeka. Three hundred people were fed a delicious meal with beef and all the trimmings. The local newspaper reported, "No dollar nor ten dollar a plate banquet ever served in the Waldorf-Astoria was enjoyed by the banqueters as was the dinner."[116]

In March 1900, Parham began to call the work "Apostolic Congregation and Bethel Divine Healing Home." Two weeks after the name was changed, Parham ordained fourteen elders and deaconesses.[117]

Parham held a second dedication of the building in early April 1900. Evidently, the event celebrated the congregation's newly acquired ownership of the building, which had been donated by George Hamaker and his wife. Hamaker was a stenographer and clerk for the Atchison, Topeka and Santa Fe Railway. The Hamakers had deeded the property to the mission with this stipulation: "If division of church or if property is used for other than church purposes to be returned to first part or $5,000 and legal interest be paid."[118]

By now, Parham had reached a place in his ministry where he claimed he did not charge for anything and did not receive collections. Instead, he said he trusted God for all the resources with which to operate the ministry. When finances were needed, he prayed and trusted God to supply them. Although he was not always faithful to this principle, his life was filled with incredible testimonies of God's faithfulness to provide.

At the building dedication, Parham declared that the structure was being dedicated to the restoration of "Apostolic Faith and Power."[119] Soon,

115. "Sunday at the Churches," *TSJ*, March 11, 1899, 6; "Sunday at the Churches," *TSJ*, April 29, 1899, 4; "Sunday at the Churches," *TSJ*, June 3, 1899, 2; "Sunday at the Churches," *TSJ*, June 10, 1899, 8; "Sunday at the Churches," *TSJ*, December 9, 1899, 3; "Sunday at the Churches," *TSJ*, December 30, 1899, 2, newspapers.com.
116. "Food for All," *TAF*, January 1, 1900, 7, KHS.
117. "Sunday at the Churches," *TSJ*, September 30, 1899, 4; "Sunday at the Churches," *TSJ*, March 10, 1900, 16; "Sunday at the Churches," *TSJ*, November 25, 1899, 4, newpapers.com.
118. "Sunday at the Churches," *TSJ*, March 31, 1900, 4; "Real Estate Transfers," *TSJ*, April 7, 1900, 3; "Phillips Wants It," *TSJ*, December 2, 1904, 1; "Santa Fe Notes," *TSJ*, October 6, 1906, 8, newspapers.com.
119. "Sunday at the Churches," *TSJ*, March 31, 1900, 2, newspapers.com.

the words "Apostolic Faith" would be heralded from coast to coast and would become synonymous with the outpouring of the Holy Spirit.

During the late summer and early fall, Parham made a faith trip from Topeka to the state of Maine. Along the way, he preached in Muscatine and in Winnipeg, Alberta, Canada. Parham had left his home in Topeka with only five dollars, but he made the five-thousand-mile trip praying and believing that God would provide the necessary finances at every stop.

Wanting to "know more fully the latest truths restored by later day movements," he visited John Alexander Dowie's work in Chicago, J. Walter Malone's Quaker school in Cleveland, and A. B. Simpson's missionary ministry in New York. The primary purpose of his trip, however, was to spend time with Frank Sanford in Durham, Maine. Sanford had built a Bible school and a commune, both operating under the name "Shiloh."

Sanford had previously visited Topeka at Parham's invitation, but the Kansan wanted to see Sanford's Shiloh in person. Parham gleaned a great deal from Sanford and would pattern much of his future ministry after what he had seen in Maine.[120]

Parham had left two holiness preachers in charge of the healing home, but during his extended absence, they took control of the work, supplanting him. Ousted from the ministry, upon his return, he accused the perpetrators of "underhanded scheming and falsehoods." Parham and Hamaker also had a major disagreement, and the latter evicted Parham and what was left of his congregation. J. Nelson, a Bible worker from Kansas City, took over the work at Fourth and Jackson.[121]

In September 1900, what remained of Parham's Apostolic Faith ministry moved to a new location on the outskirts of Topeka. That physical move and the spiritual move that followed marked a paradigm shift in the history of the Christian church.

120. "He Got Money," *TSJ*, October 20, 1900, 14, newspapers.com; S. Parham, *Life of Charles F. Parham*, 48.
121. "Stone Mansion Leased," *TSJ*, September 27, 1900, 8; "Parham Leaves," *TSJ*, January 21, 1901, 7, newspapers.com; S. Parham, *Life of Charles F. Parham*, 48.

3

THE TOPEKA
OUTPOURING

Sitting just outside of Topeka, Stone's Mansion was an impressive sight. It was called one of the most beautiful mansions in the United States. One visitor said he had never entered a "grander palace built for private use."[122]

The elaborate house had been built by a wealthy Topekan, Erastus Stone. Stone was a developer and nursery owner. He made a small fortune in the Kansas real estate business and dreamed of having the most magnificent home in the state. He bought the property in 1870 and started building in 1888. The mansion was located on ten acres where Stone planted fruit trees.[123]

Stone spent thirty thousand dollars on the home, which had twenty to thirty rooms depending on differing accounts. The house was forty feet wide, seventy-five feet long, and eighty-seven feet high at its topmost point. The exterior walls were red brick, with white stone outlining the corners and windows. Beneath the massive three-story structure was a full basement with seven "well lighted cement rooms."[124]

---

122. C. Parham, *Everlasting Gospel* (Baxter Springs, KS: Apostolic Faith, n.d.), 110; Herbert Buffum and Lillie Buffum, "Warsaw, Mo," *NM*, July 18, 1901, 5, FPHC.
123. "Patents Signed by Grants," *TSJ*, July 1, 1922, 13, newspapers.com; John W. Ripley, *An Album of 19th Century Homes of Shawnee County* (Topeka, KS: Shawnee County Historical Society, 1974), 3.
124. John W. Ripley, "Erastus Stone's Dream Castle—Birthplace of Pentecostalism," *Shawnee County Historical Bulletin*, June 1975, 42–45; "Buys the 'Folly,'" *TSJ*, July 20, 1901, 8, newspapers.com; Charles Parham, "The Twenty Sixth Anniversary of the Outpouring of the Pentecostal or Latter Rain...," *TAF*, December 1926, 2–3, originalapostolicfaith.org.

The house was patterned after an English castle with spires and cupolas. The inside was even more elaborate. The rooms on the first two floors were all finished in different kinds of wood, including cherry, knotted pine, red cedar, magnolia, juniper, black walnut, and bird's-eye maple. No two rooms or hallways were finished in the same wood. The main parlor and staircases were decorated with carved cedars from Lebanon. The third floor was finished with normal plaster and paint, Stone having run out of money before he was able to finish the house as it was originally designed. A downturn in the economy had left Stone financially embarrassed. There are conflicting stories as to whether Stone ever actually lived in the house.[125]

The property had a colorful history. In 1889, Stone bartered his house to Amanda Rowlen for $47,000 and a ranch in Greeley County. The cash price alone would be nearly one and a half million dollars at today's values.[126]

Through a series of lawsuits, the mansion ended up in the hands of a wealthy New Mexico cattleman, Charles Gause. When Gause was an infant, he was given to a poor woman named Rebecca Herald, who raised him as her own son. Gause did not forget her kindness and gave the poor woman the mansion.[127]

After sitting vacant for a season, the building fell into disrepair, and local residents began referring to the structure as "Stone's Folly." In the summer of 1901, the property was back on the market with an asking price of only $8,000 for both house and land. Through a "mortgage," ownership fell to the American Sunday School Union.[128]

125. "Payne and Thompson," *TSJ*, July 6, 1901, 7, newspapers.com; "Snap Shots at Home News," *TSJ*, March 14, 1904, 7, newspapers.com; "New Religion 'Discovered' at 'Stone's Folly Near Topeka,'" *Kansas Farmer and Mail and Breeze* (Topeka), February 22, 1901, 4 (hereafter cited as *MB*), newspapers.com; Lillian Thistlethwaite, "The Wonderful History of the Latter Rain," in *Selected Sermons by the Late Charles F. Parham and Sarah E. Parham*, comp. Robert Parham (Baxter Springs, KS: Apostolic Faith, 1941), 81; Shumway, "Study of 'The Gift of Tongues,'" 164.

126. "The Stone Mansion Sold," *TSJ*, October 10, 1889, 1, newspapers.com; https://www.in2013dollars.com/us/inflation/1889?amount=47000 (April 15, 2022).

127. "In Her Big Mansion," *TSJ*, April 20, 1892, 5, newspapers.com.

128. "Folly Is Burned," *TSJ*, December 6, 1901, 4, newspapers.com. Almost all news accounts and histories say the building was owned by the American Bible Society, but the abstract on the property says it was the American Sunday School Union (Lee Desendorf, personal interview with the author, March 6, 2021, former site of Stone's Mansion, Topeka, Kansas. Desendorf is a Holy Spirit-baptized member of the Most Pure Heart of Mary Catholic Church, which now occupies the property, and a freelance researcher with a particular interest in the history of Stone's Mansion). The American Sunday School Union's ownership is confirmed in "Light Burns Night and Day," *The Kansas Weekly Capital*, January 1, 1901, 6 (hereafter cited as *KWC*), newspapers.com.

The grandiose old mansion was perfect for Parham's equally grand personality. He rented the building from the American Sunday School Union for sixteen dollars a month and opened a Bible school there on October 15, 1900. The school, known as the College of Bethel, was at least partly patterned after Shiloh. Parham charged neither tuition nor room and board. The school was for those who were willing to forsake all and trust God for everything.[129]

Students engaged in the normal household chores necessary to maintain a home, but none had outside employment. They felt that God was not dependent on salaries. They were more a commune than a student body. One outside observer noted that most of their support came from benefactors who were not enrolled in the school, but money was never solicited. This observer also said that the company "lived well" and were as "well dressed" as average people. Though not gaudy, their appearance was also not "plain."[130]

Another visitor to the school had a slightly different opinion of the appearance of the group:

> Parham and his wife, Miss Ozman and Miss Thistlethwaite are quite intelligent, they wear clothes which fit, and have the appearance of people who frequent the bath; but the others of the "family," as Parham calls them, are about as tacky a looking outfit as one would see in a trip around the world. They may be clean spiritually, but physically they are anything but shining marks of cleanliness.[131]

When the school was dedicated to God's work, Captain Leonard H. Tuttle was a special guest. Tuttle was a decorated Civil War hero and state-representative-turned-revival-preacher. While praying over the property, Tuttle saw a vision of "a vast lake of fresh water about to overflow, containing enough to satisfy every thirsty soul."[132] Surely, the vision was

129. C. Parham, *Kol Kare Bomidbar*, 75; Shumway, "A Critical History of Glossolalia," 166.

130. "History of the Apostolic Faith Movement," *The Apostolic Faith* (Goose Creek, Texas), May 1921, 3 (hereafter cited as *TAFGC*).

131. "Parham's New Religion Practiced at 'Stone's Folly,'" *The Kansas City Times*, January 27, 1901, n.p., clipped article (hereafter cited as *KCT*), FPHC.

132. Charles Parham, "Demonology, or In My Name Ye Shall Cast Out Devils," in *Selected Sermons by the Late Charles F. Parham and Sarah E. Parham*, comp. Robert Parham (Baxter Springs, KS: Apostolic Faith, 1941), 42; "Captain L. H. Tuttle," *LDW*, June 20, 1924, 8, newspapers.com.

from God as it prophesied the great overflowing of the Spirit that was soon to come.

About forty people gathered for the opening of the school. An observer described the makeup of the diverse group in this way:

> These comprise all ages; several families with small children being now there; indeed there are over a dozen children under thirteen years of age. Besides these, there are three quite old people, and several middle aged couples; the remaining being comparatively young people, ranging from sixteen to thirty years of age.[133]

John G. Lake, a long-term associate of Parham, said the students were mysteriously drawn to the mansion by visions and revelations. According to his account, this is one such story:

> A little Quaker lady came down the street, hesitated and looked around and said, "This is the house, but there is no one living there." After a struggle with her soul she went up and rang the door bell and the fist gentlemen [sic] answered the bell and asked what she wanted. She said: "I live over in the country at such a place, As [sic] I prayed, the Spirit told me to come here to this house." He said, "Who are you?" She replied, "Just an unknown Christian woman." He said: "What have you been praying about?" She said: "About the Baptism of the Holy Ghost."[134]

The students had no textbooks but studied only the Bible. They took turns ascending to the "prayer tower" so that prayers were offered twenty-four hours each day.[135] According to Parham:

> Our purpose in this Bible School was not to learn these things in our heads only but have everything in the scriptures wrought out in our hearts. And that every command that Jesus Christ gave should be literally obeyed.[136]

---

133. "The Pathological Conditions of the Bethel School at Topeka," *TAF* (Goose Creek, TX), May 1921, 3.
134. John G. Lake, "The Calling of the Soul," unpublished, 1917, FPHC.
135. Charles Parham, "The Twenty Sixth Anniversary of the Outpouring of the Pentecostal or Latter Rain…," *TAF*, December 1926, 3, originalapostolicfaith.org.
136. S. Parham, *Life of Charles F. Parham*, 51.

By late December, the students had studied "repentance, conversion, consecration, sanctification and the soon coming of the Lord." The last week of the month, Parham had appointments to preach in Kansas City and left the students with an assignment: they were called to a ten-day fast and were asked to stay in their rooms and avoid "all unnecessary social intercourse." They were to study the book of Acts in search of any biblical evidence of the baptism in the Holy Spirit. The students were forbidden to consult with one another. Every student was "to arrive at his conclusion alone."[137]

It is hard to discern what Parham's thoughts were on this subject. In a later version of the story, he said that he told the students he believed "that any missionary going to the foreign fields could and ought to be endowed with the power to speak in the languages of the natives."[138] That claim is missing in his earlier recollections, placing the discovery with the students.

Lillian Thistlethwaite said that Parham shared the various theories about the baptism in the Holy Spirit embraced by others. Some felt it referred to sanctification; others claimed there was no definite evidence of the baptism, while still others felt the baptism was manifested in demonstrations like shouting and jumping. He encouraged the students to "see if there is not some evidence given of the baptism so there may be no doubt on the subject."[139]

There is also a testimony from student Agnes N. Ozman that some months before December 31, Parham had told the students "there was a mighty out pouring of the Holy Spirit" for them. Ozman does not say if tongues were mentioned as part of that prophesied blessing.[140]

It is certain that Parham had given some thought to speaking in tongues. He had personally heard speaking in tongues at Shiloh.[141] Also, more than a year and a half earlier, in the May 3, 1899, edition of the *Apostolic Faith*, he had reported on a woman in Jerusalem who had been gifted to speak in an African dialect. He had closed the article by writing, "Glory to our God for the return of the apostolic faith."[142]

137. Shumway, "Study of 'The Gift of Tongues,'" 167.
138. "Twenty Sixth Anniversary of the Outpouring," 3.
139. Thistlethwaite, "The Wonderful History of the Latter Rain," 83.
140. Agnes N. Ozman, "Report and Testimony of Healing," *The Pentecostal Herald*, July 15, 1922, 4 (hereafter cited as *TPH*), ifphc.org.
141. Shumway, "Study of 'The Gift of Tongues,'" 165.
142. "The Gift of Tongues," *TAF*, May 3, 1899, 5, KHS.

After three days in Kansas City, Parham returned to the school on the morning of December 31. He gathered the students at ten o'clock in the morning to hear what their studies of Acts had produced.

Each student shared their individual conclusions and opinions. To Parham's surprise, everyone, though studying privately, had reached the same verdict—the "indisputable" fact of Scripture was that every person who received the baptism in the Holy Spirit had spoken in other tongues. Although there were different manifestations on different occasions, the one thing that every account had in common was the tongues speaking.[143]

Throughout the history of the Christian church, many people had experienced the phenomenon of tongues. Most saw the experience as just another manifestation, like falling, jumping, jerking, or shouting. No one had so clearly linked speaking in tongues with the Holy Spirit baptism. These students at the College of Bethel identified, defined, and sought tongues as the one and only necessary evidence of a biblical Spirit baptism. This "discovery" birthed a spirit of renewal in the Christian church that continues to this day.

The students spent much of New Year's Eve in prayer seeking the baptism in the Holy Spirit and the "accompanying sign." This time was described by one of the students as "a determined waiting on God and not taking 'no' for an answer."[144] Another said, "The presence and power of the Lord was there in a marked way."[145]

A group of female students ascended the four flights of stairs to the small prayer room. Agnes N. Ozman was among them.[146] Ozman was no spiritual novice. She was thirty years old and had attended a Bible school in St. Paul, Minnesota, led by T. C. Horton, as well as A. B. Simpson's school

---

143. S. Parham, *Life of Charles F. Parham*, 52; Shumway, "Study of 'The Gift of Tongues,'" 166.

144. Shumway, "Study of 'The Gift of Tongues,'" 167.

145. Agnes N. Ozman LaBerge, letter to E. N. Bell, February 28, 1922, FPHC.

146. Maude J. Neer, letter to J. O. Savelle, October 27, 1954, 2, FPHC. Maude Neer was part of the Stanley family mentioned later in this chapter. She was the daughter of Thomas Stanley. Maude is mentioned in several news articles and must have played a significant role. In this letter, written more than fifty years after the event, she is incorrect about some of the details, perhaps confusing the first time Ozman spoke in tongues with the baptism on New Year's Eve.

in New York.[147] Other students considered her "the spiritual leader of the school."[148]

That evening, about seventy-five seekers gathered in the chapel for a watch-night service. The students who had found proof of the biblical evidence were seeking a Holy Spirit baptism with the confirmation of speaking in tongues. This is a very important point. Many people have experienced an odd manifestation and then searched the Bible to find evidence of it. In contrast, these individuals searched the Scriptures, found the evidence, and then sought the biblical experience. This was not a spiritual phenomenon in search of biblical affirmation; this was biblical interpretation in search of a Holy Spirit encounter.

The service began at 7:15 p.m. Time was spent in testimonies and "earnest prayer for this baptism and sign."[149] It was an "especially spiritual" service.[150] Around midnight, Ozman asked Parham to lay his hands on her and pray that she might receive the Holy Spirit baptism as believers had in the Acts of the Apostles. Previously, while praying with two other girls, Ozman had spoken a few words in an unknown language. She did not understand the manifestation but said it was "a very precious and sacred experience" that she treasured in her heart. She wanted a fuller, undeniable experience of the baptism in the Holy Spirit, so she requested prayer.[151]

At first, Parham hesitated since he had not received this experience himself. However, after being pressed, he "humbly" prayed for Ozman. Parham had prayed about three dozen sentences when the glory of God fell on Ozman. He said that "a halo seemed to surround her head and face." She opened her mouth and began to speak a language she had never spoken before. Ozman was so overcome by the Spirit that she did not speak in

---

147. Agnes N. Ozman LaBerge, letter to E. N. Bell, February 28, 1922, FPHC. This author concedes that is impossible to know the exact time of this prayer and the subsequent Holy Spirit baptism. According to one account, Ozman said she received the Holy Spirit baptism on the evening of January 1. This does not seem possible since the event was connected to a watch-night New Year's Eve service. Parham and other witnesses variously say it happened before midnight on December 31, 1900, or after midnight on January 1, 1901. This author is satisfied to say it was "around midnight."
148. Maude J. Neer, letter to J. O. Savelle, 2.
149. Shumway, "Study of 'The Gift of Tongues,'" 167.
150. Thistlethwaite, "The Wonderful History of the Latter Rain," 83.
151. Agnes Ozman, "Where the Latter Rain First Fell: The First One to Speak in Tongues," *The Latter Rain Evangel*, January 1909, 2, ifphc.org.

English for three days. When she would try to write a note to communicate with her peers, she wrote in a script that was foreign to those around her.[152]

The Christian world changed the moment Agnes Ozman spoke in tongues. In a prayer room in a stately mansion in the very middle of America, a movement was born that would sweep millions into the kingdom of God. Few divine moments have had a greater impact on the church or the world.

In either an odd quirk of history or a heavenly providence, on January 1, 1901, a Topeka newspaper ran a large photograph of Stone's Mansion under the headline, "Light Burns Night and Day."[153] The newspaper reported that prayer was continually being offered in the tower of the mansion and that a light was always burning there. The subtitle read, "Beacon Always Shining from the Tower of Stone's Folly on Washburn Road." Stone's Folly no longer stands, but from that day until the present, the light of Pentecost has continued to burn night and day all across the globe. It will burn until Christ returns.

The entire school entered a period of seeking God. On New Year's Day, Parham called for a special season of prayer from nine in the morning until three in the afternoon, the same hours Jesus spent suffering on the cross.[154]

They removed the furniture from an upstairs room, and they all gathered there to earnestly pray. Their faith was high as they humbled themselves before God. Lillian Thistlethwaite said she had never felt "so little and so utterly nothing."[155] They believed that if God could give the baptism in the Holy Spirit to one of them, He could do it for all of them.

On January 2, Parham, Ozman, and some of the other students ministered at a mission in Topeka. Ozman prayed out loud in other tongues.

---

152. S. Parham, *Life of Charles F. Parham*, 52–53; Thistlethwaite, "The Wonderful History of the Latter Rain," 83–84; Charles F. Parham, "The Latter Rain," *TAF*, Dec–Jan 1951, 3. Parham claimed the writing was Chinese. Samples were published in newspapers that covered the historic revival.

153. "Light Burns Night and Day."

154. Thistlethwaite, "The Wonderful History of the Latter Rain," 84.

155. Thistlethwaite, 85. Lillian Thistlethwaite was Sarah Parham's older sister and one of their most loyal followers. Thistlethwaite never married but gave her entire life to gospel work.

A Bohemian at the mission overheard her and said she had spoken in his native tongue. The group was encouraged to know Agnes was speaking in an actual language.[156]

For three days and two nights, the members of the Bethel community continuously cried out to God. Desperate for revival, they hardly slept or ate. They prayed personally and corporately. Finally, they got past the pleading and begging and began to worship, sing, and patiently wait on God for the promise.

Parham preached at a Free Methodist church on the evening of January 3. When he returned to the school, he heard a wonderful sound coming from the second story where a prayer meeting was in progress. He pushed open the door and saw the room lighted with a "sheen of white light" brighter than the coal-oil lamps that illuminated the room.

Among the students were a dozen preachers of the gospel from different denominational backgrounds who were all speaking in tongues. Others, including Sarah Parham and Lillian Thistlethwaite, were also filled with the Holy Spirit. Lillian testified that she "never had such a hallowed joy, such a refined joy, or such an abundance of peace."[157]

Sarah had felt unworthy to receive God's blessings, but she had still sought Him with the rest. When she prayed, "Lord, I want all You have for me," the glory of God filled her soul. She repeated the prayer until her petitions transitioned into a language unknown to her. She was so marvelously filled that she spoke in tongues in her sleep that night.[158]

Some were standing, some kneeling, some sitting, some shaking, but all who received the Holy Spirit baptism were speaking in unknown languages. Mrs. Howard Stanley, one of the students, told Parham that moments before he arrived, flames of fire had been above their heads as on the day of Pentecost. A new Pentecost had come. God was visiting His people as in the New Testament.[159]

---

156. Ozman LaBerge, letter to Bell.
157. Thistlethwaite, "The Wonderful History of the Latter Rain," 86.
158. S. Parham, *Life of Charles F. Parham*, 69.
159. S. Parham, 53; C. Parham, *Kol Kare Bomidbar*, 34; Charles Parham, "The Latter Rain," in *Selected Sermons by the Late Charles F. Parham and Sarah E. Parham*, comp. Robert Parham (Baxter Springs, KS: Apostolic Faith, 1941), 77.

Finding a secret place behind a table, Parham began to rejoice at what his eyes had seen and his ears had heard. The worshippers in the room began to sing Charles Wesley's hymn "Jesus, Lover of My Soul" in multiple languages. Parham was overwhelmed. He asked God to give him the same Holy Spirit baptism with the evidence of tongues. Parham describes his experience:

> He distinctly made it clear to me that He raised me up and trained me to declare this mighty truth to the world, and if I was willing to stand for it, with all the persecutions, hardships, trials, slander, scandal that it would entail, He would give me the blessing. And I said "Lord I will, if You will just give me this blessing." Right then and there came a slight twist in my throat, a glory fell over me and I began to worship God in the Sweedish [sic] tongue, which later changed to other languages and did so until the morning.[160]

As soon as news of the revival began to spread, newspaper reporters from near and far gathered at Stone's Mansion to get the scoop for their readers back home. Newsmen from Topeka; Kansas City; St. Louis, Missouri; and Cincinnati, Ohio, covered the events.

Bold headlines like "A Queer Faith," "Hindoo and Zulu Both Are Represented at Bethel School," "New Religion 'Discovered' at 'Stone's Folly' Near Topeka," and "New Sect in Kansas Speaks with Strange Tongues" caught the public's attention. The stories themselves gave frightening descriptions of people "jabbering a strange gibberish." Readers were told by critics that the "whole of them are crazy."[161]

Papers from other cities picked up the story. Overnight, Parham had gone from obscurity to notoriety. Thousands read the story of the Topeka Pentecost and the young preacher who had introduced it to the world.

Over the next couple of weeks, more people connected with Bethel received the Holy Spirit baptism. Before the outpouring subsided, dozens

---

160. S. Parham, *Life of Charles F. Parham*, 54.
161. "A Queer Faith," *TC*, January 6, 1901, 2, newspapers.com; "Hindoo and Zulu Both Are Represented at Bethel School," *TSJ*, January 9, 1901, 6, newspapers.com; "New Religion 'Discovered' at 'Stone's Folly' Near Topeka," *Topeka Mail and Breeze*, February 22, 1901, 4, newspapers.com; "New Sect in Kansas Speaks with Strange Tongues," *St. Louis Post-Dispatch*, January 26, 1901, n.p., clipped article, FPHC.

were filled. In the Neer family, Joseph, Saphronia, and Edward received their baptisms. Many in the Stanley family were at the school, and most, if not all, received: Howard, George, Ida, Mattie, Maude, Thomas, Emma, and Edwin. Others who were there and most likely received were Frances Dobson, Mrs. S. E. Hackman, Ralph Herrill, Samuel Higgins, Albert Horr, Joseph Horr, Mattie Horr, Mrs. Ray A. McDowell, Luella Moore, Harley Short, Mabel Smith, Opal Stauffer, Lillian Stewart, Ann Strine, and George Thomas.[162]

Some of these men and women were never heard from again. Others became heralds of the Pentecostal message. Several became ministers with the Assemblies of God. Some joined other Pentecostal organizations. Regardless of their individual futures, their experience at Topeka changed the future for millions.

A seed of revival had been sown.

---

162. Larry Martin, *The Topeka Outpouring of 1901*, Special 100th Anniversary Edition (Joplin, MO: Christian Life Books, 2000), 34–43. The author searched all available accounts of the revival to gather the names of as many people as were known to be at Topeka.

4

RIDING THE WAVE

The significance of what happened in Topeka cannot be overstated. Charles Parham had caught a big wave and was riding high. He had long seen himself as transforming the Christian church, and now he had a prominent platform for it. He thought a band of tongues-speaking missionaries would soon circle the globe winning the masses, and he was going to lead the movement.

The first fractures in Pentecostal unity came within two weeks of the initial outpouring. Two of Parham's students left the school. S. J. Riggins was the first to leave. He was very negative about the goings-on at the school and called the group "crazy." Ralph Herrill, the second to leave, was much kinder and more discreet. He hesitated to criticize the school, saying he was better for the experience but did not believe the speaking in tongues was real.[163] An overwhelming majority of the students stayed with Parham.

Capitalizing on the notoriety from the Topeka revival, on January 21, Parham took a group of students to Kansas City for the beginning of a missionary trip that would supposedly lead them to all the "principal cities and towns in the east." The itinerary would also include ministry in Canada. In perhaps one of the worst predictions in human history, the *Topeka Daily Capital* wrote, "It is not improbable that Topeka has heard

---

163. "Row at Bethel," *TSJ*, January 7, 1901, 4; "Another Deserts," *TSJ*, January 1, 1901, 3, newspapers.com.

the last about the college and the strange 'gift' which its students were miraculously given."[164]

The group held street meetings, cottage meetings, and services in a local church. The papers carried reports of salvations, healings, and Holy Spirit baptisms with speaking in tongues. A woman who had been crippled for twenty-seven years reportedly threw away her crutches and walked home from the meeting. A gentleman said physicians had given him up to die, but when prayer was offered for his healing, he got up and walked ten miles.

For a grand finale, Parham rented the Kansas City Music Hall for a massive, all-day celebration. He called it an "old-fashioned love feast" and invited "the lame, the halt, the blind, the deaf, and those afflicted with all manner of diseases" to come and be healed. One Kansas City newspaper called Parham the "Topeka Wonder."[165]

By the middle of February, Parham and his band had returned to Topeka, his extended tour obviously canceled. His dreams, however, were not diminished. He reported that some of his followers were soon to depart for China and India, where they would test their gift of tongues as a tool for missionary preaching.[166]

In March, a terrible tragedy struck the Parham family. Charles and Sarah's infant son, named after Charles, contracted pneumonia. It is a difficult circumstance for any parent when their child is sick, but when you are preaching healing as strongly as Parham did, it is a real trial. On March 16, the child experienced convulsions and died, never reaching his first birthday. The loss was devastating to the young couple. Sarah admitted she had questions and struggles but simply said, "God had seen best to take him."[167]

164. "Missionary Work," *TC*, January 22, 1901, 6, newspapers.com.

165. "Was a Pentecost," *The Kansas City Journal*, January 22, 1901, 1 (hereafter cited as *KCJ*), newspapers.com; "Throws Away Crutches as Effect of Prayer," *KCT*, February 1, 1901, 2; "Story of His Belief," *KCT*, February 4, 1901, FPHC; "At Academy of Music," *TSJ*, February 2, 1901, 1, newspapers.com; "Strange Scenes at a Revival," *The Kansas City World*, February 1, 1901, 8, newspapers.com; "Parham Leaves," *TSJ*, January 21, 1901, 7, newspapers.com; "The Gift of Seven Tongues," *The Atchison Globe* (Kansas), February 1, 1901, 4, newspapers.com; "Gift of Tongues Is Theirs," newspaper clipping, source unknown.

166. "Parham and His Work," *TM*, February 28, 1901, 1, newspapers.com.

167. S. Parham, *Life of Charles F. Parham*, 77; "Brief Bits," *TM*, March 21, 1901, 8, newspapers.com.

The next stop for Parham and his team was nearby Lawrence, Kansas. Howard Stanley established a mission there, making it the second Pentecostal church in the world.[168]

In May, Parham and his team were back in Kansas City for meetings. Parham boasted that there were five hundred Apostolic Faith believers in Topeka and thousands in other parts of the United States and the world.[169]

Also in May, Parham set up a tent at Third and Jackson streets in Topeka for weekly services. In addition, he announced a weeks-long convention and missionary training school hosted at Stone's Mansion beginning June 10. The participants were expecting to witness "scenes similar to those at Jerusalem on the day of Pentecost." The meeting never happened, and it seems that some of the "new" was wearing off of Parham and his teaching. One writer sarcastically said, "Get the genuine: delays and substitutes are dangerous; there is only one Parham; none other just as good." Another writer described him as a humbug and a religious charlatan.[170]

Parham was visiting the little town of Potwin, Kansas, on July 23, 1901, when he collapsed, presumably from "heat prostration." The unconscious evangelist was carried back to Stone's Mansion, where the Bethel students prayed for him until he recovered.[171]

In July, Parham had to vacate Stone's Mansion when it was sold to Harry Croft, a notorious hoodlum. To garner favor, Croft had told the American Sunday School Union he would use the property for a chicken ranch. In what must have been the ultimate insult to the Pentecostals, Croft converted the once-hallowed property into a roadhouse. Sitting outside the city limits as it did, the building was beyond the jurisdiction of city police, making it a perfect location for Croft's illegal activities. Gambling, drinking, prostitution, and bootlegged whiskey replaced fasting, prayers,

---

168. "Pentecostal Pioneer Called to His Heavenly Reward," *TPE*, May 22, 1955, 15, ifphc. org; "A Great Worker," *Lawrence Weekly World* (Kansas), February 14, 1901, 5 (hereafter cited as *LWW*), newspapers.com.

169. "Parham in Kansas City," *TSJ*, May 16, 1901, 5; "New Kind of Missionaries," *Honolulu Hawaiian Gazette*, May 31, 1901, 8, newspapers.com.

170. "Strange Convention," *Biloxi Daily Herald*, June 12, 1901, 1; newspapers.com; "The Gift of Tongues," *The Anaconda Standard* (Montana), June 9, 1901, 20, newspapers.com; "In Church Circles," *TC*, June 16, 1901, 11, newspapers.com; "An Easy Way to Learn Languages," *The Boston Sacred Heart Review*, June 1, 1901, 9, newspaperarchive.com.

171. "Prayed Back to Life," *TSJ*, July 24, 1901, 4, newspapers.com.

and worship. Before the end of the year, the mansion was totally destroyed by fire.[172]

The loss of the building was another blow to Parham. The dwindling band of Apostolics were forced to find much less impressive quarters at 1403 West Tenth Street in Topeka. After the summer, Parham dropped out of the news. In August, his team held meetings in Lawrence. In September, he was still holding services on West Tenth Street. By December, he had moved to Kansas City. These were very trying times for him and his family. Friends, money, and even food were in short supply.[173] Sarah repined, "Only sorrow, suffering, persecution, and hardships seemed our lot. Friends forsook us, and we often didn't know where the next meal would come from."[174]

On January 1, 1901, when the revival had begun, Parham had dreams of traveling across America and around the world to spread the news of Pentecost. At the end of the year, it seems he had gotten no further than Kansas City, only fifty miles away. Much of Parham's time must have been spent on writing his first book, *Kol Kare Bomidbar: A Voice Crying in the Wilderness*, which he published in 1902.[175]

Early in 1902, Parham was back in the news when he announced he would lead an expedition to the Holy Land to retrieve the ark of the covenant and return it to Jerusalem. Parham claimed to hold an ancient Hebrew writing that told him the location of the ark and "almost absolute directions for finding it." The story of his purported adventure was carried in newspapers nationwide.[176]

---

172. Ripley, "Erastus Stone's Dream Castle," 42; "Buys the 'Folly,'" 8; "Dens of Vice," *TSJ*, August 16, 1901, 1, newspapers.com; "'Folly' Is Burned," *TSJ*, December 6, 1901, 4. The local newspapers do not mention prostitution, but local Pentecostal historian Lee Desendorf argues there is plenty of evidence that the tenants were practicing the "world's oldest profession" (Lee Desendorf, personal interview with the author). One author said the neighbors complained that "wine, women and song were on the tap nightly." See John W. Ripley and Robert W. Richmond, eds., *An Album of 19ᵗʰ Century Homes of Shawnee County* (Topeka, KS: Shawnee County Historical Society, 1974), 1.

173. "In Church Circles," *TC*, August 11, 1901, 8, newspapers.com; "In Church Circles," *TC*, September 29, 1901, 3, newspapers.com; "Snap Shots at Home News," *TSJ*, August 8, 1901, 8, newspapers.com; "The Last of Stone's Folly," *TC*, December 7, 1901, 3, newspapers.com; S. Parham, *Life of Charles F. Parham*, 81.

174. "In Loving Remembrance," 3.

175. *Kol Kare Bomidbar* is a rough Hebrew translation of the English "a voice crying in the wilderness." It should probably be *Kol Kore Bamidbar*, which literally translates as "a voice shouting in the desert." Parham felt that he was that voice.

176. "In Search of Holy Ark," *TSJ*, January 11, 1902, 1, newspapers.com.

Parham rented a storeroom in Kansas City and started another series of revival meetings. It was a long step down from the Kansas City Music Hall. An eyewitness described it as a "humble" place with frayed carpet on the makeshift platform. The room was decorated with texts from the Bible written in "big crooked letters" on wrapping paper. The evangelist said, "He [God] has ordered this meeting, but I don't know what He wants. I am here to do as the Lord leads. I know that He has called for a great revival that will sweep the world, and it is coming, but I do not know how soon—this meeting may be simply a little meeting or it may be the great one—I cannot say."[177] Much of the wind had gone from Parham's overinflated sails.

The College of Bethel opened its spring 1902 term on March 17 in Kansas City. The school was located at 305 East Eleventh Street. Parham said, "During the coming term greater miracles and gifts are expected to fall upon the student body than at any previous period of the school's history."[178] For the evangelist, it was just another wild prediction based on nothing but wishes and dreams. Unfortunately for Parham, the wishes vanished in the wind, and the dreams disappeared with the dawn. However, a little bundle of joy came in the midst of this dark season: a fourth child, Phillip A., was born to the beleaguered family on June 2, 1902.[179]

In June, Parham was preaching at the Oak Grove School House near Lawrence. Before the summer ended, he moved his family to Lawrence.[180] He seems to have been pretty quiet for much of the rest of the year, preaching in the area around Topeka and Kansas City.

However, before 1902 ended, the evangelist received some additional unwanted publicity. He had befriended a man named George A. Francis, president of the Francis Chemical Gold Company. Francis was an alchemist and claimed that God had given him the formula to make gold. Francis attended one of Parham's meetings and told the evangelist that if he would help him, a portion of his earnings would be designated to help the College of Bethel. This certainly seems like the kind of fairy

177. "Parham Begins Meeting," *TSJ*, February 10, 1902, 5, newspapers.com.
178. "From Parham's School," *TSJ*, March 12, 1902, 4, newspapers.com.
179. findagrave.com.
180. "Stony Point," *TJG*, June 19, 1902, 3, newspapers.com; S. Parham, *Life of Charles F. Parham*, 86.

tale Parham would wholeheartedly endorse. Sure enough, Parham became his "confidant and adviser." When something seems too good to be true, it usually is, and this most certainly was. Francis swindled a slew of investors and was arrested for "obtaining money under false pretenses." This was an unfortunate and embarrassing situation for Parham as he was subpoenaed to testify at Francis's trial.[181]

It was a long, dark night for the Parhams. The year 1903 started out tough as well. If it had not been for the preacher's persistence, the flame of Pentecost might have gone out. By then, most of Parham's team had scattered. The College of Bethel had disbanded. Parham preached in the same familiar places. This was not the great awakening for which he had hoped and prayed.

During the late spring, Parham received an invitation to preach in Nevada, Missouri, in the southwest corner of the state. A woman who had attended his meetings in Lawrence had started a mission in Nevada and requested his help. Apparently, Parham also intended to start a Bible school there. When the preacher left Lawrence, a newspaper reporter wrote a most flattering description of him:

> Rev. Parham is one of the brightest, best and squarest young men we have known. He is an indefatigable worker, and will doubtless make a success of his work.[182]

As summer approached, Parham turned his attention to nearby El Dorado Springs, Missouri. El Dorado Springs was one of several cities in the United States built around a natural mineral spring. Believing that there was some medicinal remedy there, hundreds of people came to drink from the spring or to bathe in the rejuvenating waters. A town where the infirm gathered was the perfect venue for a preacher who specialized in healing the sick.

Parham and his coworkers would stand by the spring and preach the gospel. Listeners were invited to a private home where they could receive prayer for healing. One person who listened attentively to the message was Mary Arthur from Galena, Kansas.

---

181. "Could Make Gold," *The Sedalia Democrat* (Missouri), November 7, 1902, 3, newspapers.com; "Alchemist in Prison," *The Wilkes-Barre Record*, November 6, 1902, 5, newspapers.com; "Parham in Trouble," *LWW*, October 30, 1902, 5, newspapers.com.
182. "Local Briefs," *TM*, May 14, 1903, 8, newspapers.com.

Arthur had a plethora of health issues, including painful indigestion for fourteen years. She also suffered from prolepsis, hemorrhoids, and bowel problems. Her main concern, however, was her eyes. She had been practically blind in one eye since birth and was losing her sight in the other eye. She wore two pairs of glasses, one over the other. Any direct exposure to sunlight was especially excruciating. Physicians employing medical quackery treated her by raising blisters on her temples and neck and behind her ears. The treatments had brought no improvement but instead had caused her to be in constant pain for five years.

The suffering lady had spent three summers at the springs but had received no relief. She had wanted to stay home during the summer of 1903, but her husband had insisted that she try one more time. She agreed to return just to satisfy his wishes.

When she arrived at the spring, she heard gospel singing and was drawn to the service. Parham preached and invited her to a cottage prayer meeting. She attended for a few days, and then, on August 17, she asked for prayer. Parham encouraged her to leave her glasses behind as a step of faith.

She left the glasses, but the bright light of the sun hurt her sensitive eyes, so she folded her handkerchief and put it over her eyes. Her young granddaughter was with her, leading her back to her room. On the way, the child left to buy some snacks but did not return in a timely manner. In order to find the wanderer, Arthur pulled the handkerchief from her eyes. She was shocked when she saw her granddaughter a half block away. Moreover, the light did not hurt her eyes. She was even able to look upward toward the sun without discomfort. She was healed. As she began to praise God, He spoke to her, "You are every whit whole." Every affliction in her body had been healed. Arthur said she felt "like a new person."

The healing of Mary Arthur marked a definite change in Parham's ministry. Arthur and her husband invited him to Galena. He preached in their home; he preached in the Methodist church; he secured a large tent; and, when that would not accommodate the crowds, he rented a storeroom that could seat two thousand people. The meetings continued for months. More than eight hundred people were saved, and hundreds were healed and baptized in the Holy Spirit. Revival had finally come.[183]

---

183. S. Parham, *Life of Charles F. Parham*, 89–90.

On one of the coldest days of the winter, Parham baptized almost one hundred people in the chilly Spring River. Among those baptized was new convert Howard Goss. As I mentioned in chapter 1, Goss became one of Parham's coworkers and later was instrumental in organizing the Assemblies of God and the United Pentecostal Church.

The Parhams moved to Baxter Springs, Kansas, in March 1904. Having lived in small, furnished rooms for a year, they were thrilled to move into a house furnished by adherents from the city. Except for short stays in different places across the nation, they would live in southeast Kansas for the rest of their lives. Sarah was especially pleased to be settled into a home because on March 16, 1904, she gave birth to "another brown-eyed boy," Wilfred Charles.

Parham preached several meetings in the area, resulting in more converts to the Apostolic Faith. It was previously noted that, in the little town of Keelville, Kansas, the world's first Pentecostal church edifice was built. The small building still serves a Pentecostal congregation today.

The next big revival was in nearby Joplin, Missouri, in the fall of 1904. Parham raised a tent at Fifteenth and Joplin streets. With winter approaching, after a month under the tent, he rented the Roosevelt Flats, and revival continued.

Parham was seriously hurt at the altar in Joplin when a large man slapped him across the back. This injury and the strain of constant meetings took a physical toll on him. He became so ill he couldn't eat for some time. Sarah said he went down "to the valley of the shadow of death."[184] He was so weak he could not conduct meetings, so people would come to his room where he would be "propped up in his bed," and he would preach to them. His followers thought he would die.[185]

While convalescing in Baxter Springs, Parham had a visit from Tom Alley. Alley had lived in Jerusalem and had brought back pictures and clothes that had been worn by the Palestinians. He would travel the country showing the photos and costumes. Getting up in years and wearied

---

184. S. Parham, 99–103.
185. "History of Pentecost," *The Faithful Standard*, July 1922, 7, pentecostalarchives.org; "A Letter," *TAFGC*, May 1921, 5. The author of this letter is unknown. It was written by "one of the workers in 1909 and [originally] published in the *Gospel of the Kingdom*."

from traveling, Alley sold the clothes to Parham, and the items became a regular feature of his rallies. In Joplin, over two thousand people gathered to see the display and hear Parham's Zionist lecture.[186]

One of the men who was baptized in the Holy Spirit at the Galena revival was businessman Walter Oyler. He became a regular helper in the revivalist's meetings. Oyler's home was Orchard, Texas. His brother-in-law was H. H. Aylor, also from Orchard. Aylor was a railroad commissioner and a man of influence. The gentlemen rejoiced at the revivals in Kansas and Missouri and longed to see a similar move in their home state. Aylor invited Parham to bring his team to Texas.

While still in very bad physical condition, Parham heard the voice of God saying, "Go to the South-land." When Parham arrived in Orchard, he was so sick he couldn't walk and had to be carried to the home of H. H. Aylor. But within a few hours of his arrival, he received a miraculous touch and "perfect health was again restored.[187]

On Easter Sunday 1905, Parham preached his first sermon in Orchard, and a tremendous revival resulted. Entire families were saved. In fact, almost the whole town was converted. Many people were healed and baptized in the Holy Spirit. People from as far as seventy miles away were bringing their sick loved ones to receive prayer. Parham testified that it was the "grandest scene" he had seen since the outpouring in Topeka.[188]

Etta Calhoun of Houston learned about the meetings and traveled by train from her home to Orchard. When she arrived, one of Parham's team members, Anna Hall, was preaching, and Calhoun received the baptism in the Holy Spirit. Years later, Calhoun would launch the Women's Missionary Council in the Assemblies of God. This ladies' auxiliary group served Pentecostal missionaries around the world.[189]

When Calhoun returned to Houston, she told her pastor, Warren Faye Carothers, about the revival. Carothers was the pastor of a church

---

186. S. Parham, *Life of Charles F. Parham*, 104–105. Zionism was a movement to return the Jewish people to their ancestral home and establish a Jewish nation. Parham believed Jesus would return to the earth after the Jews returned to Palestine.

187. "A Letter," 5.

188. S. Parham, *Life of Charles F. Parham*, 109.

189. Barbara Cavaness, "Spiritual Chain Reactions: Women Used of God," *Assemblies of God Heritage*, Winter 2005–06, 27, ifphc.org.

called Christian Witness. He was also an attorney and a man of prominence in Houston. Carothers invited Parham and his team to the city.

The evangelist returned to Baxter Springs in May and conducted several rallies in the area. All the while, he was gathering a team of workers to accompany him when he returned to Texas to further evangelize the Southland.

In Texas, the group first went to Orchard for a July 4 rally. A downpour canceled a planned barbecue, but nothing could dampen their enthusiasm. Twenty-five workers from Kansas, Missouri, and Texas joined hands to pray as they went forth "to lay siege to the city of Houston."

The team preached on the streets and went house-to-house spreading the gospel message. For special services, they rented Calcedonia Hall and then Bryan Hall. The buildings were packed to capacity. Revival came to Houston, and Parham was riding higher than ever.

A large tabernacle was built in Brunner, two miles west of Houston. In a rare description of an early Pentecostal tabernacle, a Galveston newspaper reported:

> The shed, for it is not much more, in which it all took place is about 70 by 120 feet. The covering rests on upright posts. Across the west side are nailed several twelve-inch planks with space of a few inches between them, a protection from the ground to the eaves of the shed. These planks back up to the rostrum or platform from which the preaching is done. The remainder of the wall is actually nothing but a couple of twelve inch plank to each side, except one. This one is the east side and is wide open for all to enter and depart at their own free will. The seats are twelve-inch benches without backs, with ends touching to reach across the tabernacle. The floor is covered with shavings and the lights are supplied by big oil torches.[190]

Workers went out to all the nearby towns in Harris and Fort Bend counties to preach the Pentecostal message. Everything that Parham had hoped for in Topeka was now being fulfilled as the Lord added daily to the Apostolic Faith.

---

190. "Apostolic Fervor," *Galveston Daily News*, August 23, 1906, n.p. (hereafter cited as GDN), digitalshowcase.oru.edu.

That summer, Parham returned to Kansas for a big camp meeting in Baxter Springs. After a week of camp, the team moved to Columbus, Kansas, for several weeks of meetings. Parham's focus, however, was on the grander possibilities waiting in the great state of Texas.

One of Parham's adherents in Houston was an African-American pastor, Lucy Farrar. Farrar had been born a slave and was the niece of abolitionist Frederick Douglass. Parham employed Farrar as a cook and a governess for his children, bringing her back to Kansas with him. While she was away from Houston, it was William Joseph Seymour who took care of her congregation.[191]

In September, Parham had a close call with violence in Pittsburg, Kansas. According to the local news, he used "offensive epithets" in referring to the women and schoolgirls in the small Eastern Kansas town. The newspaper suggested "a good coat of tar and feathers" could cure his "slandering proclivities."[192] However, the revivalist was able to move on to safer and greener pastures.

In mid-October, the team boarded a train for Houston. There, the revival services were once again packed to capacity. Parham rented a large home at 503 Rusk Street to house his family and serve as a headquarters for the growing movement.[193]

Parham also conducted a twelve-week Bible school at the residence. He and Warren F. Carothers taught forty students the tenets of the Apostolic Faith. There was no tuition, and room and board were free. A strict discipline was expected of the students, and "military rule" was exacted.[194]

I mentioned previously that among Parham's students in Houston was William Seymour. Seymour, originally from Centerville, Louisiana, and the son of former slaves, was reared in abject poverty, surrounded by the worst racial hatred. He left Louisiana for the North and found employment in Illinois, Indiana, and Ohio. He also found Christ as his Savior in Indianapolis. Stricken with smallpox and near death, he surrendered to

191. Larry Martin, *The Life and Ministry of William J. Seymour and a History of the Azusa Street Revival* (Duncan, OK: Christian Life Books, 1999), 89–90.
192. "Threaten Parson with Tar and Feathers," *Pittsburg Kansan*, September 28, 1905, 1, newspapers.com.
193. Martin, *Life and Ministry of William J. Seymour*, 91–94.
194. "A Letter," 5.

God to preach the gospel, a call he had resisted until his illness. A spiritual pilgrimage had brought him to Houston.[195]

Parham saw Seymour's potential, and the two would preach together. However, adhering to strict segregationist laws in Texas, Seymour would only preach to Black gatherings. At one such meeting, Neely Terry from Los Angeles heard Seymour and was impressed by his ministry. When she returned to Los Angeles, she urged her pastor, Julia Hutcheson, to invite Seymour to the West Coast.[196]

Seymour arrived in California on February 22, 1906, but his Pentecostal message was rejected by Hutcheson's Holiness congregation. Seymour then aligned himself with a cottage prayer group at the home of Richard and Ruth Asberry and sought God for revival. On April 9, revival broke out in the little house at 214 Bonnie Brae Street. Within days, the group relocated to an abandoned church building at 312 Azusa Street. The revival that followed was remarkable. Thousands were saved, healed, and baptized in the Holy Spirit. From Azusa Street, the Apostolic Faith message began to spread around the world. Even so, as previously noted, Seymour humbly submitted to Parham as the leader of the movement and his spiritual father.[197]

With the movement growing exponentially, Parham began to organize. He appointed directors for each of the states where the work was well established. Quite possibly, much of the structural framework was planned and implemented by Warren F. Carothers, an educated professional elevated by Parham to director for the burgeoning field of Texas. Upon his appointment as state director, Carothers wrote:

> I am praying for, and I call upon all Christians to pray for a state-wide revival of Holy Ghost religion, one that sweeps clear over church lines and involves all the preachers and people in one common medley of salvation; one that shakes the foundations of infidelity and sin from the head of the government down to the humblest citizen. I am not consecrated to the "Apostolic Faith

---

195. Martin, *Life and Ministry of William J. Seymour*, 31–80. A common misconception is that Seymour was in Houston looking for his long-lost parents or some other relatives. His father was deceased, and his mother was living near where he was born in Louisiana.
196. Martin, 131.
197. Martin, 139–160.

movement" but to God, and I look ten thousand miles above man-made lines in this prayer and in this work.[198]

Beginning in April, all ministers were required to have Apostolic Faith credentials signed by Parham and the respective state directors. This was a huge step forward for the fledgling fellowship of churches and preachers. Seymour was among those who wrote and asked for credentials. Parham justified this obvious step toward organizing by reporting, "Many unscrupulous persons have palmed themselves off as our assistants simply to gain favor owing to the reputation the movement has obtained."[199]

Parham also began to set churches in order as part of his new structure. For the purpose of "strip[ping] it of all denominational semblance," he referred to the houses of worship as "Assembly Meetings" and compared them to "Old Methodist 'class meetings.'" Rules were established for the conduct of the Assemblies. They were to have a preacher and elders with well-defined qualifications and duties, a set place for meeting, and established weekly times for meetings. Despite his protestations to the contrary, Parham was well on his way to establishing a new denomination.[200]

As the revival in California was getting its wings, Parham's interest was in other fields of labor. He held a farewell rally for his troops in Texas on April 24 and headed on an "extensive tour of the North and of Canada." In actuality, it took him back to friendly territory around his home in Kansas.[201]

The evangelist stayed in Kansas for several months, holding services in most of the towns where he had had successful ministry. The family temporarily relocated to a home in Keelville, and Sarah gave birth to their fifth child, Robert Lee, on June 1, 1906.[202]

In a sermon in Topeka on July 29, Parham blamed the San Francisco earthquake on the devil, declaring that God had lifted His hand of protection from the city "because of its wickedness." Parham also issued several specific prophecies. He said that "the next governor of Kansas

198. "The Texas Work," *TAF*, March 1906, 7, Pauline Parham Collection, Holy Spirit Research Center, Oral Roberts University, Tulsa, OK (hereafter cited as HSRC).
199. *TAF*, March 1906, 4, HSRC.
200. "Assembly Meetings," *TAF*, March 1906, 7, HSRC.
201. "A Farewell Sermon," *THP*, April 20, 1906, 11, newspapers.com.
202. S. Parham, *Life of Charles F. Parham*, 147.

would be W. A. Harris and the next President of the United States Teddy Roosevelt." He also said there would be a great conflict between capital and labor similar to the "French revolution" and that Roosevelt would "assume dictatorship." Instead, Edward W. Hoch was reelected governor in 1906 and William H. Taft was elected president in 1908. There was no revolt, and, today, Roosevelt may be best known for inspiring the creation of the "teddy bear" rather than for being a dictator. It is fair to say that Parham was not a prophet.[203]

At another meeting in Topeka, Parham announced that his sermon topic would be "Where Did Cain Get His Wife?" He said his dissertation would carry the audience "in transcendent thought from the birth throes of creation through the noon of the world's night to the burst of immortal dawn." And that was just the morning service. Parham had his swagger back.

The evangelist was against drinking alcohol but was also against prohibition and the temperance movement, which he thought existed only to provide salaries for its leaders. Not surprisingly, Parham had a better idea. He always had a better idea. He suggested to a Topeka news reporter that all taxes on alcohol and all liquor licenses should be eliminated. He postulated that if everyone could make their own brew, alcohol would become so inexpensive that all saloons would be forced out of business. Once everyone was drinking their own homemade liquor, Christian influence would gradually wipe out the evil and bring "all to a higher plane of living." Some may have thought the scheme was a bit naïve, but Parham was convinced his idea would work. But again, he was always convinced his ideas would work.[204]

In August 1906, Parham returned to Texas. He saw tremendous results as he preached in more than a dozen cities. A three-week campaign was held under the tabernacle in Brunner. A reporter shared vivid images of the emotion that characterized early Pentecostal meetings:

Weeping, shouting, wailing, moaning, preaching, singly and collectively, but never in harmony…these manifestations take the form of shouts, exclamations, swinging the arms in the air, contorting

203. "Blame the Devil," *The Topeka Daily Herald*, July 30, 1906, 5, newspapers.com.
204. "He Has a New Way," *TSJ*, July 26, 1906, 10, newspapers.com.

the fingers as the dumb do, but even more rapidly, when talking…eyes closed, face upturned toward the lights, fingers, hands and arms in motion all the time, the tongue moving like an electric fan at full speed…the overwhelming force of this religion seems to take a man off his feet at times.… Toward the close they seat themselves among the shavings on the floor, throwing their arms across a long bench and resting their heads upon it. As soon as the incompetent person takes this position the workers gather around and do the laying on of hands, talking all the while in English, or "unknown tongue."[205]

The results in Brunner were phenomenal. Thousands attended, and many were saved, healed, and baptized in the Holy Spirit. On August 26, forty-four converts were baptized in White Oak Bayou. More than two thousand people attended the baptism.[206]

Parham returned to Baxter Springs in September for a camp meeting. He would continue to host the event intermittently over the next two decades. Seymour had been inviting him to California to witness the momentum there, but Parham didn't seem to understand the growing impact of the revival on Azusa Street. Perhaps it was because he underestimated Seymour; or, maybe he simply couldn't imagine the work prospering without his direct leadership. Whatever the reason, his neglect of the California field was a strategic error.[207]

While at the Baxter Springs meeting, Parham obeyed a "call" to go to Zion City, Illinois. Zion was a utopian city founded by Scottish-Australian healing evangelist John Alexander Dowie. Dowie's experiment with an ideal society in an ideal community was falling apart. Dowie was in mental and physical decline and had lost most of the control of the city to one of his subordinates, Wilbur Glenn Voliva.

From a natural perspective, the turmoil in Zion seemed like a great opportunity for Parham to establish a foothold there. Many other groups, including the Mormons and the Adventists, were making a play for

205. "Apostolic Fervor."
206. "Apostolic Faith Movement," *THP*, August 21, 1906, 7; "Thousands at Baptism," *THP*, August 27, 1906, 7, texashistory.unt.edu.
207. S. Parham, *Life of Charles F. Parham*, 155.

dominance in the chaos. From Parham's "spiritual" vantage point, God had called him to save Zion from destruction. "I will bring you out of all your difficulties if you will trust in me," he told the Zionists. The call was as dramatic and contradictory as Parham himself.

According to one version of the call, God spoke to Parham as early as May, showed him a vision of the city, and spoke clearly, "Arise and go to Zion and take up the burden of an oppressed people." In another version, Parham suffered from a "desperate" headache for many days and asked God to remove the headache if He wanted him to go to Zion. The headache disappeared "at once." Parham said that the next day, he received an invitation to preach in Zion as well as a letter with the necessary travel funds. Later in the year, he gave yet another version, saying the call came at the Baxter Springs camp meeting.[208] Whatever the reason or however the call, he headed to Zion City.

Zion being a closed city,[209] Parham could not find a meeting place, so he held meetings in a hotel room and in private homes. Almost immediately, he gained a following. F. (Fred) F. Bosworth literally converted his home into "a meeting house." Some of Zion's most prominent citizens accepted the Pentecostal message and were baptized in the Holy Spirit."[210]

Parham informed the good citizens of Zion that his work was "entirely in the spiritual interest of the city." After only a few days, he announced he would win "the entire population" in a matter of days. When Voliva sent a message asking how long the evangelist was going to stay in the city, Parham responded "'till Kingdom come."[211] Neither prediction proved to be true. Voliva declared an all-out war against Parham and his converts, and he proved to be a vicious and ruthless foe, stopping at almost nothing to destroy Parham's influence in Zion City. The ongoing conflict between the two will be discussed further in a later chapter.

---

208. "Rev. Parham's Last Vision," *Galena Evening Times* (Kansas), October 6, 1906, 4 (hereafter cited as *GET*), newspapers.com; "Zion Has a New 'Leader,'" *Los Angeles Times*, September 27, 1906, 118, newspapers.com.

209. Dowie was a theocrat, and the city was closed to any churches or religions outside his Christian Catholic Apostolic Church. He was able to enforce this proprietary arrangement because he owned everything in Zion.

210. S. Parham, *Life of Charles F. Parham*, 156.

211. "New Prophets Flock to Zion," *MNT*, September 28, 1906, 1, newspapers.com.

In a move that he had to know would further agitate Voliva, Parham took Dowie's side in the Zion rift. Parham complimented Dowie on the work he had done. While he acknowledged Dowie was "not in his right mind," he knew that if the declining leader could only be placed under his care, he would soon be "restored to his former self."

In response, Voliva called a special meeting and told the people, "You must choose either me or this intruder who has stolen into our church." He threatened that anyone who attended Parham's meetings would face expulsion from the city. He further ordered Parham to leave Zion City.[212]

Parham left with the promise that he would return before the year's end and host a huge Apostolic Faith convention that would be attended by his followers from across the country.[213] Like so many of Parham's dreams, the convention never happened, although the evangelist did return to Zion in December.

In a few months, Parham had made significant, almost astonishing, inroads into Zion City. Although he had failed to gain leadership over the city's government or church, he had succeeded in bringing hundreds into the Pentecostal movement. Many of the greatest leaders of early Pentecostalism came out of Zion: John G. Lake, F. F. Bosworth, John C. Sinclair, William Piper, Marie Burgess, and many, many others. According to Parham, in 1925, more than five hundred workers were in the field as a result of the meetings in Zion.[214]

No longer welcome in Zion, Parham decided it was time to visit the Pacific Coast and take leadership of the Azusa Street revival. Once again, God spoke to him and said, "Go to California."[215]

With the Pentecostal movement expanding literally every day, it looked as if Parham was on a trajectory that would take him to the pinnacle of fame. He turned thirty-three years of age in 1906 and was at the top of his

212. S. Parham, *Life of Charles F. Parham*, 167; "Invader Splitting Zion," *The San Antonio Daily Express*, October 4, 1906, 7 (hereafter cited as *SAE*), newspapers.com; "New Prophet in Zion," *The Wichita Beacon* (Kansas), October 20, 1906, 4 newspapers.com; "Ejected from Zion," *Independence Daily Reporter* (Kansas), November 6, 1906, 1, newspapers.com.
213. "Changes His Base," *TSJ*, November 17, 1906, 7, newspapers.com.
214. Charles Parham, "The Commandments of Jesus," *TAF*, May 1925, 5, originalapostolicfaith.org.
215. S. Parham, *Life of Charles F. Parham*, 168.

game. Could he be the next Luther, Finney, or Moody? It appeared he had everything going for him, but in actuality he didn't. He was truly riding a great wave, but trouble was brewing just beneath the surface of his sea of success. To borrow a surfing term, he was headed for a serious wipeout.

In the fall of 1906, the movement had been growing exponentially. The troops had been marching in solidarity, and Parham had unquestionably been leading the parade. Yet, by year's end, cracks had begun to appear in the unity of the movement. Within a year, fissures would become ruptures. Parham's leadership would be questioned and even rejected.

Still, 1906 was Parham's best year—by far. His ministry peaked at that point and then began a continuous decline. Parham blamed everyone but himself for his troubles, but he was wrong in his assessment of the situation. He was the reason for most of his problems. Part of the trouble was simply the man himself—his peculiarities and negative personality traits. Even greater complications arose because of what he believed and, more sadly, because of the things he did. Almost one hundred years after his death, some people are so focused on his weaknesses that they struggle to see any good that he did.

Parham's story cannot be divorced from his weaknesses and failures. As emphasized earlier, an honest accounting demands that the darker side of his life must also be explored. Later chapters will uncover many of those unpleasant details. But first we will continue to review his successes and the positive aspects of his life, particularly the remarkable miracles and divine healing that occurred throughout his ministry.

5

MIRACLES AND DIVINE HEALING

Charles Parham had a deep conviction that prayer and faith would heal the sick. Throughout his life and ministry, he never wavered from that belief. Even before the Pentecostal outpouring in Topeka, Parham advertised a ministry of divine healing.[216]

Parham was called a "divine healer," but he argued that one who prayed for the sick was no more a healer than one who prayed for a person to be saved from their sins was a savior. Parham said, "It is God who does the work in both instances, in answer to prayer."[217] Parham never claimed to have a "gift of healing," even though dramatic healing regularly accompanied his ministry.

According to his wife, Parham first prayed for the sick in his public meetings in Ottawa, Kansas, in late 1897 or early 1898. "Many" had been previously healed in answer to Parham's prayers, but only in private settings. Sarah said he "boldly" preached that Christ was a healer.[218]

---

216. As early as August 1898, Parham was advertising divine healing meetings. (See *MB*, August 5, 1898, 6, newspapers.com. The first known copy of the *Apostolic Faith* is vol. 1, no. 3, published on March 22, 1899 (see newspapers.com). In that issue, the front page contains an article on divine healing, divine healing is listed as a doctrine of Parham's Beth-el mission, and a divine healing service was conducted on Sunday afternoons.

217. "The Doctrine," *TAF*, May 3, 1899, 4, newspapers.com.

218. S. Parham, *Life of Charles F. Parham*, 33.

The results in Ottawa were amazing. This is just one of many testimonies from the meetings:

> Mrs. Ella Cook, of Ottawa, Kansas, was healed of dropsy.[219] She had been given up by physicians with only a possibility of living three days. She was carried upstairs into our meetings, in the old Salvation Army Hall. When prayer was offered the disease was instantly killed so that she fell to the floor as one dead, or like one from whom the fever had just left. The audience arose as a mob to punish us for her seeming death. Mr. Parham stepped beside her body and ordered the people to stand in their places as she was not dead, as a few minutes would prove. In a few moments she opened her eyes, smiled and we assisted her to her feet. She not only walked down the stairs alone, but walked for over a mile to her home, shouting and praising the Lord; people along the way followed to see what would take place. Neighbors came running in and until three o'clock in the morning people were getting to God and others were wonderfully healed. Her recovery was complete.[220]

Parham did not endorse the use of doctors and medicines but believed that Christians should trust God alone for their healing. Some of his theology and biblical exegesis may have been shaky, but his faith in the power of God to heal was rock-solid.[221]

In every season of Parham's ministry, people received miraculous healings following his prayers. In the earliest years, the *Apostolic Faith* newspaper regularly contained testimonies from those who were healed. The following represent some of the earliest healings as reported by the recipients and recorded by the evangelist:

> My daughter, 17 years of age, was dangerously sick with heart trouble in March, '98; was in paroxysms of suffering all night; was unable to move or turn over without throwing her in a spasm of

---

219. "Dropsy" is an antiquated term for a medical condition now known as edema. It is characterized by a buildup of fluid in the soft tissues of the body brought about by congestive heart failure. See "Medical Definition of Dropsy," medical ed. J. W. Marks, M.D., reviewed June 3, 2021, medicinenet.com/dropsy/definition.htm.

220. S. Parham, *Life of Charles F. Parham*, 33–34.

221. See chapter 7 of this book for Parham's theology of healing.

pain. The doctor gave me certain signs that would precede the final struggle. The signs developed and we sent for Bro. Parham. She was gasping in the agonies of death when he entered the room. Her death was but a question of a few seconds, had she not been anointed in the name of Jesus. The prayer of faith saved her and the Lord raised her up. (James 5th chapter.) She was suffering so with pain about her heart she could hardly whisper. She at once got up, dressed, ate breakfast and went to school, and has had no return of the disease since. (Mrs. J. A. Grove, Massasoit Street, Ottawa, Kan.)[222]

I had been also troubled with catarrh for twelve years.[223] I heard Brother Parham tell of God's wonderful power to heal, and on the 20th day of last March the Lord graciously healed me. Since that time I have enjoyed good health, life, joy and peace in the Holy Ghost.[224]

I lost my hearing so that I could scarcely understand a sermon unless I sat close to the minister. I was baptized the 30th of April by Bro. Parham and another brother. I had only come out of the water when I felt a queer sensation ringing in my deaf ear. Inside of two hours I heard Bro. Parham preach at the mission; it was the first sermon I had heard distinctly for 35 years. Thank God for his healing power. (Maggie Gosney, Desoto, Kansas).[225]

I want to praise the Lord for his wonderful love and mercy to me, [sic] For about three months last summer my baby had chills and fever almost every day, and would lie for hours in a stupor apparently lifeless. We did everything possible, had the best doctors in town, but he got no better, and we had about given up hopes of his recovery when as a last resort we took it to the Lord in prayer.

---

222. "Healed When Dying," *TAF*, August 1905, n.p., originalapostolicfaith.org; *TAF*, March 22, 1899, 5, newspapers.com.
223. "Catarrh," or "catarrah," is a buildup of mucus in the back of the nose, the throat, or the sinuses. It can be characterized by cough, fever, and excessive secretions. See Amanda Barrell, "What Is Catarrah?" June 11, 2020, medically reviewed by Cynthia Taylor Chavoustie, MPAS, PA-C, https://www.medicalnewstoday.com/articles/catarrh; Sylvain Cazalet, "Catarrh," Old Disease Names, http://www.homeoint.org/cazalet/oldnames.htm.
224. *TAF*, March 30, 1899, 7, newspapers.com.
225. *TAF*, May 23, 1899, 7, newspapers.com.

Bro. Parham prayed for him, and he never had another chill from that day, and now is a strong healthy baby, for which I give God all the praise. (Mattie L. Slausen, 1016 North Jackson Street, North Topeka, Kansas)[226]

Our little daughter was wonderfully healed through prayer by Bro. Parham. She had catarrh, which affected her lungs, also an enlargement of her tonsils, nearly choking her at times; her bowels had been so badly diseased that for two years scarcely a day passed without a cathartic,[227] and then nothing seemed to help her, and a passage seemed impossible. Two days after she was prayed for about two dozen small tumors passed from her; they seemed to come off like you would shell corn. (Mrs. L. A. Lucas, Morris Avenue, Lowman Hill, Topeka, Kansas)[228]

Probably the most consequential miracle in Parham's ministry was the healing of Mary Arthur from Galena, Kansas. Arthur's testimony is related in chapter 4 of this book. Her healing led to the great revival in Galena, as well as the spread of the Pentecostal movement to Texas and eventually to the world. A number of significant miracles were reported during that season. The following is one example:

Getting up at the usual hour, I was taken deathly sick I managed to get down stairs. I thought that my time was almost run. My husband laid hands on me and prayed. I wanted a doctor. My husband said he would get Bro. Parham to come and pray for me. My husband prayed for me again. Bro. Parham laid hands on me and prayed for me. I felt somewhat better at the time he left. I asked him to pray for me again at 12 o'clock; he said he would. At the hour set for prayer my husband came and laid his hands on my neck and side, which felt almost paralyzed. We prayed. God healed me then and there, soul and body. (Mrs. Jennie Wells, 421 Lake Street, Topeka, Kansas).[229]

---

226. *TAF*, May 3, 1899, 8, newspapers.com.
227. A "cathartic" is a laxative. See Merriam-Webster.com Dictionary, s.v. "cathartic," https://www.merriam-webster.com/dictionary/cathartic.
228. *TAF*, July 12, 1899, 7, newspapers.com.
229. "Spinal Meningitis," *TAF*, August 1905, n.p., originalapostolicfaith.org.

Not only was Parham seeing answers to his prayers, but he was also sending out disciples preaching the doctrines of the Apostolic Faith. Below are excerpts from the testimony of Theophilus W. and Annie E. Oyler. The Oylers became faithful followers of Parham and were partially responsible for his invitation to take the message to Texas.[230]

> My husband's health began to fail, and for two years he gradually grew worse. The Dr. in charge said that he was a very sick man.... Dr. Smith who had the case in charge, examined my husband, and found that he had cancer of the stomach, floating kidney, sciatic rheumatism and heart trouble....
>
> My husband often spoke of dying....
>
> Then we felt in our heart to have prayer meetings in our home, and the Lord wonderfully blessed the meetings and we soon heard of a man in Webb City holding a meeting and praying for the sick, and he also spake in tongues.... This minister had attended some of Bro Parham's meetings and he came to our cottage prayer meetings and we found that he had got the light of the "baptism," and Divine healing through Bro Parham....
>
> ...One night at our home, when the sick were being prayed for, my husband and I went down before the Lord for healing.... When the Saints laid hands on us, anointing us with oil in the name of the Lord, and prayer was offered to God, we were healed.... My husband's kidney trouble, sciatic rheumatism and heart trouble was healed; and he was prayed for several times after, and in a month the cancer of the stomach was gone.[231]

Not only was Parham commissioning ambassadors to pray for the sick, but he was also mailing handkerchiefs to infirm individuals who requested them. Parham wrote, "We bless hundreds of handkerchiefs continuously and mail them out to all parts of the world."[232] The idea of praying over a cloth is taken from the New Testament account of believers taking pieces

---

230. Annie Oyler was the sister of Henry Aylor, who brought Parham to Orchard, Texas. As the revival grew at Azusa Street in Los Angeles, the Oylers traveled to California to help give oversight.
231. *TGK*, n.d., 6, ifphc.org (document 2 of non-dated issues).
232. *TAF*, April 1927, 4, originalapostolicfaith.org.

of clothing worn by the apostle Paul, who had been performing miracles, and sending them to the sick so they would be cured.[233] Here is just one testimony of a person healed by a prayer cloth through Parham's ministry:

> About five years ago I became convinced that Jesus Christ died on the cross just as much for the healing of our bodies as He did for our salvation. I threw away all the medicine I had in the house and have taken Him as our Physician, and He has proven a wonderful Physician in every case.
>
> I suffered some terrible attacks of gall stones, and believing the doctors could not heal them, I turned the case over to the Lord. The last attack came this summer. My side was so sore I could scarcely walk or turn over in bed. I wrote Bro. Parham for an annointed [sic] kerchief which I applied with prayer for my healing. Although I had more pain all that night than I had been having, I trusted and praised His name. The next morning the pain and soreness were all gone. (Mrs. Ira B. Watson)[234]

As time passed, the paper contained fewer individual testimonies than general reports of the meetings of Parham and others. However, healings remained an important feature of Parham's ministry. As his travels carried him from one end of the nation to the other, miracles continued to occur. This testimony came from the West Coast in 1912:

> With thanksgiving and praise to God I give my testimony of victory through the precious blood and broken body of our Lord, trusting it may help and comfort some weary suffering one. Some fifteen years ago I turned from earthly physicians to the Lord when all earthly help had failed. The Lord healed me many times of many diseases, yet one terrible trouble remained (tumor of the bladder). It had been cut out and burned out by doctors and surgeons. Last time operated on was twenty-three years ago. When Bro. Parham called the fast for ten days for any thing we desired to be wrought out in our lives, I entered in, spirit, soul and body. I wanted healing and all God had for me to get me ready to meet The King

---

233. See Acts 19:11–12.
234. *TAF*, January 1929, 15, originalapostolicfaith.org.

in His glory. Glory to God! I was not disappointed in my healing. The third day of the fast He healed me wonderfully. O! how I praise Him! And that is not all. My soul is filled day and night as never before. Joy bells are ringing continually, because he has done so much for me. Now my faith looks up to Him for still greater blessings. O! how I praise God that He ever sent Bro. Parham to California to teach us this gospel of the Kingdom. (Mrs. S. Finney, 223 E 61st Street, Los Angeles)[235]

The April 1914 edition of the *Apostolic Faith* featured an article about a meeting in Webb City, Missouri. The dispatch contained this brief but remarkable report:

Among the notable healings, a few only can be mentioned. The sick came from a radius of 200 miles and miracles were almost a daily occurence [*sic*].

A lady was healed from consumption in the last stages.

A young man from seven years of epilepsy.

A young lady of two years blindness in one eye.

A school teacher of a withered hand.

A drummer of Bright's Disease.[236]

Such results were the norm in Parham's meetings. In the last five years of his ministry, the *Apostolic Faith* added more healing testimonies to its reports. The following are a few of the glowing accounts from across the United States:

Among the wonderful Healings in New York I mention three. A lady whose left ear was affected by a cancerous condition, losing her hearing. The ear drum was completely healed so that a new ear drum was formed, hears perfectly. A man stone deaf has been healed till he can hear the quietest conversation. A woman who had been in bed two months was healed, got up and come to the meetings and has been coming ever since. She was given up by

235. *TAF*, May 1912, 5, originalapostolicfaith.org.
236. "Locals," *TAF*, April 1914, 9, originalapostolicfaith.org.

the doctors but now does all her own work and is rejoicing also in salvation.[237]

He has healed me when I was sick and saved my life three times.

The Lord healed me when I was taken seriously ill with severe cramps in my limbs, I could not sit up or lie down, I never thought any one could live in such pain.

About nine o'clock that night my wife sent my son to Corona, a near by town where Brother Parham was holding meetings and about the time they prayed I was completely delivered and went to bed and rested well. Praise the Lord for his wonderful healing power. (Wm. H. Creswell).[238]

For about 20 years I was a wretched, miserable sufferer with little hopes of ever finding relief. For like the woman mentioned in the Bible who had an issue of blood. [sic] I sought to many physicians and spent hundreds of dollars, but grew no better, at times I was able to drag around and attend to my household duties. But most of the time I was far from able to do anything and was never free from pain. At times, too my mind refused to work, and a great fear of insanity came upon me, so that I would cry unto God, Oh, don't let me loose [sic] my mind. I often wished for death to end all my suffering.

I was a strong Luthern [sic]. Yet in my heart I longed for a closer walk with God. One day, about four years ago while in Cheney, Kans., I saw a large tent and as I passed by I read: Hear Chas. F. Parham, Old time Salvation and Healing for the body. I said, that sounds good I believe I'll go in. The sermon impressed me as the most powerful one I had ever heard and as the minister emphasized the fact of an experience for everyone, witnessed to by the Holy Spirit, a freedom from sin…and oh, how I needed healing! So when the call was made for those who were sick to be prayed for, according to Jam. 5–14 I went forward, and when the man of

---

237. Charles F. Parham, "Miracles in New York," *TAF*, March 1927, 19, originalapostolicfaith.org.
238. *TAF*, November 1927, 13, originalapostolicfaith.org.

God laid hands on my head and in a few words prayed for me. [*sic*] I felt the healing touch of God. But was not perfectly healed at that time. I prayed nearly all that night, and never before had I felt the reality of God as on that blessed night. At the next meeting I went forward again, and praise His Holy Name I felt the healing touch go through and through my whole body and was wonderfully healed from the crown of my head to the soles of my feet. (Mrs. Philip Stoehr, Cheney, Kansas)[239]

After ten years of suffering and misery and having spent large sums on doctors and medicine they finally told me there was no hope. But in less than one week after Bro. Parham prayed for me I was entirely well of Sugar Diabetes in the third stage, so that now after two weeks I have not had the least Symptoms of the disease. My eyesight was so poor that I had to be led around and now I can go any where and see quite well and that is getting better daily. (Mr. A. Keyes, 1110 Wash Avenue, Lansing, Michigan)[240]

I want to thank our Lord Jesus for hearing prayer for me in the time of my great need, for truly I was very sick with flu and I suppose pneumonia for my lungs were very sore and fever very high. I felt that truly I had passed into the valley of the shadow, so did others, they sent Brother Parham a telegram to Compton, Calif., and one to Wm. Bacon, (my son) at Houston, Texas, and called Sister Parham on phone.... About the time they were all in prayer for me the fever left. My lungs were not sore any more and the healing began from that moment. (Mrs. F. M. Stoner, Wyandotte, Oklahoma)[241]

Not all testimonies concerned healing of a physical malady. Here is the engrossing story of a woman delivered from drug addiction in Parham's meeting in Lansing, Michigan:

In my eighteenth year, I became sick, and a young lady came into my room and gave me a white powder, to place on my tongue, followed by a glass of water. I did so, not knowing what it was and

---

239. *TAF*, August 1925, 13, originalapostolicfaith.org.
240. "Testimony," *TAF*, September 1925, 7, originalapostolicfaith.org.
241. *TAF*, February 1926, 12, originalapostolicfaith.org.

it made me feel so well, that I dressed myself and went on with my duties, but oh. [sic] how little I dreamed where it was leading me. Of course in due time, I found out that I was a drug fiend and would go to most any length to obtain it and the many times I have suffered and humbled myself, begging on my knees to doctors for it, would fill a book. I would actually go without eating, if short for money. Oh, how we should pity the poor helpless wretches, until they find God.

I would get disgusted with myself and would try to quit it at home, also at hospitals under doctors orders and go thru the torments of the damned, until I would give up in despair and take it again. Then I would continue to go through the same experience again and again, and that has been my life for nineteen years, fighting the demon drug.

In those years I took anything I could get, morphine, heroin, gum opium, laudlum [sic], cocaine and smoked hop, took it by mouth, shot it with the needle, also sniffed it up into the nose.

In four years time I took eight so called cures for drug, but they only obtained my money and I was left with the over powering desire for drug.

...God was leading me to Him, step by step through my husband's sister. God told me to go to her home and get healed through the blood of Jesus, which I did. Praise His Holy Name.

Brother Parham was conducting some meetings at Lansing, Mich., where we went regularly, and from the first I have not taken any drugs whatever. (Mrs. F. Albro).[242]

The following testimonies were recorded by someone who attended Parham's meetings in Elsinore, California, in 1925. According to the extraordinary report, nine out of ten people prayed for in the meeting received a healing miracle. Here is a sampling of those healings:

One of the most remarkable healings of years is that of Mrs. Sol Owens of Lake Elsinore. Sister Owens was examined by different

---

242. "Delivered of Drug Addiction of Nineteen Years Standing," *TAF*, September 1925, 7, originalapostolicfaith.org.

physicians who discovered a large inward growth which was pushing the organs of her body out of their normal position and caused her a great deal of pain and suffering. One of her limbs would at times draw up and she could not straighten it out to walk upon it. On attending the meetings there she came up for prayer and after Brother Parham prayed for her she was completely healed and is now well and strong and preaching the gospel in that place.

Dr. Durham, a German lady who is a noted physician, having been graduated from many different Medical societies in Germany, South America and America, and who practiced in Argentine [sic] and many other places, came into the meetings in Elsinore. She had been injured in an accident 8 years ago and one hip and knee so badly injured that the consulting physicians of New York City said that she could never be benefited in any way. The knee cap had been broken and she was unable to kneel, or climb a stairway or raise her foot upon a step of any kind without taking the injured limb in her hands and lifting it up. After the first time in the prayer line she was wonderfully healed and can now kneel, climb stairs and walk with comfort and ease. Dr. Durham is a Roman Catholic but afterwards on talking with Brother Parham stated that she did not now need her beads to pray as she had God in her heart.[243]

Finally, here are a few of the testimonies that Parham found among the most outstanding he had witnessed:

The wife of a man who operated a laundry in North Topeka, Kansas, being afflicted with cancer was brought to our healing Home. The second day after prayer had been offered, she gave birth to a cancerous mass, weighing 7 and one-half lbs. This cancer was of the octopus type, with long tentacles which buried themselves in different parts of her body. The foot of one of these had laid hold upon her liver. A portion of her liver was as smooth cut away as tho done with the knife of a surgeon. We kept this cancer with its portion of liver in alchol [sic] and it was viewed by hundreds of people...who were astounded at the miracle....

---

243. "Some Special Healings at Lake Elsinore, California," *TAF*, January 1926, 10–11, originalapostolicfaith.org.

Mrs. Judge Anderson of Galena, Kansas, who had a terrible cancer upon her face was so completely healed, that it did not leave even a scar. In this Galena meeting which lasted three months, hundreds of people were healed of almost every disease known....

While holding a meeting in Houston, Texas, in 1905, a little boy was brought to the meeting on crutches, which he had used for five years. One hip was so drawn up that he was unable to sit down. The child had also a large hunch upon his back. I laid my hand over this and began to pray which in a moment was entirely gone, and as my hand passed down his back, the hip also came down to its proper place. Taking the crutches and simply leading the child, he walked to his mother....

While holding meetings in San Angelo, Texas about the year 1910. [*sic*] A blind man who was...led about by a little boy, heard of the miracles of healing taking place at the meetings. He asked the boy to lead him to the auditorium. He was unsaved, smelled fouly [*sic*] of liquor and tobacco, yet we prayed for God to not only save him, but heal him. God wonderfully saved his soul, and rejoicing he said, "If I get nothing more I am fully paid for coming." He was led to his room and laid down for a sleep, two hours later he arose with perfected eyesight....

A man came down from the mountains with a broken leg, that had been improperly set, though he walked with crutches this limb dragged the floor. About 75 people were in line to be prayed for before his turn would come. As he neared the front, Satan kept speaking to me in a tormenting way, saying, "Now that man will not be healed, and the faith of this audience will all be blasted" [*sic*] mentally I answered him, "I am going to pray for him whether he is healed or not, it is none of my business whether he is healed." At last his turn came. After prayer I did not even open my eyes, for I heard him drag that foot away. Directly I heard a shout. [*sic*] and a terrible clatter as he threw the crutches half way across the room. And there he was, shouting and leaping over the seats.... At last shouldering his crutches he walked from the meeting.[244]

244. Charles F. Parham, "Healings That I Have Witnessed," *TAF*, April 1927, 2–4, originalapostolicfaith.org.

This is just a small representation of what Parham said were the "scores of thousands" of healings he had witnessed.[245] When reading multiple testimonies like these, it can be easy to forget that each account is a story of relief from real pain and suffering.

In the majority of cases, more than a hundred years have passed since these miracles took place. Being so far removed by time and with limited records, it would be impossible to investigate each person and substantiate the individual stories. However, we should keep in mind that most of the accounts were posted contemporaneously with the healing miracles. In Parham's time, each healing or deliverance story could be scrutinized and verified.

Skeptics may question the testimonies. For some people, the accounts might seem impossible to believe. It may be that these people's theological framework does not allow for a God who heals the sick and afflicted today as He did in the Gospels and the book of Acts. To them, the days of miracles have passed, having died with the last apostle. "God does not heal the sick today," they pessimistically proclaim.

There was the same type of skepticism in Parham's day, but Parham ignored the skeptics. He believed that God would heal, and God abundantly answered his prayers of faith. Thus, despite his shortcomings, Parham was used mightily in the alleviation of the suffering of thousands.

---

245. C. Parham, "Healings That I Have Witnessed," 4.

6

THE REVEREND
MISTER PARHAM

There was more to Charles Fox Parham than a magical pulpiteer. This Pentecostal preacher from Kansas was a very complex person. He was both loved and despised, respected and rejected. Taking a deeper dive into his life and ministry might help to answer the question, who was the real Charles Parham?

Some mental-health professionals affirm the existence of a syndrome called the "Napoleon complex," while others deny that such a syndrome exists. Those who advance the idea suggest that men who are small in stature feel inferior or inadequate and therefore overcompensate by developing distinctive (sometimes aggressive) personality traits. The syndrome is named after the French general who was small of stature but large in narcissism.

Charles Parham was a small man. He was only five feet four inches tall, with a slight frame.[246] William Seymour referred to him as a "little man."[247] If Parham had a Napoleon complex, he would certainly seem to have overcompensated for his height in other areas of his life. One could argue that examining Parham's personality would be a classic case study in the authenticity of the syndrome, whether it exists or not.

---

246. Passport application, 1908, ancestry.com.
247. Klaas Brower, "Origin of the Apostolic Faith Movement on the Pacific Coast," *TAFGC*, May 1921, 6.

COMPLICATED AND PARADOXICAL

Saying that Parham was "complicated" and "paradoxical" is actually a serious understatement. He made a strong impression on most people he met. Many thought he was the world's greatest preacher; others considered him to be a charlatan. Fortunately, a number of those who knew him or at least met him recorded their impressions. Here is a selection of descriptions from his contemporaries, some friend and some foe, from various periods of Parham's life, which help to demonstrate the mixed impression he made:

Parham is a ranter, and no one believes in his sincerity. He used to live here but he did not cut much ice.[248]

Mr. Parham is a slightly built, spare man, extremely delicate looking.... His face is pale and earnest looking, while masses of brown hair cover his remarkably shaped head. Parham is the possessor of such a wonderful personality that some have accused him of hypnotizing his followers.[249]

Short of stature and thin of chest, with the face of the dreamer of new cults.[250]

Parham is a short man with glossy black hair and black eyes. He has a weak voice and is a poor speaker, but his emotion and evident sincerity carry conviction and he is rapidly making converts.[251]

...a nervy little preacher who does not wear a plug hat and sport a gold headed cane. Rev. Parham is a young man, scarcely a voter, but he has convictions and the nerve to back them up.[252]

Parham is described as a powerful speaker, a hard hitter, who is both humorous and pathetic.[253]

---

248. *LDJ*, July 30, 1906, 4, newspapers.com.
249. "Wonderful Cures in Kansas," *TAF*, July 1912, 2, originalapostolicfaith.org.
250. "Changes His Base," *TSJ*, November 17, 1906, 7, newspapers.com.
251. "Parham to the Front," *TM*, October 4, 1906, 8, newspapers.com.
252. "Rev. Parham Should Be Encouraged," *TJG*, February 22, 1894, 2, newspapers.com.
253. S. Parham, *Life of Charles F. Parham*, 317. Sarah is quoting a newspaper in Spokane, Washington.

This much will be hazarded, that if asked the question [about fanatical followers] point blank, Parham would look at you with wide-open gray eyes, and smile and smile—and then smile some more, as blandly as a child; that is unless he has changed in recent years, which is not likely. And as likely as not the only answer you would get would be in parables.[254]

Charles Parham, who never tires, but preaches day and night and jokes during all intervals.[255]

Mr. Parham does not impress one as being a peculiar man. Indeed his is a right good fellow and earnest in his work.[256]

He [Parham] believes he has started a movement which will bring about the millennium, and thinks his is a second voice crying in the wilderness, and preparing the way for the second advent of Christ. His talk and manner, in public and private, are those of a sincere and extremely optimistic fanatic.[257]

One night in a watch-night service back in Galena, I had heard him preach to a large audience for five hours without stopping, and no one moved or left the service until he had finished.[258]

There is nothing remarkable in the meetings of the evangelist. He is not even an unusually gifted speaker—at least, he was not last night.[259]

He is a small man with simple, unassuming manners and an air of earnestness and strength.[260]

254. "Holy Rollers," *TJG*, September 5, 1906, 7, newspapers.com.
255. "Another Week," newspaper article clipping, unknown source, n.d., HSRC.
256. "A Great Worker," *LWW*, February 12, 1901, 3, newspapers.com.
257. "Was a Pentecost," *The Kansas City Journal*, January 12, 1901, 1, FPHC.
258. Ethel E. Goss, *The Winds of God* (Weldon Spring, MO: Word Aflame Press, 1958), 134.
259. "Prayer Is His Cure," newspaper article clipping, unknown source, n.d., HSRC.
260. "In Tower of Babel," *The Inter Ocean* (Chicago, Illinois), January 27, 1901, 37, newspapers.com.

He is a small man and when he speaks he stretches his body and raises his voice to a high pitch. He laughed and related humorous incidents in the course of his address.[261]

The whole appearance of the man is repulsive. In speaking, his favorite movement is walking backward, paddling his open hands like boat oars. His voice has mixture of bark and growl, and coming from such a small person sounds most peculiar.[262]

Mr. Parham is below medium height, pleasant looking, has a fine reddish brown beard, a voice like a pirate and manners as brusque as a janitor in a flat. He is a native of Kansas and talks at the rate of 250 words a minute, and if it is a matter of doubt about his having the gift of tongues, he has at least the gift of one.[263]

It is no more than fair to state he never inspired confidence here and people were always suspicious of him, although his conduct so far as learned was above reproach.[264]

He has a pleasant and convincing manner that makes his discourse almost irresistible.[265]

He was a narrow, bigoted fellow, and did not make many friends. He was not regarded here as being trustworthy.[266]

He believes in, and prays and preaches for pungent conviction, clear and powerful conversion and a holy, sanctified life here and now.... Young as he is, but few surpass him in the work of an evangelist. In his pleasant, smiling, winning way, and his strong faith in God, he is a wonderful soul-winner for God.[267]

261. "Apostolic Rally," *THP*, August 20, 1906, 10, texashistory.unt.edu.

262. "Parham a Devil Worshipper?" *Zion City Herald* (Illinois), September 6, 1907, 1 (hereafter cited as *ZCH*), newspaperarchive.com.

263. "Are from Kansas," *TAF*, July 1912, 7–8 (reprinted from the *Kansas City Journal*, July 1901), originalapostolicfaith.org.

264. "Parham in Trouble," *LWW*, October 30, 1902, 5, newspapers.com.

265. Gordon P. Gardiner, *Out of Zion into All the World* (Shippensburg, PA: Companion Press, 1990), 3. The quote is from *The Daily Gazette* (Waukegan, Illinois), n.d., n.p.

266. "Parham Sect Tortured," *LDJ*, September 21, 1907, 2, newspapers.com.

267. J. H. Pracht, "Burns," *WM*, June 6, 1895, 4, newspapers.com.

While we may not have always approved his course since he has been among us, there is one thing at least that can be said to his credit, and that is, he has the courage to preach his convictions of what he believes to be right, whether it pleases his congregation or not, which we think is very commendable, to say the least.[268]

Mr. Parham is no wild-eyed, long-haired crank or fanatic, but is a highly cultured, intellectual man, one who has made it a life study to look into existing evils, and suggesting proper remedies.... The preacher is fluent and eloquent with a remarkable tact to cudgel the hypocrit [sic] and an adeptness to produce confidence and hope in the sinner.[269]

He clings to no creed or doctrine, whence, then does he get the title of Reverend? And without creed or doctrine he must be a sort of cackling rooster who lays no eggs.[270]

This new prophet is by name Charles F. Parham. He left Kansas for Zion after having had two convincing visions showing that Voliva was a false prophet and a sorcerer and that Parham was the cheese.[271]

Charles F. Parham is a man who has gone over the Bible with a microscope. He knows every nook and corner of it. After the meetings he permits questioning, and the questioning reveals his knowledge of the book. From Genesis to Revelation he has the Bible practically at his finger ends.[272]

The language was simple, but the strange Interpretation of the Bible teachings was original and puzzling.[273]

Parham has left a bad record in every place that I know of him working and I am compelled to say I consider him as an unsafe

268. Richards, "Hell for the Wicked."

269. "From Brownwood, Texas," *TGK*, n.d. (about January 1911), 3, ifphc.org.

270. "Religious Thimble-Riggers," *The Catholic Advance* (Wichita, Kansas), October 31, 1903, 4, newspapers.com.

271. "With the Long Bow," *The Minneapolis Journal*, October 1, 1906, 14, newspaperarchives.com.

272. "Pentecost in Toronto? Preacher Says So," newspaper article clipping, source unknown, n.d., Pauline Parham Collection, HSRC.

273. "Parham Returns," newspaper article clipping, source unknown, n.d., HSRC.

man; he was when I knew him. Try his spirit and I am convinced you will find him a hypocrite and an Anti-Christ. Yet we know not whether he may have repented or not. But if he has, there is much for him to do that he has not done in straightening up the past. He was a liar, and also a dishonest business man in Topeka.[274]

All who know Bro. Parham will bear me witness that he is a man of strong and uncompromising convictions, but equally strong in his love and forbearance for those who differ with him.[275]

Parham admits that he is a "startling pulpit speaker" and his known proclivities for speaking plainly his opinions on all subjects from love, marriage and religion and politics to all other subjects commonly dwelt on by public speakers, bear him out in his admission that he is a startling pulpit orator.[276]

Mr. Parham is a pulpit orator of great ability and his intellectual force and exhaustive study of the scriptures has brought thousands of converts to the faith.[277]

Parham is still a middle aged man, genial, possessed of a captivating delivery even while almost every one of his doctrines are repellant and offensive to a wholesome interpretation of Scriptures.[278]

Elder Parham speaks straight out from the shoulder and deals in facts. He does not hesitate to call a spade a spade and to handle social ills and economic problems in a manner that clearly defines his position thereon.[279]

Brother Parham, can make his audience see the man Jesus as no other man I have ever heard in the pulpits of Europe and America.[280]

274. "He Reflects on Parham," newspaper article clipping, source unknown, n.d., HSRC.
275. "Unity Prevailed," *TAF*, September 13, 2–3, David Allan Hubbard Library, Fuller Theological Seminary, Pasadena, CA (hereafter cited as HLFTS).
276. "He Has a New Way," *TSJ*, July 26, 1906, 10, newspapers.com.
277. "The Apostolic Meeting," newspaper article clipping, source unknown, n.d., HSRC.
278. Shumway, "A Critical Study of 'The Gift of Tongues,'" 171.
279. "Mr. Parham Tells the Truth," *TAF*, June 1925, 18, digitalshowcase.oru.edu. The quote is from a Wichita, Kansas, newspaper.
280. "Twentieth Annual Birthday Celebration," *TAF*, May 1926, 2, digitalshowcase.oru.edu. This description is by John G. Lake.

While there are many records of people's public impressions of Parham, very little is known about his private family life. It is abundantly clear that Sarah was a devoted wife and Parham's most vocal supporter. Parham was away from home for months at a time preaching. It would probably be fair to say that he was seldom at home. Not only was Sarah tasked with raising the couple's children and maintaining the family household, but she also bore much of the burden of leading the local ministry.

Parham paid a well-deserved compliment to his faithful companion in the *Apostolic Faith*:

> When I depart from home wife does not follow me to the door begging me not to go, but with her shoulder to the gospel wheel and her hand to my back, her parting remark is, "God speed you and bring you back safely some time."[281]

One tiny glimpse at their relationship comes in a postcard Charles sent Sarah when she was living in Tonganoxie, Kansas. He addressed her as "Dear Wife" and wrote:

> Your letter came [*sic*] all O.K. am on run these days so I can get home for as long as possible before I have to strike the Eastern trail [*sic*] The money is coming in fine [*sic*] I am having great meetings everywhere... Sunday all folks ask for you [*sic*]

Parham signed the card, "yours, C.F.P."[282]

For a greater understanding of Parham's personality beyond these general, conflicting impressions, we will examine some of his dominant character traits.

INDIGNANT AND CONTENTIOUS

Parham may have had a loving and peaceful relationship with his wife, but he had problems getting along with his superiors in the Methodist Church. He had issues with the Methodist congregation he pastored. One observer put it kindly, saying, "His relations with the church membership

281. *TAF*, March 1907, 13, Parham Collection, Apostolic Faith Bible College, Baxter Springs, KS (hereafter cited as AFBC).
282. Charles F. Parham, postcard to Mrs. Charles Parham, date indiscernible, AFBC.

was not the pleasantest."[283] He had conflicts with his coworkers at the Bethel Healing Home. He had issues with the leadership in Zion, Illinois. He had issues with the way the Apostolic Faith in California was functioning. He had issues in his relationships with members of the Apostolic Faith in Texas. Could it be concluded that he simply had issues?

A city official in San Antonio described Parham as having "great indignation."[284] Perhaps that is a most fitting characterization. Every battle Parham fought, and there were many, was a battle for justice. Right or wrong, he was always right. He was always the offended party and could be quite belligerent about it even though his own words and actions were often what offended. There are many suitable examples, but perhaps just one will suffice.

The story revolves around Parham's ministry in Los Angeles in 1908. The Women's Christian Temperance Union had been most kind to him. When Parham had been in California in 1907, the W.C.T.U. had allowed him free use of their auditorium for a full week. The next year, when Parham arrived in the city, the W.C.T.U. gave him a new suit of clothes. The superintendent of the Temperance Temple, Mrs. S. E. Wemple, said she was a friend of Parham and "felt sorry for him." Still, even with the kindness and empathy extended toward him, a serious rift fractured the relationship between the evangelist and his hosts in the city.

According to Parham's side of the story, he was only trying to help the poor when the W.C.T.U. put demands on him that his conscience would not allow him to accept. He said he was feeding soup to the unemployed on the sidewalk outside the building and collecting money each night to apportion to the impoverished souls who attended his meetings. In his view, he was a valiant crusader for the needy.

Mrs. Wemple saw it quite differently. She said the building was not a kitchen and should not be used for one. She simply asked Parham not to serve soup in the building. She would allow bread in the auditorium but not soup. The request seems reasonable enough. Still, the men brought their food into the building, and Parham apparently did not try to stop them. In addition, Parham's own congregation complained about the street people sitting near them in the services.

---

283. "Holy Rollers."
284. "St. Voliva Springs a Sensation," *Lake County Independent* (Illinois), August 2, 1907, 1 (hereafter cited as *LCI*), newspaperarchives.com.

The W.C.T.U. building was also the living quarters of a number of single women. Wemple said it was "quite unpleasant" for the ladies to come through a crowd of homeless men every night when they returned from work.

Despite the challenges, Wemple tried to accommodate Parham, asking him to control his crowd and seat the vagrants on one side of the building. Parham not only refused to compromise, but he also took the platform of the Temple to attack the W.C.T.U. members and their motives. He publicly chastised the W.C.T.U. for not caring for the less fortunate. Wemple was rightly offended and wanted to counter the unwarranted charges. When she stood to defend her organization, Parham turned the lights out on her and prevented her from speaking.

Mrs. Wemple noted, "When the Rev. Mr. Parham was denouncing the W.C.T.U. as not favoring the unemployed, which, of course, is wrong, he was wearing a suit of clothes which the women of that society had helped buy him."[285]

EGOTISTICAL AND VAINGLORIOUS

Parham loved favorable press. He once stated that what the newspapers said about him was "a matter of indifference."[286] Perhaps not. Since most of his wife's biography of her husband consists of quotes from newspapers, he must have clipped and kept every news article that he (and perhaps Sarah) read that placed him in a positive light. It is quite possible that one could track where Parham had been and what he had been doing during almost every month of his adult life through news accounts. He needed the applause of men.[287]

When Parham was nineteen years old, he held an extended revival in the Pleasant Valley School House near Lawrence, Kansas. At the close of the meeting, several of the men of the community gave him a letter stating their appreciation. Parham kept that letter until he died. With all the moves he made from one house to another and from one community to

---

285. "Pastor and Women Tell Their Sides," *Los Angeles Herald*, February 19, 1908, 9 (hereafter cited as *LAH*), chroniclingamerica.loc.gov.
286. "Are from Kansas," newspaper article clipping, *KCJ*, HSRC. A handwritten note appears to date the article as "Feb 1901."
287. "Texas Newsboy Preacher," *The Beloit Daily Call* (Kansas), October 14, 1921, 5, newspapers.com.

another, that seems quite remarkable and might be a striking example of how dependent he was on the affirmation of his fellow citizens.[288]

His desire for attention did not escape the notice of the press. One newspaper publisher, recognizing Parham's love of publicity, wrote, "The press agent of the Rev. Chas. F. Parham must be on a vacation as nothing has been heard from that gentleman for two or three days."[289] Other papers wrote, "[Parham] cannot fail to make himself heard in either good or evil respect" and "We understand he loves notoriety."[290] Parham was such a hot item with the press that one newspaper even reported when he shaved his beard.[291]

The evangelist also liked titles. He assigned titles to himself, and he was given titles by others. Here are just some of the appellations ascribed to him:

"Dr. Parham."[292] Parham had no degrees and no licenses but was often called Dr. and never seemed to object.[293]

"World Famed Evangelist." This might have been an appropriate title if it had been given him by an outsider, but this was how Parham described himself in his own publicity.[294]

"Projector." This was probably his title of choice, as in the "projector of the Apostolic Faith Movement."

"Divine Science Physician." This is how Parham described his occupation in the 1900 United States Census.[295]

"Elijah III." When Parham went to Zion City to try to wrest control of the city from Wilbur Voliva, he was called "Elijah III," John Alexander Dowie being the second Elijah.[296]

---

288. S. Parham, *Life of Charles F. Parham*, 19.

289. "Snapshots," *TSJ*, October 6, 1906, 15, newspapers.com.

290. *LDJ*, September 23, 1907, 2, newspapers.com; "Heraus Mit Ihm," *Cherokee County Republican* (Baxter Springs, Kansas), September 19, 1907, 1, newspapers.com.

291. "On Second Thought," *TC*, August 23, 1901, 8, newspapers.com.

292. Throughout this list, titles and other designations have been capitalized for consistency.

293. "Claim to Be 'Cured,'" *Delphos Republican* (Kansas), January 8, 1904, 3, newspapers.com; "Happening in Houston," *THP*, June 27, 1916, 7, newspapers.com.

294. *TAF*, August 1925, 20, originalapostolicfaith.org.

295. ancestry.com.

296. "Ejected from Zion," *Independence Daily Report* (Kansas), November 6, 1906, 1, newspapers.com.

"Apostle of Unity." This title was another of Parham's favorites, but unfortunately he was often the opposite.[297]

"Prophet." When Parham was accused of wrongdoing, his supporters in Houston said, "He cannot sin," because he was a prophet. The truth is, Parham prophesied often, but his prophecies seldom found fulfillment.[298]

"The Messenger with the Seal of the Living God." Parham believed that the baptism in the Holy Spirit was the seal given to the 144,000 servants of God mentioned in Revelation 7 and that he, the projector of the movement, was the messenger who brought the seal.[299]

"A Voice Crying in the Wilderness." Parham thought that as John the Baptist preached and prepared the way for Christ's first coming, he himself was the second voice crying in the wilderness, preparing the way for the second advent and the millennium.[300]

"The Original Exponent of Pentecostal Restoration." Parham used this title in a flyer he published in Los Angeles in 1907 after some people claimed William Seymour had started the Pentecostal movement. The same flyer took an obvious swipe at Azusa Street, showing Parham's contempt for the meetings there by saying, "Avoid erroneous teachings of ranting fanatics."[301]

"Most Persecuted Evangelist of the Day." This description came from an advertising blurb in the *San Antonio Gazette* after Parham was arrested in the city. It is a definite peek into the way he saw himself.[302]

A DREAMER

One of the above descriptions of Parham was that he had "the face of a dreamer." And a dreamer he was—a big dreamer. The problem was that he announced his dreams with spectacular intensity and promoted them with the passion of a zealot, but many of these dreams, if not most, never came true.

297. "He's an Apostile [sic] Now," *LDW*, July 6, 1906, 2, newspapers.com.
298. "Parham Is Rallying Forces," *THP*, May 22, 1907, 5, texashistory.unt.edu.
299. "Pentecostal Papers," *TGK*, April 1910, 2, ifphc.org.
300. "Parham in Kansas City," *TSJ*, January 23, 1901, 8, newspaperarchive.com.
301. "Seventh Annual Watch Night Memorial," flyer, digitalshowcase.oru.edu.
302. *San Antonio Gazette*, July 24, 1907, 2 (hereafter cited as *SAG*), newspaperarchive.com.

He dreamed of building a mission in Jerusalem from which he could speak to all nations. He dreamed of having the returning Jews hear the message of Jesus in their own language. It was only a dream.[303]

Early in his ministry, he was fascinated with the ark of the covenant. He believed that despite the fact there were many learned and experienced archaeologists in the world, he was the only person who knew exactly where the ark was. Of course, he had never been within five thousand miles of the purported site. He announced on numerous occasions that he would go, find the ark, and bring it back to Jerusalem. He first announced that he would go to Palestine in 1895, but "pressing need of labor at home detained him."[304] Over the years, he made many plans to visit the Holy Land but was only able to go to Palestine near the end of his life, when he spent four months there.

Parham believed that once he had singlehandedly restored the ark to the Holy City, the Jews would begin to flock to Palestine from every nation of the world, triggering the second coming of Christ. He alone would be responsible for the restoration of Israel and the second coming. He even claimed finding the ark "[will] cause the world to fall at the feet of the Nazarene, will put to flight infidelity and skepticism, and give to the world a truth that cannot be gain-sayed."[305] Quite a dream.

His often-repeated, highly publicized, starry-eyed dreams of finding the ark earned him the scorn of at least one newspaper. In a pasquinade, the publisher suggested Parham would live on sandwiches "made from the bread of the prophets and fresh cuts of green cheese from the moon." His satire continued with the claim that Parham would return from Palestine with Evelyn Baldwin (a famous polar explorer) and with "the North pole over his shoulder."[306] On another occasion, Judge J. T. Botkin, the assistant secretary of state, buffooned Parham in an article about the cost of

---

303. "Baptism of the Holy Ghost, Gift of Tongues and Sealing of the Church and Bride," *TAF*, July 1905, 4, HSRC.

304. "The Latest Version," *EN*, March 28, 1895, 2, newspapers.com.

305. "After Holy Ark," *The News-Courant* (Cottonwood Falls, Kansas), February 6, 1902, 1, newspapers.com; "Parham Appeals to His Followers," *LCI*, September 4, 1908, 8, newspapers.com.

306. "As Seen by the Other Fellow," *The Topeka Plaindealer*, March 21, 1902, 1, newspapers.com.

shipping the ark from Palestine to Kansas.[307] Parham never apologized for his long string of broken promises, and nothing slowed him from publicizing his next preposterous scheme.

He also believed he would find Noah's ark in Asia. Although many explorers who were familiar with the region had tried, Parham would be the person to find it and prove to the world that the biblical story was true. He said that finding the ark would "do more for Christianity than the support for a lifetime of a thousand preachers."[308]

One of Parham's greatest dreams was connected with the baptism in the Holy Spirit and speaking in other tongues. He believed that tongues-speaking missionaries would not have to learn the languages of the world to preach the gospel. If, on the day of Pentecost, the audience understood the glossolalia, then people who spoke other languages should understand all those who speak in tongues. Although there are a number of remarkable testimonies about foreigners understanding the words of someone who did not know their language but spoke in tongues, those examples are not the norm. Parham continued to hold to this belief even after it was proven invalid by hundreds of Pentecostal missionaries.[309]

Parham also announced trips to India and China.[310] He planned trips to England, Australia, and South Africa.[311] Early in his ministry, he claimed he was "led from the limited confines of church organization and the hampered position of a denominational minister into wider fields, where the world became his parish."[312] Despite his big dreams, he left North America only once, and that was to travel to Palestine near the end of his life. His often-proposed adventures were so ridiculous that they were once met with this sarcasm by a local newspaper: "The Rev. Chas F. Parham with a band of his followers will start around the world the first of next July. This is the

307. "Not Listed," newspaper article clipping, source unknown, n.d. HSRC.
308. Shumway, "Study of 'The Gift of Tongues,'" 171; "Noah's Ark and the Ark of the Covenant," TAF, November 1913, AFBC.
309. "New Kind of Missionaries," The Honolulu Advertiser, May 31, 1901, 15, newspapers.com.
310. "Parham and His Work," TM, February 28, 1901, 1, newspapers.com.
311. "The Call to Regions Beyond," TAF, September 1927, 15, originalapostolicfaith.org.
312. "Apostolic Band and Their Creed," newspaper article clipping, source unknown, n.d., HSRC.

first time since last winter that the Rev. Mr. Parham has announced his intentions to go around the world."[313]

Parham always wanted the *Apostolic Faith* to be a weekly paper. Although he often spoke of making this change and frequently promised to do so, he published a weekly only for a few months in 1899. For the rest of his life, producing a weekly was merely a dream. The fact is, he often lacked the resources to get the paper printed on a monthly basis.[314]

The evangelist also dreamed of establishing a world headquarters in San Antonio. He boasted about all he would build in the Alamo City. He envisioned a Bible school to train workers, a printing plant to spread his teaching around the world, and a "'temple of healing,' where the lame, the halt and the blind" would come and be healed. It would be a second edition of Zion City. However, it never happened. It was a dream—or perhaps just an empty promise to placate his followers during a most trying time.[315]

Parham dreamed of gatherings that would be the "greatest since the days of Pentecost."[316] They weren't. They not only didn't live up to the hype, but some never even happened. He announced long road trips that fizzled after the first stop. He dreamed of churches that were never built.[317] He dreamed of himself as more than he was. He most certainly had "the face of a dreamer."

A PROPENSITY FOR EXAGGERATION

Reading Parham's accounts of his life, one would suspect that he had a tendency to stretch a good story. In a rare moment of honest confession, Parham wrote, "Beloved, I crossed the river Jordan some years ago, but Canaan experience to me has been one of warfare, for I have had a time with the enemies there.... I have battled a spirit of exaggeration that had always been in my life."[318]

---

313. "On Second Thought."
314. *TAF*, March 1907, 3, AFBC.
315. "San Antonio the Capital of Parham's Spiritual Kingdom," *SAG*, July 31, 1907, 6, newspaperarchive.com.
316. "The Gift of Tongues," *Anaconda Standard* (Kansas), June 9, 1901, 20, newspapers.com.
317. "A Splendid Improvement," *TSJ*, March 21, 1900, 5, newspaperarchive.com.
318. *TAF*, April 14, 1899, 4, KHS.

Parham exaggerated claims about his health. On various occasions, he said that his body had been sanctified when he was twenty-four years old and that he had "scarcely had a pain in his body."[319] On another occasion, he said he had been sick only three times but had received immediate healing.[320] This does not seem to square with his other reports.

Several times, he was seriously ill. He collapsed in Potwin, Kansas.[321] He was sick in Cheney, Kansas. He was sick when he went to Orchard, Texas.[322] He was sick almost to death when he had the vision to go to Zion City.[323] He was sick in the Holy Land.[324] He was sick in the weeks leading to his death.[325]

Apparently, he also exaggerated his lack of any formal religious experience in his youth. He said he recalled hearing only one or two preachers before reaching the age of thirteen. He preferred to claim that he developed his theology with little or no religious training or experience, writing:

> Thus with no preconceived ideas, with no knowledge of what creeds and doctrines meant, not having any traditional spectacles upon the eyes to see through, I scarcely knew anything about church and Sunday School. These facts are stated to show that any early Scriptures were entirely unbiased.[326]

Yet this does not seem to have been the case. Information on the faith of his mother is not available, but, as previously mentioned, his father and stepmother were both active members in the Methodist Church, as were his maternal grandparents. His father once told him, "Charlie, you know I have always been a good church member."[327] The editor of the *Western Methodist* called Parham "the boy preacher" and said he "is the son of our esteemed patrons and friends, Brother and Sister W. M. Parham of

319. "Another Milestone," *TAF,* June 1925, 20, digitalshowcase.oru.edu.
320. "Personal Testimony of Chas. F. Parham," 16.
321. "Prayed Back to Life."
322. "A Letter," 5.
323. "Parham's Last Vision," *The Columbus Weekly Advocate* (Kansas), October 11, 1906, 3, newspapers.com.
324. S. Parham, *Life of Charles F. Parham,* 382.
325. S. Parham, 408–413.
326. S. Parham, 3.
327. S. Parham, 288.

Cheney, in this conference."[328] Another account said Parham's childhood home had "a pervading spirit of gracious Christian faith and practice."[329]

It seems that a "good church member" and "esteemed patron" of the Methodist Church would have taken his son to church more than twice in the first twelve years of his life.

It was mentioned previously that on the night of his conversion, Parham hummed a hymn as he walked home. At the third verse, he had a deep spiritual experience. The relevant question is how did someone so totally without church experience know a hymn so well as to sing three verses, especially since he did not list a hymnal among the few books the family owned? It is very hard to square these two distinctly different narratives.[330]

Parham also exaggerated the extent of his education. The oft-repeated story was that he was educated for the ministry at Southwestern College. It is true that Parham attended the school, but he only took preparatory classes. According to the college catalog, "It is the aim of the following course to furnish a thorough preparation for the work of the College; and at the same time, to give such an excellent discipline of mind as to prepare well for most of the professions, and for business in case a college course cannot be taken." The catalog intimated that the preparatory school would be comparable to "a good High School course" if the student substituted another course for the required Latin studies.[331]

On the junior level of the prep school, Parham took classes in language and math. The next level of study was "middle," and Parham took courses in math and history. On the senior level, he took one civics class. He did not actually enroll in ministry training and apparently only took one college-level class. He was not ranked at an academic level but was enrolled in "Selected Studies." That class was in modern languages and not ministry related.[332]

---

328. "Brevities and Personals," *WM*, March 15, 1894, 8, newspapers.com.

329. "A History of Kansas Just Published in Five Volumes," *TAF*, June 1928, 8, originalapostolicfaith.org.

330. S. Parham, *Life of Charles F. Parham*, 3–5; C. Parham, *Kol Kare Bomidbar*, 14–15. Parham explained that he tried to sing the song but did not have a talent for singing until God gave it to him at a later date.

331. *Southwest Kansas College*, 1892–93, 37, SC.

332. Transcripts, SC; *Southwest Kansas College*, 1890–91, 73, SC; *Southwestern Kansas College*, 1892–93, 66, SC; George Hindman, Southwestern College registrar's office, email message to author, March 2, 2021.

Parham also exaggerated his ministerial connections with the Methodist Church. He is often mentioned as having been ordained, but he was only licensed with the church. Most accounts say he received credentials when he was seventeen, but, at least once, Parham said he received an exhorter's license at the age of fourteen.[333] There are no records to confirm this claim. He also spoke often of being a Methodist pastor in Eudora, Kansas. This is only partly true. Parham was appointed as a "supply" pastor. This would be similar to what today might be called an interim pastor. There are no records indicating Parham was ever officially the pastor.

When preaching on temperance at a rally in Kansas City, Parham bragged he had once closed all the "joints" in a Kansas town. He did not name the town except to say it was a German town. Not only did he say he had closed all the establishments that served alcohol, but he also apparently singlehandedly kept them closed. Cheney, Parham's hometown, had a large German population, but the boy preacher left there before his twenty-first birthday. From the evidence available, this "notable feat" was not mentioned again.[334]

These are but a few examples of exaggeration from Parham's early years. His inflation of facts and circumstances never totally ceased. It seems the gifted preacher was especially skillful in the "gift of exaggeration."

INCONSISTENT AND CONTRADICTORY

A deep look into Parham's life reveals many inconsistencies. He often spoke of the loftiest ethical goals for his life and ministry. Unfortunately, he did not always live by the code he hoped to follow. Perhaps, like the apostle Paul, he wanted to do right but fell short. According to Scripture, Paul, too, was conflicted at times, writing, "For the good that I would I do not: but the evil which I would not, that I do" (Romans 7:19).

Indeed, the biggest contradiction in Parham's life was a moral one. It was large enough to dwarf every other inconsistency. That issue is so huge it demands special attention and will be dealt with in a later chapter. But there are a number of other incongruities in his conflicted life.

333. "Apostolic Rally"; Francis Lyons, Reference Archivist, General Commission on Archives and History, United Methodist Church, email message to author, March 1, 2021.
334. "Parham in Kansas City."

Parham often stated that did not believe in defending himself against attacks.[335] Yet he always fought back, often in mean and ugly ways. At one point, many of the ministers in Texas had broken with Parham over moral charges. Parham sent a letter to all the workers in the state clarifying his position:

> Feeling that the "machine rule" in the state of Texas is practically broken, and that all opposing forces on this score are breaking down, I feel free that there will be no chance for it to be said that I am in anyway [sic] making a fight, but....[336]

That little "but" is the key to understanding Parham. While maintaining the highest thoughts on love and charity, he was brutal to those who fought him. Apparently, his high-minded principles served him well only when it was convenient for him. Parham continued by making it clear that even though he *wasn't* going to fight, he most certainly *was* going to fight:

> ...at the same time I feel the time has come again to do all I can to once more restore order, and to unify the work, and once more establish it on the original principles, free from all rules, ecelesiasticism [sic], systems &c and to bring it again to the simple teaching of the Apostolic Faith.[337]

Parham's reputation as a fighter was such that one of his defenders wrote to the *Houston Post* to convince readers that this was not the case, stating, "Please allow me to say that this man is generally classed as a 'fighter' against churches, seeking a following of his own, tearing down; this is untrue."[338]

When legal charges were brought against him in San Antonio, he swore he would not fight the charges, but, of course, he fought the charges. He fought W. F. Carothers, one of his own lieutenants, over moral charges that Carothers brought against him, as well as associated leadership issues; he fought William Seymour over control of Azusa Street; he fought

---

335. See, for example, "St. Voliva Springs a Sensation."
336. Charles Parham, letter "To the Workers, and missions, of the state of Texas," May 15, 1907, Center for the Study of Oneness Pentecostalism, Florissant, MO (hereafter cited as CFSOP).
337. Charles Parham to the workers, and missions, of the state of Texas.
338. "A Pentecostal Campaign," *THP*, March 2, 1908, 6, texashistory.unt.edu.

William Durham, another Pentecostal leader, over the doctrine of sanctification. There seemed to be no limit to how far he would go to sully the reputation of any who opposed him. He even seemed to take pleasure in his opponents' deaths.[339]

One of Parham's supporters said he "has not had to move a pen in defense of himself."[340] How blind could one man be? Parham lifted many a pen and anything else he could get his hands on to defend himself.

It has already been noted that the evangelist liked to call himself the "Apostle of Unity," but he was always a divider. He boasted that he was not against other churches and sought only their cooperation. One of his supporters claimed, "This campaign is not in connection with any church, or denomination; neither is it a fight against them; it is only a revival move, seeking to get men and women saved and leaving them in the hands of God to unite with any church as they may choose."[341] Yet, Parham very frequently verbally castigated other churches. Here are but two such examples:

> In the course of his talk he found it necessary to rail at every form of religion save his own, to assure those who clung to other creeds that Hell was their portion and Heaven his.[342]

> This little "Mistake on earth" had the gall to get up at the park Monday night and give the people a worse scoring than will St. Peter give the poor Galenaites when they seek admittance to the celestial abode. He even went so far as to say that all preachers and members of other churches in this city "were not fit for kindling wood to start a fire in hell."[343]

Parham was also seriously conflicted over finances. He loved to boast that he trusted God to meet his needs and that he never solicited money.

---

339. "Leadership," *TAF*, June 1912, 5–7, originalapostolicfaith.org; Charles Parham, "Durham Is Dead," *TAF*, September 1913, 11, FPHC. Parham goes so far as to say Durham committed "the sin unto death" and compared his death to Ananias and Sapphira's deaths in Acts 5.

340. Klaas Brower, "God's Work Here," *TAF*, May 1912, 11, originalapostolicfaith.org.

341. "A Pentecostal Campaign."

342. "Disrupter of Zion is in Los Angeles," *Bisbee Daily Review* (Arizona), November 16, 1906, 2.

343. "Heraus Mit Ihm."

He claimed, "I have never lacked money to do the things the Lord directs me to do.... Financial difficulties never harass me."[344] But the whole truth is that he always solicited money, and his needs were not always met. He professed this about money:

> There was a time when we charged the sick ones that came to our home for healing, board; took collections; did some soliciting and were always in debt. But when we decided to utterly abandon ourselves to practice the word of God, "to owe no man anything but love; and freely ye have received freely give," have payed [sic] our bills never to go in debt for a cent's worth, and have had hundreds to use where we formerly had tens.[345]

Unfortunately, this bold faith statement was not the reality in which Parham often lived. In 1917, he borrowed money to buy a car and was soliciting help because he was behind in the payments.[346]

While trying to raise money for a trip to the Holy Land in 1908, he sent out a long appeal letter to his followers:

> Personally, an appeal to even my children, my brethren or friends is a thing that I have never before made, and it is a thing that I have shrank from and looked upon as a thing I should not do: but....[347]

Once again, that word "but" got in the way of Parham's higher ideals. He goes on to explain that he is not only justified in making the appeal, but it is also in the "Divine order."[348] After sending out the letter asking for support, he reported, "I am not collecting money for the ark plan, but if people wish to give me any aid in the search I do not refuse it."[349]

Parham visited Zion City just before his planned trip and distributed "thousands" of cards with Acts 19:11–12 on one side:

344. "Parham Home," *KWC*, February 12, 1901, 3, newspapers.com.
345. "Forsaking All and All Things in Common," *TAF*, September 1905, 13, originalapostolicfaith.org.
346. "The Auto Fund," *The Everlasting Gospel*, August 1917, 10 (hereafter cited as *TEG*), FTSL.
347. "Parham Appeals to His Followers."
348. "Parham Appeals to His Followers."
349. "Parham Says the Charges Are False," *LCI*, December 11, 1908, 1, newspapers.com.

And God wrought special miracles by the hands of Paul: so that from his body were brought unto the sick handkerchiefs or aprons, and the diseases departed from them, and the evil spirits went out of them.

Beneath the Bible text, Parham wrote:

If you prefer, inclose [sic] a money order on Jerusalem and we will purchase a handkerchief there, pray over it and mail it to you as a souvenir blessing from the Holy City.[350]

While reporting about these cards, a Zion-area newspaper included this disclaimer: "It is said that this is the only request for money in any way or shape that Parham, the leader of the Gift of Tongues sect, makes of his people." Unfortunately, that may have been "said," but it was not the case. Parham also sent out "typed circular letters" soliciting donations for the trip.[351]

When he planned the same trip in 1927, he solicited funds by saying, "Now I am not soliciting means for this venture *but* [emphasis added] many have asked to have part in this trip and for me to let them know when I could arrange to go."[352] Perhaps he did not see the contradictions in his non-soliciting solicitations.

As he prepared to go South and West in 1912, he suggested that those who had written and said "they had some of the Lord's money for this trip" should get it in the mail.[353] Somehow, in Parham's mind, this was not soliciting funds since the donors had previously offered to contribute to the trip.

Calling for a great meeting at the San Francisco World's Fair, Parham hoped to raise a million dollars and recruit five hundred workers. He suggested, "Everyone should make all possible sacrifice for this work of unity, for, never since the early days of this movement, when women gave their jewelry and even their hair, and men their all, has there been a work of such promise, freighted with such import, as the campaign now ahead of us."[354]

---

350. "Blessings Given with Kerchiefs," *Waukegan News-Sun* (Illinois), December 8, 1908, 1 (hereafter cited as *WNS*), newspapers.com.
351. "Digging for the Ark," *Confidence*, October 1908, 21–22, ifphc.org.
352. "The Call to Regions Beyond," 16.
353. *TAF*, August 1912, 11, originalapostolicfaith.org.
354. "The Fall and Winter Campaign," *TAF*, September 1912, 14, originalapostolicfaith.org.

Friends in Kansas provided Parham with a home in Baxter Springs. He proceeded to ask followers to send him trees, bushes, and seeds for the yard, and books for a library. He said he could not procure these things on his "small income." But, of course, he was not soliciting.[355]

Is it wrong for a preacher to raise money? No, even the apostle Paul solicited funds. It is wrong to be hypocritical about it. Claiming not to solicit funds while doing that very thing might be the definition of a double standard. Moreover, Parham scorched other preachers for raising funds:

> There is no Bible authority for salaried preachers, settled or stationed pastors, and no man can be a minister and follow Jesus in the true sense of the word and belong to a denomination, take collections, beg, or accept funds from stews, festivals, fairs, etc.[356]

The evangelist also lived short of the prosperous life he claimed. Once, when a reporter informed him that it was "intimated" that he canceled a tour because of a lack of finances, Parham replied, "I've never lacked money to do the thing that the Lord directs me to do."[357] But he did lack money. At times, he did not know where his family would get their next meal. While he was on the road, his wife rented rooms in their home to "buy groceries." He asked his supporters to send them linens for the beds.[358]

Parham asked people who wanted him to answer a letter or pray over a prayer cloth to include the handkerchief and stamps because "I am often without funds to secure them."[359] Many months, he could not publish the *Apostolic Faith* because he did not have the money.[360] He did not have the finances for his big dreams and schemes.

One of the most glaring examples of his contradictory claims about money appears in the January 1914 issue of the *Apostolic Faith*. Parham wrote, "When I first took this way I was getting from five to seven hundred dollars a year in a Methodist pulpit; I now get from five to seven thousand dollars a year."[361] At the time of this writing, adjusting for inflation, that

---

355. "Circular Letter," *TAF*, March 1912, 12, originalapostolicfaith.org.
356. *TAF*, September 1913, 8, FTSL.
357. "Parham Home."
358. *TEG*, October 1917, 8, FTSL.
359. "Notice," *TAF*, February 1914, 16, originalapostolicfaith.org.
360. "Christmas Greetings," *TAF*, December 1914, 10, originalapostolicfaith.org.
361. "Address," *TAF*, January 1914, 2, originalapostolicfaith.org.

would be the equivalent of a very comfortable income of between $140,000 and $200,000.[362] Just a few months later, he wrote, "Three or four times this winter I had to take money we needed for the necessities of life for the family to get the paper out."[363] Could he not see how the statements were at variance with each other?

The *Apostolic Faith*, by the way, was always sent out free—with the exception that Parham often made it clear that those who wanted to receive it should send an offering to pay for it.[364] At times, he was so bold as to suggest that "some will have to give into the hundreds."[365] Those who didn't contribute were sometimes the object of his scorn; Parham said he hoped the readers would be awakened "to feel your responsibility."[366] In another issue, he asked, "Does not God appeal to you…?"[367]

Finally, Parham was quite adamant that he never wanted to start a church organization. He was supposedly against denominations and did not want to be part of one. He repeatedly made that stance abundantly clear. For example, he said, "Now, we don't come to establish another church. We are not a new sect. We haven't anything for you to join."[368]

However, from the revival at Topeka through the rest of his life, he sought to establish and lead a movement. He rejoiced with the planting of each new mission.[369] He boasted continually of the growth of the Apostolic Faith. He worked tenaciously for its success. He established himself as leader of the movement, never surrendered that position, and fought anyone who rose in leadership or questioned his authority. He was a nondenominational denominationalist.

Yes, Charles Fox Parham was a conflicted person—perhaps *oxymoronic* is a better word. Parham could have been a much better person if he had been the man he wanted to be and often claimed to be. Sad to say, he was not always that man.

---

362. in2013dollars.com (May 3, 2022).

363. "Locals," *TAF*, April 1914, 9, originalapostolicfaith.org.

364. See, for example, "Review," *TAF*, June 1925, 8, digitalshowcase.oru.edu. There are dozens of additional examples in the papers.

365. "Editorial," *TAF*, April 1925, 4, digitalshowcase.oru.edu.

366. "Christmas Greetings."

367. "Locals," 4.

368. "Apostolic Rally."

369. "Rev. Charles Parham Here," *GET*, June 18, 1904, 5, newspapers.com.

Parham at about six years of age.
Courtesy of *The Apostolic Faith Report*

Parham (far left) and his father and
siblings after the death of his mother.
Courtesy of *The Apostolic Faith Report*

Southwest Kansas Conference College. The Larry Martin Collection

Student body about 1890. The younger-looking student near the top on the right-hand side may be Parham. The Larry Martin Collection

A very early photo of Parham preaching, location unknown. Courtesy of *The Apostolic Faith Report*

Charles and Sarah Parham, wedding portrait.
Courtesy of *The Apostolic Faith Report*

Eudora Methodist Church (Kansas)
and Media Presbyterian Church
(Kansas), both pastored by Parham.
Courtesy of the Kansas United
Methodist Assistant Archivist,
Baker University Library

Stone's Mansion.
The Larry Martin Collection

"Modern Babel of Tongues in Kansas," with depictions of Agnes Ozman and Charles Parham, published in the *Cincinnati Commercial Tribune* (Ohio), January 20, 1901. The Larry Martin Collection

Some of Agnes Ozman's writings in tongues.
The Larry Martin Collection

Parham, Sarah, and their children with Lillian Thistlethwaite, Sarah's sister, at top right, in 1906. Courtesy of *The Apostolic Faith Report*

Parham in his office. Courtesy of *The Apostolic Faith Report*

Parham baptizing new converts in Orchard, Texas, about 1906. Courtesy of *The Apostolic Faith Report*

Top: Parham's team at Brian Hall in Houston. Courtesy of *The Apostolic Faith Report*

The team with costumes from the Holy Land. Courtesy of *The Apostolic Faith Report*

The Bible Training School on Rusk Street in Houston. Courtesy of *The Apostolic Faith Report*

Brunner Tabernacle.
Courtesy of *The Apostolic Faith Report*

Parham with Warren F. Carothers,
Texas State Director.
Courtesy of *The Apostolic Faith Report*

William J. Seymour, pastor of the
Azusa Street mission.
Courtesy of Dr. Gary W. Garrett,
Apostolic Archives International

The Azusa Street mission.
Courtesy of the Center for the Study
of Oneness Pentecostalism

A cartoon depicting Parham and Seymour's division at Azusa Street, published in the *Burning Bush*, February 21, 1907.
The Larry Martin Collection

A cartoon showing Parham racing out of town, source unknown. Courtesy of *The Apostolic Faith Report*

A cartoon showing Parham fleeing a mob, source unknown.
The Larry Martin Collection

Parham's family on the way to church. Courtesy of *The Apostolic Faith Report*

The Parham family at home with their livestock, about 1914.
All photos courtesy of *The Apostolic Faith Report*

The Parham home in Baxter Springs, Kansas. Courtesy of *The Apostolic Faith Report*

Parham at a tent meeting later in his life. Courtesy of *The Apostolic Faith Report*

Parham street preaching, locations unknown. Courtesy of *The Apostolic Faith Report*

Parham with Fred Campbell, a frequent soloist at his meetings.
Courtesy of *The Apostolic Faith Report*

A promotional flyer for one of Parham's camp meetings.
The three Ks at the bottom were printed in red for emphasis.
Courtesy of Dr. Gary W. Garrett, Apostolic Archives International

Images of two Ku Klux Klan
booklets belonging to Parham.
The Larry Martin Collection

Parham with his trunk, prepared to travel.
Courtesy of Dr. Gary W. Garrett, Apostolic Archives International

Parham baptizing in the Jordan River. Courtesy of *The Apostolic Faith Report*

The last photo of Charles Fox Parham, newspaper clipping, source unknown.
Courtesy of *The Apostolic Faith Report*

Parham's funeral. The Larry Martin Collection

Parham's grave marker, sculpted like a pulpit with a Bible on top.
Courtesy of *The Apostolic Faith Report*

7

A FLAWED FOUNDATION

Charles Parham considered himself a groundbreaking theologian. He never finished his formal theological training, so he built an eclectic faith system that was both borrowed from others and concocted in his own vivid mind. His dangerous dogma provided a very poor foundation for the newly formed Apostolic Faith movement. Within five years, the most outlandish of his views had been totally rejected by the movement he had founded.

In fact, most elements of Parham's theological framework were never adopted by even the most devout of his followers. As more studied men aligned themselves with the new Pentecostalism, they bent the tenets of Apostolic Faith toward a more orthodox theology largely in the Wesleyan Holiness tradition.

Some of Parham's more unconventional biblical interpretations are discussed only briefly in his writings and not given the attention needed to fully understand them. Without being able to speak to him to further clarify the nuances of his beliefs, it is difficult to comprehend most of his positions, let alone explain them to others. Perhaps some of the things Parham taught never made sense anywhere except in his own mind.

Parham relies on quotes from the Apocryphal books of 1 and 2 Esdras; the Jewish historian Josephus; the spurious Gospel of Barnabas; George Washington; and even Leo Tolstoy. Much of his theology is borrowed from others and put together in a practically incoherent mishmash. It would take an encyclopedia to fully explore and explain Parham's doctrines and the underlying reasoning that formed them. Such a task is far beyond the scope of this work. The following, however, is an abbreviated look at some of his doctrines.

CREATION

A six-day creation, as described in Genesis, was far too simple for Parham. First, he believed that each day represented one thousand years. Parham also believed that God created animals and man on the sixth day, and then He rested, in line with the Genesis account. However, this, too, was far too simplistic for the amateur theologian. He claimed that on the *eighth* day, God formed "Adam" and a special class of animals that lived only in the garden. Parham was quite convinced that the imaginary lost city of Atlantis was Eden and that all that remained of it was the West Indies.[370]

Besides this, Parham makes a great distinction between inferior human beings who were "created" on the sixth day and superior human beings who were "formed" on the eighth day. He said that after Adam sinned, God promised him a Savior, but the "created" ones never received any such promise.

He further postulated that after Cain killed his brother, he married a woman from the "created" race. Because their intermarriage polluted the "formed" race, God sent the great flood to destroy the world. The entire "created" race died in the flood, as did the entire mixed race, as well as the created animals, including the dinosaurs. Only the clean animals supposedly formed on the eighth day and placed in the garden were allowed on the ark.

In an apparent attempt to explain the difficult passage of 1 Peter 3:18–20, Parham also believed that Jesus Christ, between His crucifixion and resurrection, went to the heart of the earth and preached to the unfortunate "created" beings that had died without hope. Since they had had no

---

370. "God's Plan of the Ages," *The Everlasting Gospel (TAF)*, April 1916, 1, FPHC. For a short time in 1916 and 1917, Parham changed the name of his periodical to *The Everlasting Gospel*. He then returned to the original title.

previous opportunity for salvation, hearing the gospel after they were dead was their first chance to be saved.[371]

DEMONS

Without offering a hint of biblical corroboration, Parham apparently believed and taught a fictional story from the Quran that says after God created mankind, He sent out an edict that all the angels should come before Him, bow, and acknowledge His great handiwork. As the angels appeared and bowed before Adam, Lucifer refused to obey. He thought it demeaning to bow before a creature he felt inferior to himself. This led to Lucifer's rebellion, with the result that Lucifer and his followers were kicked out of heaven. They then declared war on the men of earth.

Parham believed that these fallen angels were joined by a host of demons, of unknown origin, that also harassed men. He thought that these imps of darkness were behind every preacher who didn't teach truth. He also taught that all "such diseases as cancers, tumors, consumption, catarrh, rheumatism, all fevers, epilepsy, fits and spasm, whooping cough, St. Vitus dance, insanity and all nervous disorders are the direct result of tormenting demons."[372]

THE GOSPEL OF THE KINGDOM

Parham's definition of "the gospel of the kingdom" was probably closer to Pentecostal orthodoxy than any of his other claims. He believed the eternal gospel of Christ has three essential elements. First, it gives remission of sin. Second, it destroys the works of the devil in sickness and affliction. Finally, it offers a baptism in the Holy Spirit.

These points are very close to the four fundamentals of the Assemblies of God, the International Church of the Foursquare Gospel, and other classical Pentecostal denominations. The exception is they would add the second coming of Christ as one of their essential tenets.[373]

---

371. C. Parham, *Everlasting Gospel*, 81–85.

372. Quran 2:34, https://corpus.quran.com; C. Parham, "Demonology, or In My Name Ye Shall Cast Out Devils," 39–43.

373. C. Parham, *Everlasting Gospel*, 38.

FULL REDEMPTION

Parham also had a relatively orthodox view of salvation from sin. He believed in a born-again experience. However, he also believed in another level of salvation that he called "full redemption," or "maturity of redemption." His scheme sounds more like something birthed in the "Twilight Zone" than a doctrine born of sound biblical hermeneutics. Claiming he had seen a vision or a dream of an earthy friend encased in a glistening form, Parham received a "new revelation" about redemption that he called the "Church all of gold," to distinguish it from the rest of the church. Only the seed of Abraham, those "of His own blood," could be part of this exclusive body.

He believed that the full redemption would be accomplished when the present church came into unity with the historical church. Living believers, as well as some of the resurrected dead, would make up the church of gold, or, as he also called those who belonged to it, "the elect."

Only Parham was given the plan to bring the church into unity. He was to divide the church into the twelve tribes of Israel and then "they would gather as one man." It is not clear how this unification would be accomplished, but Parham said the time was coming when the church would have the same mind and the same judgment, and believers would all speak the same things. This would bring about the church's full redemption.

The fully redeemed would be miracle-working super-Christians. They would go forth according to Parham's dogma to preach the gospel, and multitudes would be saved and healed. These redeemed would be able to appear and disappear as needed. A glimpse of the state of the full redeemed could be seen in the transfiguration of Christ. Jesus draped in His glory was a type of the redeemed. Those fortunate to be part of this church of gold would enjoy all the attributes of Christ in His post-resurrection appearances.

Parham took many biblical texts that his contemporaries usually connected to the rapture or the resurrection of the dead and applied them to the fully redeemed. For example, in 1 Corinthians 15:51, where Paul told the Corinthians that not all would die but some would be "changed," Parham saw them changed not into raptured saints in heaven but into the fully redeemed on the earth.

There was no other way, according to his reasoning, to evangelize the world. Present methods had failed to reach the multitudes, so God would employ the elect to reach the lost millions. The redeemed would be led by the "true Elijah" who would bring them to unity. Parham stopped short of giving the identity of this "true Elijah"; however, considering his view of his own self-importance, it doesn't take much imagination to venture a guess.[374]

WATER BAPTISM

Parham was a Trinitarian—believing in one true God who has revealed Himself as embodying the principles of relationship and association as Father, Son, and Holy Ghost. However, he rejected the triune baptismal formula as recorded in Matthew 28:19, instead choosing a baptism in Jesus's name alone. He finally settled on "baptized in the name of Jesus, into the name of the Father, Son and Holy Ghost."

The formula is not as unorthodox as was the logic that led Parham to this baptismal scheme. Parham said that while he was waiting upon God for an answer regarding how to baptize, the Holy Spirit spoke to him and said, "We are buried by baptism into His death." Parham said he had known that truth for years, so the Holy Spirit explained further, "God the Father, and God the Holy Ghost never died."

Concluding that a believer "could not be buried by baptism in the name of the Father, or in the name of the Holy Ghost" because the Father and the Spirit had never died or been resurrected from the dead, as Jesus had been, Parham amended his baptismal formula.[375]

SANCTIFICATION

As one of the principal tenets of the Apostolic Faith, Parham believed in a complete sanctification as a second and last work of God's grace, the first work being salvation. According to the evangelist, conversion gave you probationary membership in the church of the living God, but sanctification made you a full member.

---

374. C. Parham, *Kol Kare Bomidbar*, 69–80; Charles F. Parham, "The Everlasting Gospel," *The Everlasting Gospel*, July 1916, 17, FPHC.
375. C. Parham, *Kol Kare Bomidbar*, 21–24.

While he believed that holiness grew in the life of the believer, sanctification was instantaneous. Sanctification does not deal with sins committed but with inbred sin. Every person is born with a sinful nature, but sanctification removes that propensity toward sin. Conversion does not remove this sin nature, but a sanctified individual no longer has the old nature that causes them to sin or leads them into sin. All "inherited passions, appetites and lusts" are removed from a sanctified life.

According to Parham, sanctification makes a believer holy. He is one with Christ. This is an action of "God's free grace."[376]

One of the requisites for attaining sanctification was a full consecration. Parham did not believe in giving God only a tenth of one's bounty; he believed in giving God all of it. Yes, that is what he taught, saying, "The entire increase of your possessions at the end of the year, unless absolutely needed in the furtherance of your business or occupation, shall be turned over into the service of the Lord."[377]

Although early Pentecostals did not adopt all of Parham's views on sanctification, the idea that it was a second work of grace was almost universally accepted until 1910. Chicago evangelist William H. Durham introduced the "Finished Work" doctrine, declaring that sanctification was part of the work of Calvary and was received at conversion. By Durham's definition, the baptism in the Holy Spirit is the second work of grace. Parham, Seymour, and others vehemently opposed Durham. However, within a few years, Durham's view became the dominant view among Pentecostals and remains so today.

THE BAPTISM IN THE HOLY SPIRIT

As emphasized throughout this book, Charles Parham was the first to teach that, in the New Testament, the baptism in the Holy Spirit was always accompanied by speaking in an unknown language. He empathically stated, "[N]o one has the Holy Spirit unless he speaks in tongues."[378]

---

376. Charles Parham, "Sanctification," in *Selected Sermons by the Late Charles F. Parham and Sarah E. Parham*, comp. Robert Parham (Baxter Springs, KS: Apostolic Faith, 1941), 51–59.
377. C. Parham, "Sanctification," 51; *Everlasting Gospel*, 104.
378. C. Parham, *Everlasting Gospel*, 63.

His view of tongues speaking, or glossolalia, has become known to Pentecostals as the "initial physical evidence."

In his first sermon on Pentecost following the outpouring at Topeka, Parham said:

> This promise, when fulfilled was followed by such unmistakable evidence that no one can doubt it who has received it. Thousands of Christians profess this sealing as well as the Baptism of the Holy Ghost, yet the Bible evidence is lacking in their lives....
>
> Now all Christians credit the fact that we are to be the recipients of the Holy Spirit, but each have their private interpretations as to His visible manifestations; some claim shouting, leaping, jumping, and falling in trances, while others put stress upon inspiration, unction and divine revelation.[379]

Throughout the remainder of this sermon—and indeed throughout the rest of his life—Parham continued to make the case that speaking in tongues was the only biblical evidence of the Holy Spirit baptism. He said, "All Scripture upon this subject agree; only modern teachers disagree."[380]

Parham believed the baptism in the Holy Spirit was the sealing of the bride of Christ, which, as will be discussed in a subsequent section, he erroneously believed to be the 144,000 servants of God mentioned in the book of Revelation. As previously mentioned, the evangelist also believed that speaking in tongues would enable missionaries to preach in other nations without learning the indigenous languages. Again, except for some notable examples, this has not proven to be the case.[381]

HEALING

Parham believed that divine healing was available to all believers all the time. He declared that the healing of the sick "is as much a part of

---

379. C. Parham, *Kol Kare Bomidbar*, 27–28.
380. C. Parham, *Kol Kare Bomidbar*, 37–38.
381. C. Parham, *Kol Kare Bomidbar*, 25–38; Charles F. Parham, "The Baptism of the Holy Spirit," in *Selected Sermons by the Late Charles F. Parham and Sarah E. Parham*, comp. Robert Parham (Baxter Springs, KS: Apostolic Faith, 1941), 64–74; C. Parham, *Everlasting Gospel*, 63–69.

the gospel as telling…of heaven."[382] He further taught that a fully sanctified person would be sanctified in both spirit and body and would have no
"taint of disease."[383]

Consequently, all sickness was either inbred, acquired because of a
predisposition to illness, or a result of sin, either by omission or commission. Many Christians, he taught, were sick because of their sins. He called
sickness a "filthiness of the flesh" and believed that healing would come
through sanctification, particularly through the cleansing of the blood of
Jesus.

Parham saw a difference between infirmities and sicknesses. The former
were the maladies brought on by aging, while the latter were acquired. He
also declared that half of all sickness was imaginary and "existed only in the
mind of the individual."[384]

The evangelist had an amazing ability to diagnose sicknesses described
in the Bible, or at least he thought he did. Job apparently had smallpox, and
David had rheumatism.

As stated earlier, Parham testified that at the age of twenty-four, he
experienced the full triumph of Christ in his life, which enabled him to
become completely sanctified. The sanctifying power reached every part of
his body, "destroying the very root and tendency to disease."[385]

Parham stood in total opposition to the medical profession. He did not
believe in seeing a physician or taking any medicines. He taught that "medical science and her practicers" were mentioned in both biblical testaments
in connection with those "guilty of vilest sins against God and humanity."
He claimed, "The more proficient in relieving pain a system becomes, the
more anti-Christian is its influence." He called prescription drugs "poison"
and the medical field the "octopus-god Molloch."[386]

In one article, he hypothetically asked, "Why don't you use medicine;
does the Bible forbid its use?" His answer, "Yes, most emphatically YES."

382. C. Parham, *Everlasting Gospel*, 30.
383. "The Days of Noah," *TAF*, December 1914, 19, originalapostolicfaith.org.
384. C. Parham, "Demonology: In My Name Shall Ye Cast Out Devils," 42.
385. C. Parham, *Kol Kare Bomidbar*, 19, 52.
386. Charles F. Parham, "Healing," in *Selected Sermons by the Late Charles F. Parham and
Sarah E. Parham*, comp. Robert Parham (Baxter Springs, KS: Apostolic Faith, 1941), 25;
C. Parham, *Kol Kare Bomidbar*, 40–41.

He then took Jeremiah 30:13 and Jeremiah 46:11 completely out of con-text, applying them universally: "Thou hast no healing medicines," and "In vain shall thou use many medicines, for thou shalt not be cured." Without giving the slightest biblical evidence, he went even further to say, "The New Testament is most positive in the construction of its denounciation [sic]."[387]

Thanks be to God, many suffering people received physical healing in Parham's meetings, but his teachings on medicine were rejected by the vast majority of Pentecostals as too extreme.[388]

BRITISH-ISRAELISM AND THE LOST TRIBES OF ISRAEL

Parham was a strong believer in a doctrine known to theologians as British-Israelism. The false theory claims that there is archeological, his-torical, and biblical proof that the Anglo-Saxon people of the British Isles are the people of ancient Israel. In other words, the Brits are really Jews.

Laying out his case, Parham said that Jeremiah the prophet moved to Ireland after his cousin Zedekiah released him from prison. Jeremiah brought with him the scepter of David and the Stone of Scone from the temple in Jerusalem. Supposedly, every king of Judah was coronated on that stone, and it followed that the royalty of Ireland, Scotland, and then England were all installed on the same stone. Therefore, Edward VII, the ruling monarch at the time when he expressed this theory, was actually sitting on David's throne. (Sound ridiculous? It gets worse.)

Going to great lengths, Parham traced the lineage all the way from Adam to Victoria to prove a "direct and unbroken line of ancestry." Parham further believed that the British people were from the tribe of Ephraim, one of the ten "lost tribes" of Israel; the Danes were descended from the tribe of Dan, and those who lived in the United States came from the tribe of Manasseh. What proof did he offer? Well, for starters, Manasseh was a son of Joseph, and Joseph was married to an Egyptian. Furthermore, the great seal of the United States has an eagle with an olive branch on one side and a pyramid on the other. The eagle is an emblem of Israel, and the pyramid is a symbol of Egypt, signifying the "same hybrid origin."[389]

---

387. *TAF*, September 13, 1899, 7, KHS.
388. C. Parham, *Kol Kare Bomidbar*, 39–52.
389. C. Parham, *Kol Kare Bomidbar*, 91–108.

Parham felt that since they were not among the lost tribes, "the Black race, the Brown race, the Red race, the Yellow race" were still all "nearly heathen" despite all the missionary efforts to reach them. Only at the "dawning of the coming age" would these ethnicities "be given to Jesus for an inheritance."[390]

Parham's unsubstantiated claims about British-Israelism and the lost tribes of Israel might be innocent enough or even amusing if they were not also tied to ideas of racial and spiritual superiority, topics we will discuss in the next chapter.

WAR

Like many early Pentecostals, Parham was a strict pacifist. He did not believe in the shedding of blood, even in a "just cause." Christians, according to the evangelist, should "not fight." "He that taketh the sword," he paraphrased Matthew 26:52, "shall perish with the sword."[391] With no apology, he labeled brave young men who volunteered for military service in the great war "self-appointed murderers."[392]

In a 1914 sermon, Parham postulated on the reason for war:

To murder a fellow-creature! To receive therefore even less than thirty pieces of silver, and perhaps live to receive the plaudits and honor of a more cowardly country and imbecile nation; for the nation is imbecile which retains its existence through the struggling exploits of war. We hang our head in shame to see Christian nations and individuals yield themselves to the embrace of the Moloch-God, Patriotism.[393]

Unfortunately, F. Rolland Romack, Parham's printer for many years, was drafted in World War I and was killed on a battlefield in France. Romack had applied for an exemption from combat service on religious grounds, but it was denied by the War Department.[394] Parham's last letter

---

390. C. Parham, *Kol Kare Bomidbar*, 107.
391. S. Parham, *Life of Charles F. Parham*, 273.
392. C. Parham, *Kol Kare Bomidbar*, 59.
393. C. Parham, *Everlasting Gospel*, 82.
394. S. Parham, *Life of Charles F. Parham*, 272–273.

to Romack, expressing his prayers, love, and respect, was mailed on the day the reluctant soldier was killed. The letter was returned with the stamp, "Deceased, Verified."[395]

DIVORCE AND REMARRIAGE

Parham was more lenient on remarriage after divorce than many early Pentecostals were. He said, "It is a question never yet settled whether an innocent party in a divorce case has a right to marry, and a mission cannot always say that a couple is living in adultery just because they are twice married, for if the innocent party is allowed to marry, they must answer to God and if God blesses them, the mission must keep their hands off."[396] He may have adopted this tolerant position because his stepmother was the victim of divorce.

THE END TIMES

The evangelist often took on himself the role of prophet, forecasting things that were supposedly "soon" to come upon the earth. Apparently, in 1896, he prophesied that the world would end in two years.[397] A few years later, he was forecasting the coming of the Lord by 1925.[398] His view of the seven seals of Revelation is typical of his prophetic prognosticating.

In an article he wrote for a local newspaper in 1896, Parham gave his explanation for the seven seals. His interpretation did not come only from what he believed was a careful exegesis of the Scriptures; he said he also received revelation after waiting on the Lord, who "graciously bestowed upon me the meaning." His overall view was that the seals represented the period of time from Christ until the end. The white horse in the first seal represented purity, and therefore the first seal represented the pure preaching of the gospel from Christ to Constantine. The second seal described a time of persecution and inquisition, from Constantine until the "settlement of America." The balances held by the rider of the black horse in the

---

395. Charles F. Parham, letter to Francis Rolland Romack, September 13, 1908, AFBC.
396. "Questions and Answers," *TAF*, March 1913, 15, FTSL.
397. "Additional Locals," *The Burns Citizen* (Kansas), 4 September 1896, 2, newspapers.com.
398. Shumway, "A Critical Study of 'The Gift of Tongues,'" 166.

third seal indicated the age of reason. Parham said this period lasted until 1893.

According to the evangelist, in 1896, the world was living during the time when the fourth seal was open. He saw this period as a time of war, hunger, and death. The fourth seal would end with the "first resurrection," the restoration of Palestine to the Jews, the revelation of the Antichrist, and the first half of the tribulation. Parham claimed the Antichrist was already in the world. He saw the fifth seal as celestial and not terrestrial, describing latter-day martyrs in heaven.

The opening of the sixth seal marked Christ's return to the earth, the battle of Armageddon, and the millennial reign, which Parham called the "Sabbath reign" or "Earth Jubilee." He believed that there was an overlap in the opening of the seals and that the Earth Jubilee would begin in 1900.

Parham also believed the seventh seal would be opened after the "Sabbath" and would be poured out on the resurrected wicked. He admitted he was still "dissecting" the seventh seal.[399]

Over the years, Parham became a bit more cautious in date setting, but here is an example of how he prophesied about world events in 1917:

> To give you a little note of what will soon come according to my light on prophecy, I submit the following: After a short time the demand for men and war taxes the nation to utter bankruptcy, which will cause the masses to refuse to support the war. If you do not believe this from the prophetic standpoint, just listen to what is already rumbling among the masses in all nations, and all the power of rulers or lawmakers will not be able to stem the rising tide of objections to this awful war. The masses will demand that they settle this thing and DO IT NOW, and if they do not one and all the ruling powers will be wiped off the face of the earth by the enraged masses, whose homes and loved ones and even their food has been taken to gratify this Moloch or God of War—Mars.
>
> The lodges, churches and unions are all going to fall and the rich will be killed in the streets. A period of terrible and awful anarchy

---

399. Charles F. Parham, "The Seven Seals of Revelation," *TM*, February 7, 1896, 4, newspapers.com.

will follow in which the Pope will call the Catholics of the world to stand for order, and he being the only one who can control sufficient of the consciences of men, will re-establish order. A great teacher will then arise with a system of ethics similar to Socialism. The Pope will be compelled to accede to the general clamor and will appoint ten men as a commission to rule the world. This will be the ten-horn, ten-king, ten-toed kingdom of Daniel and Revelation. Out of this will arise this great teacher, the little horn of Revelation, as the universal dictator—the Anti-Christ—who will establish a universal autocracy and a world-wide union so that no one can buy or sell without his name or number.[400]

Unfortunately for Parham, but good for the rest of humanity, World War I ended with victory for the Allies. The rich were never murdered in the streets, and the pope never ruled the world, but Parham continued to prophesy.

THE BRIDE OF CHRIST

The bride of Christ, according to Parham's interpretation, was not all Christians or the full body of Christ but a select group of believers who were chosen from out of His body. As Adam's bride came out of his body, Christ's bride must come from His. Every member of the bride would have "Israelitish" blood and be baptized in the Holy Spirit with the evidence of speaking in tongues. Parham did allow that the blood of Abraham could be in all races because of intermarriage. The bride would be made of both living saints and those who had died but had been "found worthy."

Parham also believed that the bride would gather in Jerusalem in the end times and then flee into the "wilderness" for the last three and a half years before the second coming of Christ. The wilderness, according to Parham's teaching, was the land of Bashan (in modern-day Syria) mentioned in the third chapter of Deuteronomy. Parham claimed that all sixty cities of Bashan were built by giants and had been discovered by explorers. He said they were uninhabited but had been "preserved and protected" by God since the days of Moses, ready for reoccupation.

---

400. "An Open Letter to the Rulers of Europe," *TEG*, October 1917, 4–5, FTSL.

The bride, according to Parham in his interpretation of the book of Revelation, gave birth to a man child.[401] This special company of believers, chosen from among those who were worthy to be the bride, had reached the "highest perfection attainable for human beings." The man child would be taken to heaven like Enoch and Elijah were caught up to heaven in the Old Testament. This catching away was Parham's only belief in a "rapture." Only this exclusive numbered group with Abraham's blood and sealed by the Holy Spirit would be caught up to heaven.[402]

THE RETURN OF THE JEWS TO ISRAEL

As mentioned previously, Parham was a strong proponent of the Zionist movement of his day. He believed and taught that it was required by Scripture that the Jews return to the promised land. In fact, he predicted that once the "Jewish Congress"[403] met in Jerusalem and declared Israel to be a nation, Jesus would literally set his feet on the Mount of Olives in seven years. Israel became a nation in 1948, and, to date, Parham's prediction is off by more than seventy years.

Since the Jews were not coming back to Palestine as quickly as Parham had wished, he believed the only way to hasten their return was by bringing the ark of the covenant back to Jerusalem. Restoring this precious relic to the Holy City would cause the Jews to "flock like birds to the window." Through his "most laborious search," Parham believed he had located the ark and was charged to find it and return it to its rightful home.[404]

THE ANTICHRIST

The Antichrist, as Parham saw it, would be a man who was an "exact imitator and promulgator of the life and teaching of Jesus." He would first appear in the "closing days of the Bolshevik revolution" and after the pope had rallied all Catholics and restored order to the world. He would establish his government in a restored Babylon. The Antichrist would capture

---

401. See Revelation 12:5, 13.
402. C. Parham, *Kol Kare Bomidbar*, 86–90.
403. "National Jewish Congress," *San Jose Mercury-News* (California), January 9, 1901, 3, cdnc.ucr.edu.
404. C. Parham, *Kol Kare Bomidbar*, 101–104.

the world's attention and ultimately gain power by writing a book about "socialistic democracy." The masses, "with enthusiasm such as the world has never seen," would overthrow the Catholic rule and establish a kingdom for the Antichrist. While attending a "World's Fair" type of gathering in Jerusalem, this world leader would be murdered by the sword. Life would come back into his body, but he would be "animated by another spirit entirely." The spirit that possessed the Antichrist would be none other than that of Judas Iscariot.

Parham believed that Judas was the devil in the flesh. He stated that Judas was as much Satan incarnate as Jesus was God incarnate.

For some unexplained reason, after the leader is possessed by Judas Iscariot, the Jews will accept him as their Messiah, and the pope and reunited "churchanity" will accept him as the Christ. He will then become an autocrat, an absolute dictator.

According to Parham's interpretation, the Antichrist will order the whole world to take the mark of the beast. This will be accomplished through a worldwide union organized by "fanatical patriotic followers." One would not be able to buy or sell without the mark, so those who refused to receive the mark would either starve or be killed by the Antichrist. The only way to escape death would be to be sealed by having received the baptism in the Holy Spirit with evidentiary tongues.[405]

THE STATE OF THE WICKED DEAD AND THE LAST JUDGMENT

According to Parham, the dead wait in the grave until the judgment. He believed that only those who were born again possessed a spirit. The lost had a body and a soul, but the soul lies dormant in the tomb until the "general resurrection."[406]

The judgment, as Parham defined it, would last for one thousand years because every person would individually take their turn standing before God. God would be on the throne, and Parham's redeemed would serve as a jury. Strangely, Parham did not believe the judgment would be based on

405. C. Parham, Kol Kare Bomidbar, 119–123; Everlasting Gospel, 33–36.
406. "The Devil, Evil Spirits or Disembodied Spirits," TAF, September 1913, 13, FTSL.

whether a person received or rejected Christ. Each person would be judged by their works alone.

Babies, the heathen, and the unconverted church members would all be judged. A person who never knew the law would not be judged by the law, but every person would be judged fairly. Those who passed the muster would be welcomed into the coming kingdom and have "everlasting human life" as Adam enjoyed in the garden of Eden.

Hypocrites and others who failed to pass God's test would be thrown into the lake of fire.[407]

HELL

Eternal life, as defined by Parham, is the "gift of God" and belongs only to believers. God did not make Adam with an eternal soul, and thus all human beings who came after him were born without an immortal soul. Men inherited a sinful nature, not immortality, from Adam. Therefore, hell is only a place of temporary torment. The wicked will be burned up like garbage consumed in a fire. Sarah Parham wrote, "When we make a bonfire, it is to destroy that which is worthless. Is that not God's purpose?"[408]

Parham blamed the doctrine of hell on the Catholic Church and boldly proclaimed, "The teaching that all men have immortal souls denies the Divinity of Christ, makes him a liar and an imposter, and all His claims to bring life and immortality to men through His death are false."

Both Parhams used God's love as a reason to deny the existence of an eternal hell. Sarah wrote, "Would it be possible for a God of love to subject His creation to endless misery, eternal torment giving them life...only to suffer, yet with no hope of their betterment...?"[409] Charles took this idea even further and expressed it in much more graphic terms:

> We are supposed to believe in a God who, after bringing creatures into existence, will cast them into [sic] lake of eternal torment; who is possessed with such a diabolical character that He is able to sit

---

407. C. Parham, *Everlasting Gospel*, 98–100.
408. Sarah E. Parham, "Immortality," in *Selected Sermons by the Late Charles F. Parham and Sarah E. Parham*, comp. Robert Parham (Baxter Springs, KS: Apostolic Faith, 1941), 104.
409. S. Parham, "Immortality," 93–95.

upon the throne of His glory, listen to their howling and screeching, and view them sizzling, stewing, frying and browning, without surcease throughout the countless cycles of Eternity.[410]

Sarah Parham also believed that the idea of an eternal hell was derived from a misunderstanding of New Testament parables.[411] For example, the Parhams believed that the parable of the rich man and Lazarus was a fictitious narrative that had nothing to do with death or eternal judgment; rather, Jesus was talking about the Jews in exile.[412]

A FINAL WORD

Critics of the Pentecostal movement will look at the whole of Parham's doctrine and label him as a theological nutcase. In a number of instances, they may be right. Many critics, however, may go further. They may be tempted to paint all of Pentecostalism with a wide, Parhamite brush, claiming that the entire movement rests on a faulty foundation.

Such an assessment would be decidedly incorrect and a disservice to multitudes of Pentecostals in both the past and the present. The Pentecostal movement rejected Parham's extreme positions. They rejected them completely and almost immediately. Some of his theology was Bible-based and sound. A wise discerner of truth can reject what is false without also dismissing what is true.

Martin Luther brought some great truths to the church. His realization that "the just shall live by faith"[413] changed the Christian church and, to a great extent, all of human history. Yet Luther embraced some doctrines that the evangelical church has rejected today. His ideas of consubstantiation in regard to the Lord's Supper are not embraced by non-Lutherans. Should everything Luther believed and taught be labeled heresy because he was wrong on some issues? Of course not.

---

410. C. Parham, *Everlasting Gospel*, 111.
411. Sarah E. Parham, "Earnestly Contend for the Faith Once Delivered to the Saints, Jude 3," in *Selected Sermons by the Late Charles F. Parham and Sarah E. Parham*, comp. Robert Parham (Baxter Springs, KS: Apostolic Faith, 1941), 21.
412. S. Parham, "Immortality," 107–108; C. Parham, *Everlasting Gospel*, 115.
413. See, for example, Romans 1:17.

In another example, the American Declaration of Independence declares that "all men are created equal." Yet, the United States Constitution allowed slavery for more than seventy-five years, and it clearly did not treat all men equally. Should the entire document be rejected? Should our founders be defamed because they tolerated slavery and even owned slaves? Our new "tear it down" cancel culture says yes. Proponents want to destroy anything that doesn't fit perfectly into their "woke" mindset. Wiser and more mature Americans will realize you can separate the meat from the bones. Having some things wrong does not mean having everything wrong.

Of course, this does not excuse the fact that Parham was wrong, very wrong, about a lot of things. Neither does it answer the question of how he could have been wrong about so much and have been right about the baptism in the Holy Spirit and speaking in tongues. The critics might say it is impossible. They might argue that Pentecostals drink only from a bitter spring.

Yet, among the estimated six hundred and fifty billion Pentecostals and charismatics in the world today, it would be difficult, perhaps impossible, to find even one single person who embraces the totality of Parham's teachings. Millions have accepted his teaching that speaking in tongues accompanies the biblical baptism of the Holy Spirit but would soundly reject his unorthodox doctrines.

In 1912, one of Parham's strongest advocates wrote, "I knew in 1906 that he was a chosen vessel and that he and his teaching would stand until redemption. I have often said, time will tell."[414] This man was right about one thing: time did tell. Parham's strangest teachings have been thoroughly discarded by most Pentecostals.

So, how did Parham glean a particular biblical truth that has changed the Christian church? There is an old saying, "Even a blind crow occasionally finds an acorn." Perhaps Parham was the blind crow, and the Holy Spirit baptism was his acorn.

Or perhaps not. The truth is that Parham did not "discover" the gift of tongues. Before the outpouring in Topeka, he had heard people speak in tongues at Sanford's Shiloh campground. Even in Topeka, it was the students who finally formalized the biblical connection between tongues

414. Brower, "God's Work Here."

speaking and the New Testament baptism in the Holy Spirit. Remember, these students were not spiritual novices. Some were mature Christian workers. They were totally immersed in prayer, fasting, and Bible study. It was in this atmosphere that the biblical truth about the baptism was rediscovered and reintroduced to the church. It was not Parham but Agnes Ozman who first received the gift of speaking in other tongues as a definite evidence of the Holy Spirit baptism. Perhaps Parham merely rode the wave.

At the same time, as emphasized earlier, one cannot dismiss the influence of God's sovereign works. God often chooses weak or flawed vessels to accomplish mighty things. People often quote the adage, "God is not looking for ability but availability." Charles Parham was available. If God had chosen someone with a more traditional theology, would they have had an open mind to something as unorthodox as speaking in tongues as the evidence of Holy Spirit baptism? They almost certainly would not have. In fact, history makes that case. In Parham's time, thousands rejected this idea. Whole denominations rejected it. They still do. It doesn't fit into their closed theological framework.

Charles Parham, with all his flaws—and there were plenty—was open to a new interpretation of an old truth. He was a vessel of clay, available and moldable. Like chaff in the wind, most of his teachings have blown away with the passage of time, but this one truth that he taught has endured and has changed the world.

8

PLAYING THE RACE CARD

American society's attitudes toward race have changed a lot in the one hundred and fifty years since Charles Parham was born. Mindsets and language that were acceptable in Parham's lifetime are by no means acceptable today. The word *racism* did not even appear in *Webster's Dictionary* until after Parham's death.

Many people, including this author, have, at times, used these changing mores to give Parham a pass on some of his racial views. The defense goes something like this: "Parham would be considered a racist by today's standards, but not by the standards of his day."

The truth is that racism was just as wrong in Parham's day as it is today, regardless of how society tolerated it at the time. To use an illustration, smoking cigarettes was once accepted, if not applauded, by American culture. Medical doctors advertised the benefits of smoking. Some great preachers were smokers. Yet despite the approval of society, smoking tobacco was just as deadly and destructive then as it is now when it is widely condemned.

It is the same with racism. A culture winking at racism or turning a blind eye toward it does not make racism any less an evil. Racism is wrong—it always has been and always will be.

The dictionary defines racism as "the belief in or practice of racial superiority."[415] By this definition, or by almost any other definition of racism, Parham was undeniably a racist. Racism was interwoven through his theological framework. Believing as he did that Anglo-Saxons were Jews from the lost tribes of Israel, he perceived his race as superior.

Some of Parham's racial comments are almost too ugly to repeat. Merely quoting his ill-informed racial reasoning is painful. Reading what he said must be especially agonizing for people of color. No Christian should ever think or speak as Parham did about race.

This excruciatingly dreadful account written by one of Parham's associate editors and published in the *Apostolic Faith* shows the worst of the evangelist's prejudice:

> Negro rapists meet summary punishment at the hands of enraged mobs, and yet how much better is the white lust fiend who alienates the affections of another's wife, or the reptile who creeps in and steals a daughter's virtue? The negro is usually a monstrosity with small brain capacity, and so near the brutes of the lower order that really their acts should create no great surprise. But the white male knows better and because of his reasoning faculties, his guilt is the more glaring.[416]

I deeply regret that any Christian ever made a statement like that. I apologize to people of color.

Some people believe that to be a racist, one must hate people of other races. That erroneous view misses the true definition of racism. A person can be a racist and show kindness to other races. For the most part, Parham was not hostile toward other races; he may even have "loved" them. At least, he was concerned about their eternal destiny. Blacks were welcome in his meetings, albeit often separated from whites.

Parham also welcomed people of color to his annual camp meeting in Baxter Springs. He once exclaimed, upon observing the diversity of his

---

415. *The Doubleday Dictionary for Home, School, and Office* (Garden City, NY: Doubleday and Company, 1975), s.v. "racism," 599.
416. H. W. Schermer, "Leaves by the Wayside," *TAF*, May 1913, 13, AFBC.

audience, "We had the Gospel in black and white and red all over."[417] One year, a black man received the baptism in the Holy Spirit at the camp meeting and spoke in German.[418]

Parham shared preaching opportunities with William Seymour. Early in their relationship, he was nothing but kind to Seymour. As mentioned previously, he helped to pay Seymour's train fare to Los Angeles. Parham also spoke sympathetically of Seymour and R. A. Hall, another Black minister from Houston, saying, "I feel pledged to help these brethren in every possible way. They need a lot because of the peculiar difficulty they have in securing meeting places."[419]

Parham didn't "hate"; he just thought he and his entire race were better—much better. He looked down on people of color, again, not in a specifically malicious way but in an extremely condescending way. Thus, as best as can be determined, Parham didn't think all of his Black brothers and sisters were particularly bad; he just didn't think they were his equals. For example, Lucy Farrar was good enough to be a cook for his team and a governess for his children. She received the Holy Spirit baptism in Parham's home in Kansas. But he referred to her as "a very light colored."[420] It is unlikely he would have given her a position of leadership in the organization. He could send her to California to help Seymour with the African American saints in Los Angeles, but he almost certainly would not have let her lead white workers.

Similarly, Seymour could preach with Parham on the streets of Houston, but only to Blacks. He might be considered fit for leadership, but only leadership of a "colored" branch of the Apostolic Faith. When two more Blacks joined the movement in 1906, they were described as "splendid negro preachers." W. M. Viney was called "capable of managing any field," but he was made "Director of the work in the Houston district among *his* people [italics added]."[421]

---

417. "Reports of the Thirteenth Annual Camp Meeting," *TAF*, September 1913, 3, FTSL.
418. "At the Camp Meeting," *TAF*, October 1913, 19–20, FTSL.
419. *TAF*, March 1906, 10, HSRC.
420. "A Critical Analysis of the Tongues Movement," *TAF*, June 25, 3, digitalshowcase.oru.edu.
421. *TAF*, May 1906, 15, originalapostolicfaith.org.

Sad to say, Parham was probably never self-aware enough to recognize his own racism. Yet the following sections further reveal the outworking of his racist beliefs.

RACIST DOCTRINES

In the previous chapter, Parham's peculiar beliefs about the bride of Christ were outlined. He believed that every member of the bride would be physically born with Jewish blood. Although he said that, because of intermarriage, there "seemingly will be people of all races" within the bride, his "all races" apparently did not include Blacks.[422] Both Parham and Glenn Cook "almost discouraged" Lucy Farrar by telling her that Blacks could not be part of the bride of Christ.[423] Discouraging, indeed.

Parham also developed a strange doctrine on interracial marriage. Again, he believed that the flood during Noah's time was caused by the intermarriage of people who were "created" and people who were "made." This was one of the reasons he was totally opposed to intermarriage between whites and Blacks.

With no Bible or facts upon which to base his opinions, the evangelist claimed that intermarriage always causes plagues and incurable diseases. He argued that if interracial marriages continued between "whites, the blacks and the reds in America, consumption and other diseases would soon wipe the mixed bloods off the face of the earth."[424]

RACIST LANGUAGE

In his sermons and publications, Parham referred to African Americans as "darkys." In one issue of the *Apostolic Faith*, he included the story of a "darky" preacher who was asked to pray for a white man. The preacher's prayer, which was originally published in the *Roanoke News*, was clearly intended to mock the man's intelligence:

O, Lord, gib him de eye of de eagle dat he spy out sin afar off. Glue his hands to de gospel plow. Tie his tongue to de line ob truth.

---

422. C. Parham, *Kol Kare Bomidbar*, 86.
423. Brower, "Origin of the Apostolic Faith Movement on the Pacific Coast," 6.
424. C. Parham, *Everlasting Gospel*, 3.

Nail his ear to de gospel pole. Bow his head way down between his knees, and his knees way down in some lonesome, dark and narrer valley, where prayer is much wanted to be made. 'Noint him wid de kerosene ile of salvashun and sot him on fire.[425]

The *Apostolic Faith* printed this piece of ridicule more than once. A search of the available issues of the paper gives several other examples of inappropriate caricatures of African Americans.[426]

Parham often ridiculed African American church services. In his publications, he reprinted statements that compared religious fanaticism to the "old fashioned negro worship of the south."[427] In one sermon, he told the audience that if they had not seen "an old fashioned darky camp meeting in the south," they had missed half their life. He went on to say, "That is the way they worship God, but what makes my soul sick, and makes me sick at my stomach is to see white people imitating unintelligent, crude negroism of the Southland, and laying it on the Holy Ghost."[428] On another occasion, he criticized the churches in Texas for worshipping "God after a negro fashion, thus making themselves ridiculous in the sight of all sane and reasonable people."[429]

Parham had no problem using the "n-word" and other racial slurs in his publications. In the March 1912 *Apostolic Faith*, he published a sarcastic attempt at humor entitled "The American Circus." It was a tongue-in-cheek appeal for Mexicans to come to America, while enumerating all the reasons why they shouldn't come. Among the problems the author saw in the United States was "'n------' can vote and women can't."[430]

In a December 1912 article, the evangelist wrote:

> For instance, in a meeting in Oakland, Cal., where the leader (a lady) took great pains to tell how "they loved each other SO MUCH!" In speaking of a Negro who was visiting them, she told how they all loved him so, and just made him love them; "in fact,

425. "A Darky's Prayer," *TAF*, December 1905, 7, originalapostolicfaith.org.
426. *TAF*, April 14, 1899, 3, KHS; *TAF*, September 1926, 15, originalapostolicfaith.org; "Tithing—Thanksgiving Ann," *TAF*, October 1926, 11, originalapostolicfaith.org.
427. "Editorial," *TAF*, September 1914, 9, originalapostolicfaith.org.
428. "Sermon by Chas. F. Parham," *TAF*, April 1925, 10, originalapostolicfaith.org.
429. "Change of Plans," *TAF*, October 1912 Supplement, n.p., originalapostolicfaith.org.
430. "The American Circus," *TAF*, March 1912, 3, originalapostolicfaith.org.

we will not let anyone stay in our house unless they love us all, and we just love each other more and more and all the time, etc., etc.,"

This lovely talk went on until it was actually sickening. An outsider would have thought that this was another bunch of n----- lovers and free lovers; but they were not, oh no, but were a very esteemable [*sic*] class of Christians.[431]

An even worse piece appeared in the *Apostolic Faith* in May 1913:

Another Apostolic (?) preacher hobnobbed with the "n------" in Houston, Texas, until trouble arose, and he was unmercifully beaten by the c----. It was disgusting to hear him shout and praise God for persecution for righteousness sake.[432]

In August, another piece selected for the paper said, "The spirit of 'hero worship' is rife, and whether it is combat a buck n----- or find the North Pole, the public mind is fickle and bestows its favoritism where it will."[433]

Parham has many apologists, but there is no way to rationalize such ugly language. These were no slips of the tongue (although that, too, would be inexcusable); they were part of an article written for publication. These words were intentional.

SEGREGATION IN THEORY

Although Parham did not write much about segregation, he definitely had strong feelings against integration. In the *Apostolic Faith*, he allowed the publication of these almost unbelievable comments by Warren Carothers:

God has made the two races, African and Caucasian, and manifestly intended that each should be preserved in their racial purity. God's plan for preserving this racial purity was originally by geographical separation. He intended for each people as a race to occupy its own country, just as he does for families to occupy separate homes. The white man, for selfish purposes, stole the colored

---

431. Charles Parham, "Free-Love," *TAF*, December 1912, 4, FPHC.
432. *TAF*, September 1913, 14, AFBC.
433. "Leaves by the Wayside," *TAF*, August 1913, AFBC.

man from his native home, and we have in the South, the unnatural condition of two peoples of unmixable blood trying to occupy one and the same land, contrary to God's racial plans, as proven in the cases of all other nations of the earth. Now, to meet the unnatural, unheard of condition God has resorted to the next best expedient and through his Holy Spirit has intensified the racist impulses between the white and black men as the only remaining possible barrier to the miscegenation of their respective races. This intensified racial impulse is mistaken by many outsiders for prejudice, or a work of the devil, when in truth it is the work of God's Holy Spirit, and as such is binding upon all Christians. Out of this has grown unwritten laws on the "race question," which we as Christians must respect. They forbid purely social intercourse between the races; they forbid their worshipping together in the family altars and in the public congregation upon terms of social equality and trust, therefore, that our evangelists and workers from the North will not forget this condition of affairs and embarrass the work South by well means but mistaken efforts to disregard them. Take the word of a native Southerner who through the sanctifying grace of Jesus Christ is incapable of prejudice, loving the colored man's soul equally as much as the white man's and let the race question alone until you have been South long enough to know by experience what it seems impossible for our Northern brethren to learn through other sources. They continually say to me: "Why up North where there is no prejudice against the negro, we have no race question." True enough, possibly. Neither do Texans have any race question with the Mexicans and why? Simply because the body of the Mexican people is across the Rio Grande, and the few thousands who struggle over here are regarded as visiting neighbors. It is exactly so with the negro in the North—the great body of the race being South of the Mason and Dixon's line, the North is delivered the race question. Dump the body of the Mexican people into Texas and wipe Mexico off the map and there would at once arise a "race question" between us and them, and, whether you may have thought so or not, the transfer of the great body of the negro race out of the South into the North would blot out the race question and so-called prejudices in the South and raise it in the North. God is giving us splendid negro preachers for their work in Texas, let us help them all we can, assured that this will fully meet the case.[434]

SEGREGATION IN PRACTICE

During Parham's ministry, segregation was the law of the land. In most Southern states, the unjust "Jim Crow" laws made it illegal for Blacks and whites to congregate together. When Parham preached at the Majestic Theater in San Antonio, Texas, he announced that "the gallery is open to colored people."[435] Such announcements and separation of the races were typical for the times. But Parham, who never missed the opportunity to fight a battle for "truth and justice," seemed to have no problem with the laws that separated the races.

The evangelist seemed to have a particular prejudice against Blacks and whites praying together, writing:

I have seen meetings where all crowded together around the altar, and laying across one another like hogs, blacks and whites mingling; this should be enough to bring a blush of shame to devils, let alone angels, and yet all of this has been charged to the Holy Spirit.[436]

Parham's most deplorable comments regarding racial integration were in his description of the Upper Room in the Azusa Street mission. He remarked:

...men and women, whites and blacks, knelt together or fell across one another; frequently a white woman, perhaps of wealth and culture, could be seen thrown back in the arms of a big 'buck n-----' and held tightly thus as she shivered and shook in freak imitation of Pentecost. Horrible, awful shame![437]

---

434. "The Race Question in the South," *TAF*, March 1906, 10–11, HSRC.
435. "Revival Gathers in Interest," *SAL*, June 29, 1907, 3, newspaperarchive.com.
436. C. Parham, *Everlasting Gospel*, 72–73.
437. "Free Love," *TAF*, December 1912, 4–5, FPHC.

Another example of Parham's practice of segregation is the matter of William Seymour's attendance at the Bible School in Houston. Again, prior to going to Los Angeles in 1906, Seymour studied at the school for several weeks. It seems he was separated from the other students. It is hard to know exactly what the arrangement was since some eyewitnesses put him in the classroom and others put him in the hallway outside the door. Regardless of the exact circumstances, it is all but certain that Seymour was not treated the same as the white students.[438]

RACIST AFFILIATIONS

Although never a member of the Ku Klux Klan, Parham spoke sympathetically of the group. The Klan made a strong resurgence in America in the 1920s and found considerable success in Southeast Kansas. It is estimated that forty thousand Kansans joined the "invisible empire." The Klan in Kansas was as evil as in any other place in the country. They "tarred and feathered" and otherwise intimidated citizens who opposed them, and a group of Klansmen flogged a Catholic mayor who spoke against the secret organization.[439]

Drawing on the popularity of the Klan, Parham announced his meetings with the letters "K K K" on the bottom of his advertisements. In smaller letters, he posted, "K—onvincing; K—onvicting; K—onverting."[440] He also came far short of criticizing the Klan when he mentioned the organization in a sermon at his interstate camp meeting in 1925:

They ask me why K. K. K.'s wear sheets and pillow cases? You ask the wives. They do not get to their business until 11:00 P.M. or 2:00 A.M. and she hides their clothes, and all they can grab to wear is sheets and pillow cases. A few of them do scare the Jews mightily. Some people say, "I tell you that the K. K. K.'s are of the

438. B. F. Lawrence, *The Apostolic Faith Restored* (St. Louis: Gospel Publishing House, 1916), 64. Howard Goss said he clearly remembered Seymour coming to the classes. Mrs. Parham said, "He was given a place in the class." Another witness said Seymour was "a regular attendant, taking his seat in the classes." E. Goss, *Winds of God*, 73; S. Parham, *Life of Charles F. Parham*, 137; "A Letter;" Shumway, "Study of 'The Gift of Tongues,'" 173.
439. "Kansas Battles the Invisible Empire," *Kansas Historical Quarterly*, Autumn 1974, 393–409, kshs.org.
440. *TAF*, September 1925, 20, originalapostolicfaith.org.

devil." We are aware it came up so fast, and swallowed so many things it had to have a house cleaning, and then they use a little formaldehyde on a few of its members, it will be a pretty decent organization, but they will need some formaldehyde. Think of it, in a few years an organization of eight million has been accumulated. It has something to do with the closing of the age.[441]

It is hard not to notice that Parham, while saying that the Klan scared the Jews, failed to mention fear among Blacks, who were the primary object of Klan hatred. What, except prejudice, would cause that to escape his attention and mention?

In another sermon, Parham was encouraging the audience to love their enemies. He joked, "If I could get the police force and the Ku Klux Klan to help me I would round up all the Pentecostal preachers in the State and have a foot washing." The audience laughed, but it was most likely an all-white audience.[442]

In 1927, as Parham was planning a great rally in Alma, Michigan, he received an offer from the Klan "to back the meeting." Parham said they "happified [*sic*] everybody by telling them that we wanted all the possible help we could get, the more the merrier, and were truly grateful for the offered help."[443]

The Klan was very popular in Michigan in the 1920s. One estimate said that as many as one in ten Michiganders belonged. Their meetings drew crowds reaching into the tens of thousands. A klavern was proposed for Lansing, Michigan, that would accommodate twelve thousand people.[444]

Immediately after leaving Alma, the evangelist accepted an invitation to speak at a Klan rally at the klavern in Saginaw, Michigan. Klansmen had

441. "Prophecy," *TAF*, October 1925, 6, originalapostolicfaith.org.

442. Charles Parham, "Present Reality and Future Rewards," *TAF*, November 1925, 2, originalapostolicfaith.org.

443. "Alma, Michigan," *TAF*, January 1927, 7, originalapostolicfaith.org.

444. Rachel Greco and Krystal Nurse, "It Doesn't Go Away: Remembering the KKK's Legacy of Hate in Michigan," *Lansing State Journal*, August 7, 2021, lansingstatejournal. com; "Klan to Build Meeting Hall," *The News-Palladium* (Benton Harbor, MI), August 22, 1924, 3, newspapers.com. The term "klavern" was used to describe both a local Klan group and the building where they met.

traveled to Alma to extend their invitation to Parham.[445] Over three thousand men and women had marched in a parade celebrating the opening of the klavern in Saginaw. Rev. Fred Ross, a Christian Church pastor, spoke at the dedication, declaring that the Klan was an "organization of white, Protestant, native born Americans." He emphasized that other races and religions were not allowed, referring to Blacks and Jews as "c---s and k---s." It was clear where the Saginaw KKK stood on the matter of ethnicity.[446]

In a report on this meeting in the *Apostolic Faith,* he called on Klan members to "give their time and strength and money" to spreading the gospel, but he had no unkind words for the "Empire." He called the Klansmen "splendid men" who were using their efforts "to make the world better on lines of reform and moral suasion." He lauded their "high ideals for the betterment of mankind" while recognizing their need for conversion.[447]

In Parham's scrapbook, passed down to Pauline Parham, the wife of his youngest son, Robert, there were several articles on the Klan that the evangelist had clipped from newspapers and kept. Also among his personal mementos were two Klan booklets, "Ideals of the Ku Klux Klan" and "The Ku Klux Klan: Yesterday, Today and Forever." If there was ever any doubt that Parham knew who and what the Klan was, the first full page of the former booklet sets the tone for the entire piece of propaganda:

> This is a white man's organization, exalting the Caucasian Race and teaching the doctrine of White Supremacy. This does not mean that we are enemies of the colored and mongrel races. But it does mean that we are organized to establish the solidarity and to realize the mission of the White Race. All of Christian Civilization depends upon the preservation and upbuilding of the White Race, and it is the mission of the Ku Klux Klan to proclaim this doctrine until the White Race shall come into its own.[448]

445. Charles Parham, "Leaves by the Wayside," *TAF,* March 1927, 5, originalapostolicfaith. org; "Evangelist Ends Meetings Sunday," *The Alma Record* (Michigan), January 27, 1927, n.p. This article was clipped by the Alma Public Library.

446. "Crowd Gathers at Klan Park Meeting," *Saginaw News Courier* (Michigan), May 29, 1924, 8 (hereafter cited as *SNC*); "Klan Plans Parade, Ceremonies Friday," *SNC,* May 28, 1924, n.p.; "Klan Ceremony Is Staged Here," *SNC,* May 31, 1924, 1. All three articles are from records on microfilm, the Library of Michigan, Lansing, MI.

447. Charles Parham, "Leaves by the Wayside," *TAF,* March 1927, 5, originalapostolicfaith.org.

448. "Ideals of the Ku Klux Klan," n.d., 3, HSRC.

The booklet goes further to condemn interracial marriage, calling for purity of the white blood. It says that the United States was established by white men and for white men. It sees citizens of all other races as only "permitted to reside" in the white man's country. The Klan booklet wraps all this bigotry and hatred in a patriotic love for America, the flag, and Christian ideals.[449]

The Klan's philosophy toward Black Americans was also clearly set out in the second booklet:

> The Ku Klux Klan is not the enemy of the negro. It opposes and will continue to oppose the efforts of certain negro organizations and periodicals which are sowing the seeds of discontent and racial hatred among the negroes of this country by preaching and teaching social equality.... Yet we hold it is obligatory upon the negro race, and upon all other colored races in America to recognize that they are living in the land of the white race and by courtesy of the white race and that the white race cannot be expected to surrender to any other race, either in whole or in part, the control of its vital and fundamental governmental affairs....the white race IS the ruling race by right of inheritance and that it does not intend to surrender this right or to compromise it with any other race— black, red, yellow or brown.[450]

The Ku Klux Klan was and still is a deplorable organization. From out of its dark soul, members have spewed hatred, terrorized people of color, and brought division wherever the Klan has raised its ugly head. Some Pentecostal historians, trying to put the founder of the Pentecostal movement in a better light, have tried to justify Parham's friendship with the Klan. For example, Eddie and Susan Hyatt have argued that the Klan of this period hid its racist views and presented its members as "guardians of morality, patriotism and the Protestant faith."[451] Yet any person look-

---

449. "Ideals of the Ku Klux Klan," 5–7.

450. William Joseph Simmons, "The Ku Klux Klan: Yesterday, Today and Forever," n.d., 4, HSRC.

451. Eddie Hyatt and Susan Hyatt, "Charles Parham's Contributions to the Inter-Racial Character of Early Pentecostalism," unpublished manuscript. Eddie Hyatt is otherwise an excellent Pentecostal historian, but this author respectfully disagrees with his views on Parham and racism.

ing for the facts during that period in history would only need to have scratched the surface of the Klan façade to know they were a hate group.

The Hyatts also attempt to neutralize Parham's Klan affiliations by reporting that Justice Hugo Black and Senator Robert Byrd were Klansmen.[452] The fact that these men were associated with the Klan is no less despicable than the fact that Parham was. All Klan sympathizers should be equally condemned.

Certainly, not everyone in Parham's day condoned the Klan. Governor Henry Allen of Kansas strongly opposed the group. He signed a proclamation making the wearing of a mask in public illegal. He brought a suit before the Kansas Supreme Court that eventually ousted the Klan. Allen said that the KKK "introduced in Kansas the greatest curse that can come to any civilized people, the curse that arises out of the unrestrained passions of men governed by religious and racial hatred." Allen recognized the Klan for what it was. With typical Midwestern common sense, Allen said if the Klan stood for Christianity and the protection of womanhood, why "do they have to wear a mask for that?"[453]

For years, the Klan tried to infiltrate Kansas politics, but they were eventually defeated. When the group requested a charter in Kansas, the corporation commission denied the request, saying the Klan "stirred up religious hatred and racial prejudice and it created dissension, discord, and ill feeling in every community of the state."[454] The commissioners knew what the Klan represented.

When legislation friendly to the Klan was defeated in the Kansas House of Representatives, the Kansas chapter of the National Association for the Advancement of Colored People sent newly elected governor Ben Paulen a letter thanking him for his "courageous stand" in "defeating the Ku Klux Klan Bill."[455] The Black citizens of Kansas recognized what the Klan was and the racism that defined it.

Men of conviction who wanted to know the truth about the Klan saw through its flimsy cloak. Parham could have too. The fact that any

---

452. Hyatt and Hyatt, "Charles Parham's Contributions."
453. Simmons, "The Ku Klux Klan: Yesterday, Today and Forever."
454. "Kansas Battles the Invisible Empire."
455. The National Association for the Advancement of Colored People to Mr. Ben S. Paulen, Governor of Kansas, March 13, 1925, kansasmemory.org.

servant of Jesus Christ would bestow favor on a group born of pure hatred is indefensible.

BULLYING AND CONDESCENSION

As illustrated previously, Parham had a low opinion of African American worship and spoke about it in patronizing terms. He wrote, "A negro camp meeting can get all 'worked up' and get the 'power,' and God not be within a thousand miles of the place."[456] This condescending manner of thinking also had an effect on his relationships with Blacks.

As noted, when William Seymour was in Houston and was subordinate to Parham, the two worked well together. They preached together on the streets of Houston, Seymour attended Parham's school, and Parham raised train fare for Seymour's trip to California. Yet when the revival at Azusa Street exploded and Seymour's role began to eclipse that of Parham's, there was a dramatic shift in the relationship.

Again, Seymour showed the utmost respect for Parham. When the Azusa Street mission printed its first edition of an *Apostolic Faith* newspaper, Parham was heralded as the founder and leader of the movement. On the Azusa Street stationery, Seymour was recognized as pastor, but Parham's name also appeared with the title "Projector." The Azusa pastor wrote W. F. Carothers requesting Apostolic Faith credentials. Seymour called Parham his spiritual "father" and repeatedly invited him to come to California and speak at the mission. He was expecting God to shake the city with a spiritual "earthquake" when Parham arrived. Seymour could not have been more loyal and could not have esteemed Parham more highly.[457]

How did Parham respond when he arrived in Los Angeles? Before he ever entered the Azusa Street building, he claimed to hear "chattering, jabbering and screams." Before he could be introduced, Parham walked to the front of the mission, greeted Seymour, and said, "God is sick at his stomach."[458]

---

456. *TAF*, November 1913, FPHC.
457. S. Parham, *Life of Charles F. Parham*, 154–155; J. G. Campbell, "History of the Apostolic Faith Movement: Origin, Projector, etc.," *TAFGC*, May 1921, 7.
458. Shumway, "Study of 'The Gift of Tongues,'" 178.

For the rest of his life, Parham criticized the Azusa Street Revival. He claimed it was a "cross between the old fashioned Negro worship of the South and Holy-Rollerism."[459] He called the work "hypnotic" and said it had "all kinds of fanatics." If that was not enough, he said it was "a hotbed of wildfire" with "religious orgies outrivaling scenes in devil or fetish worship." According to Parham, the Azusa Street worshippers were "barking like dogs, crowing like roosters, etc., trances, shakes, fits and all kinds of fleshly contortions with wind-sucking and jabbering."[460]

The leaders at Azusa Street were deeply offended. A. G. Osterberg, an Azusa Street worshipper, said, "We didn't like it that he told us that he was above us." Finally, the congregation had had enough. Two of the elders at the Azusa Street mission asked Parham to leave, and Seymour "closed the door" against him.[461]

Parham started competing meetings at the Women's Christian Temperance Union building. He planted another Apostolic Faith mission in Los Angeles and drew away many of the Azusa Street faithful. The "Apostle of Unity" caused the first split at the Azusa Street mission.[462]

Was Parham's reaction warranted? Thousands of witnesses would say no.

For example, George Studd, the brother of famed missionary C. T. Studd, attended the meetings and saw none of the fanaticism that Parham claimed had possessed the meeting he attended. Studd taught a class at the Azusa mission and spoke glowingly of the services: "Though I have lived and labored with spiritual workers and very prayerful people in many places for twenty years, I have never seen such praise and such worship as among these Pentecostal people—never."

Studd went further to say:

> For myself I can only say that after being in the closest touch with these dear people and the work of this Pentecostal movement for a full year, my convictions are stronger and deeper than ever;

---

459. C. Parham, "Free-Love"; C. Parham, *Everlasting Gospel*, 116.
460. Charles Parham, "Leadership," *TAF*, June 1912, 7, originalapostolicfaith.org.
461. Martin, *Life and Ministry of William J. Seymour*, 270; Campbell, "History of the Apostolic Faith Movement," 6; S. Parham, *Life of Charles F. Parham*, 163.
462. S. Parham, *Life of Charles F. Parham*, 163–64.

and it is a joy for me to give this testimony. I have many opportunities of witnessing to these convictions in public and private, and as I do so God certainly does bless my soul as never before.

Surely this is the mighty work of God.[463]

A. S. Worrell also attended the meetings in Los Angeles. He had preached for Parham in Topeka before the Holy Spirit outpouring. Worrell's credentials were a mile long. He taught biblical languages in three colleges and was the president of at least three more institutions of higher education. The scholar wrote at least eight books and translated the New Testament. His perception was much different from Parham's. Worrell wrote, "There are real gifts of tongues here in Los Angeles." He said he asked God for discernment "to distinguish between the false and the true" and, after investigating the facts, "found nothing to regret."[464]

It is true that many people did not approve of the Azusa Street meetings. Some said they were of the devil and even worse, but those critics were fighting *all* Pentecostals, not just the good people at Azusa Street. Among Pentecostal leaders, it seems only Parham felt the meetings were so dramatically out of order.

Even if there were some serious issues that needed to be addressed, Parham's overreaction tells more about Parham than it does about the problems at the mission. A good leader would have called Seymour aside and privately counseled him. Seymour was a humble and loyal servant. Surely, he would have listened to and accepted godly counsel from the man he called father. Yet Parham was not interested in saving Seymour's work; he wanted to destroy it. The condescending way Parham treated his fellow worker was shameful.

Even Seymour recognized that Parham's attitude toward Azusa Street was not about fanaticism at the mission. E. S. Williams, an Azusa Street participant who later served as General Superintendent of the Assemblies of God, remembered Seymour saying, "You know, it is my color." Williams

---

463. George P. Studd, "My Convictions as to the Pentecostal Movement Irreverently Called 'The Tongues,'" Bedford, England, tract, n.d., FPHC.
464. A. S. Worrell, "The Movements in Los Angeles, California," *Triumphs of Faith*, December 1906, 256.

also reported that this was the only time he ever heard Seymour make a comment about race.[465]

Today, the world celebrates William Seymour and his work. *Church History* magazine named him one of the ten most important church leaders of the twentieth century. *Life Magazine* said that the Azusa Street Revival was one of the top one hundred events that changed the world in the last millennium. However, Parham seldom if ever said a kind word about the man behind that revival or his work. He called this glorious revival celebrated by millions the "sewage of Azusa."[466] Think about those words. Charles Parham was small in so many ways.

Historians mark the Azusa Street Revival as the seminal event that catapulted Pentecostalism to the world. In contrast, Parham claimed the movement would have appealed to hundreds of thousands more "had it not been for the wildfire and fanaticism, spiritualistic and hypnotic forces with a lot of the old fashioned negro performances which were dubbed Pentecostal manifestations that accompanied nearly every Christian worker that went out from Azusa street in California."[467] If Parham was truly so blinded by his own overinflated ego and racial prejudice to actually believe this nonsense, he was surely one of the few people on earth who did.

As expressed earlier, many people have tried to excuse Parham's racism as typical of his times. Perhaps it was. However, a man of God should do better than reflect the sins of his culture. Racism was rampant in early twentieth-century America, but that is no excuse for Parham's views or behaviors. He came from an all-white town and likely had little or no interaction with African Americans while growing up. Most likely, he did not form his racist views from some unpleasant interaction with African Americans. His opinions seem to have grown from his biblically and historically erroneous views of British-Israelism. He truly believed that Caucasians were superior to other races. Racial pride influenced his conduct. He was wrong. His actions deeply hurt people of color. Merely knowing about his actions still does. Christ demands better of His people.

---

465. Ernest S. Williams, interview with James Tinney, November 8, 1978, FPHC. Tinney was a professor at Howard University and was considered an authority on Black Pentecostalism.
466. C. Parham, "Free-Love."
467. Charles F. Parham, "The Latter Rain," *TAF*, August 1926, 1, originalapostolicfaith.org.

9

THE BESETTING SIN

Late in life, Charles Parham reflected on the struggles he had faced and the battles he had fought. In a few statements that were extremely candid for Parham, the aging preacher shared a rare glimpse into his own personal demons. Perhaps by acknowledging that everyone had conflicts, he felt it was safe to admit that he, too, had struggles. As someone who never hesitated to use the personal pronoun "I," Parham cloaked these confessions in the plural "we":

> Well, all of us have our special trials; we have all had things, some more than others, to fight in our lives. We have dealt with most of them and conquered but perhaps one thing, the thing that we struggled with, dealt with and sometimes conquered, sometimes not. Fought and then gave in and said, "Well it is natural for one to be thus and so; or it is a birthmark with me; or it is my besetting sin, or it is 'my thorn in the flesh' etc."—It may have been temper, habit, passion or lust. But all have had their fights and won or lost thru the years. I too have fought on....[468]

He continued by comparing life's battles to camping out in the open and being frightened in the night by creatures prowling about the campsite. Or, while at home, being anxious about vermin that you hear scurrying

---

468. S. Parham, *Life of Charles F. Parham*, 395.

about your bedroom at night. Fear that one of these dreaded pests might jump on you while you are asleep makes you "sore afraid to rest in peace." Parham said such night crawlers disappear when you turn on a light or with the rising of the morning sun. These vivid illustrations make it clear that Parham knew what it meant to be frightened and tormented. He admitted that he had been the victim of this fearsome anguish. And he rhetorically asked, "Did they exist? Oh yes, all affirming or denying or mental process could not have destroyed them."

To finish these unusually straightforward ruminations, Parham returned to the first person singular, saying, "Praise the Lord, all fear is gone. I dwell in His Presence and sin and disease and that *one thing* [emphasis added] is gone, as flees the creatures of the night when the morning dawns."[469]

To what battle did Parham refer? This "besetting sin" that so tormented him was certainly more than one of the normal battles that every man faces. What was that "one thing" that had finally fled like the creatures of the night? He does not say. There is a limit to his candor. A full confession is not forthcoming. The reader is left to speculate about Parham's besetting sin.

Speculation, nevertheless, is not difficult. Throughout his early ministry, rumors of misconduct followed Parham. It was not gossip about financial improprieties or even adultery that hovered like a dark cloud over Parham's life and work. Parham was frequently accused of homosexuality. It was considered the worst of sexual sins. It was an abomination. Homosexuality was chief among "acts against nature"; it was considered to be a mental illness. And not only was homosexual conduct sinful, but it was also illegal and often punishable by imprisonment.

To be accused of homosexuality in the post-Victorian era was as rare as it was damaging. Homosexuality was in the closet, far back in the darkest recesses of the closet. In decent society, it was only whispered about. There was little tolerance for same-sex relationships in society as a whole, and absolutely zero tolerance for them among conservative Christians.

Did Charles Parham, the founder of Pentecostalism, struggle with homosexuality? Absent a clear confession, we may never know for certain.

469. S. Parham, 395.

It is highly unlikely that he ever embraced a homosexual lifestyle. It is probably safe to say that he did not. Whether he had same-sex attraction and homosexual tendencies is another question altogether. However, the circumstantial evidence is quite convincing.

There were rumors. There were always rumors.

Parham himself said, "Wherever I have gone my enemies have followed me with these slanderous stories."[470] A relative and friend lamented, "Christians are not burned at the stake these days, but it would be far more merciful to do so, than to drag one's reputation through the mire and filth, concocted from slander, hatched in the very pits of hell!"[471]

Rumors alone prove nothing. Yet it is often said that where there is smoke, there is fire. In Parham's life, there was enough smoke to indicate there may have been at least some fire.

The gossip about sexual deviancy started early in Parham's ministry career, even before he was credentialed. Jonathan Perkins and Charles Parham were both former students at Southwestern College. Perkins attended the school several years after Parham did. According to Perkins, he was "closely associated" with Rev. R. L. George, a Methodist minister who pastored the campus church. Perkins described George as "deeply spiritual," and he said that George had described Parham as a "man with a brilliant mind but unscrupulous character."

George went further to tell Perkins that Parham "left Southwestern college in deep disgrace over having been caught in acts of Sodomy with little boys." George said Parham was a very capable leader, but his "debauchery had greatly shaken the Methodist Church in Winfield."[472]

Did these incidents really happen? It seems unlikely. Perkins definitely had an axe to grind with the Pentecostal movement. He began his ministry as a Methodist. After receiving the baptism in the Holy Spirit, he was credentialed by the Assemblies of God. Perkins rose in the denomination and became the associate editor of the *Pentecostal Evangel* in Springfield,

470. "Sensation at San Antonio," *The Houston Chronicle*, July 21, 1907, 14, San Antonio Public Library.
471. S. Parham, *Life of Charles F. Parham*, 199.
472. Jonathan Perkins, unpublished life story, 40, provided to the author by Perkins's mother, Leatha Perkins Dahlgren.

Missouri.[473] He wrote a book called *The Brooding Presence* for Gospel Publishing House. The book was considered a best seller, went through four printings, and sold as many as fifty thousand copies.[474]

However, Perkins later soured on the Pentecostal movement, renounced the Holy Spirit baptism with speaking in tongues, and became a fierce critic. His later book, *Pentecostalism on the Washboard*, was an all-out attack on Pentecostalism, especially the Assemblies of God.

Perkins said that when he found out that Parham was a Pentecostal preacher and claimed to have founded the movement, it "put the damper on my appreciation of the Pentecostal movement and shook me up greatly, within." He continued to write that he was "bothered about facing the world on the Baptism of the Spirit with a man of Parhams [sic] reputation in relation to Sodomy."[475]

Pedophilia was a very serious charge with considerable prison time for a guilty party. If minor children were involved, it seems reasonable that law enforcement would have been notified. Yet religious authorities have often covered up equally egregious charges to protect their own reputations and the reputations of their institutions.

So, we repeat the question, did these incidents really happen? There are no records of these events at Southwestern College, but records from that time period are extremely sparse.[476] The rumor can be neither confirmed nor totally denied. All the players are long deceased. However, with Perkins's animosities, the allegations seem suspect. If there were no other charges against Parham, this weak accusation would probably be rapidly dismissed as mere hearsay by a disgruntled denigrator.

Not long after Parham left the college, he received ministry assignments in Methodist churches. Unless the matter was quietly swept under the rug, it seems impossible that the Methodists would have put confidence in someone with such a tainted reputation.

---

473. *TPE*, July 12, 1924, 4, ifphc.org.
474. Robert C. Cunningham, letter to Leatha Perkins Dahlgren, August 22, 1980. Cunningham was the editor of the *Pentecostal Evangel*.
475. Perkins, unpublished life story, 41.
476. Mary E. Blake, letter to Leatha Perkins Dahlgren, April 2, 1990. Mary Blake was the executive assistant to the president, Southwest College, Winfield, KS.

If anything could add credibility to the charge, it is that Parham often described his spiritual condition at the time in the worst terms. He spoke of being totally backslidden and refers to himself as "a hopeless degenerate."[477] Is that enough to indict him? Probably not, but one hundred and thirty years after the fact, the rumor will not go away.

Parham's ministry in Zion, Illinois, was also marked by whispers of sexual impurity. *The Waukegan Daily Gazette* hinted at the rumors in January 1907. The story, more gossip than news, said, "A report comes from Zion City, that Prophet Parham is being tracked by persons holding a warrant over his head. What the charge is or whether the statement is correct is not known as the *Gazette's* informant merely heard the report on the street."[478]

At that time, a bitter religious war had broken out among John Alexander Dowie's followers and Parham and his followers. It is not surprising that charges of all kinds would be raised in such a volatile environment. Since the accusations are not recorded in detail, they cannot be answered, but the rumors remain.[479]

Another accusation comes from Bert Hamilton Doss. Doss was a pioneer Pentecostal preacher. Here is a portion of a letter he sent to the Assemblies of God:

> I would like to say just a few words about Brother Parham. I am sure you know him—so do I. Also I know that Brother Birdsul [Birdsall] who started that news on Brother Parham. Now notice, I am sure that Brother Birdsul [sic] told the truth about Bro. Parham. I was at Baxter Springs, Kans. At Charles Parham meeting, and as there was a great crowd, it fell on my lot to sleep with him. I am sorry to say he tried that same thing on me. I was sure surprised to think a man who was telling us how to live and trust God could do such a thing as he was doing. This broke our fellowship in the spirit. I talked to no one but my wife, not even my son Loren Doss. But now I am telling you that he belongs to that class the Apostle Paul spoke about in Romans 1:27. Is this clear to you? He is guilty.[480]

477. Charles F. Parham, letter to Howard Goss, February 13, 1907, CFSOP.
478. "To Arrest Parham," *Waukegan Daily Gazette*, January 22, 1907, n.p., FPHC.
479. "Sensation at San Antonio."
480. B. H. Doss, letter to Assemblies of God, April 23, 1956, *TPE* files at FPHC. The author was surprised to find another copy of the letter in the Pauline Parham Collection at the HSRC.

The original letter is not known to exist. Only a typed transcription of this portion of the letter remains. The transcriber had added, "(evidently E. G. Birdsall)." Accompanying this transcription was a typed explanation of who B. H. Doss was. According to the summation, Doss was eighty-two years of age; lived in Fair Oaks, California; and had been a pioneer Pentecostal preacher holding revivals in the Springfield, Missouri, area as early as 1906. Doss's son Loren D. Doss was an Assemblies of God minister in Chicago.

There are two different accusations in this letter. The first involved Elias Gerow Birdsall (or, at least, the person who transcribed the account believed the letter was referring to Birdsall). According to Doss, Birdsall had started rumors about Parham's making a homosexual advance toward him. Outside of this letter, nothing exists of Birdsall's charges.

Birdsall was one of Parham's earliest followers. Parham and W. F. Carothers ordained him as a missionary on May 1, 1906. He was ordained as an evangelist by Carothers and D. C. O. Opperman on March 25, 1909. Just two days later, he was ordained as a minister by Opperman, Howard Goss, E. N. Bell, and Archibald P. Collins. When the Assemblies of God met to organize in Hot Springs, Arkansas, Birdsall was ordained as an elder by Goss and Bell on June 12, 1914. With names like Parham, Carothers, Goss, Bell, Opperman, and Collins on his credentials, it is obvious that Birdsall associated with the highest echelons of the Pentecostal movement.[481]

Birdsall later renounced Pentecostalism and became a long-term Baptist pastor in Dallas, Texas.[482] Was it an unpleasant experience with Parham that had caused his transition away from Pentecostalism?

Without further evidence, it is impossible to know if Birdsall really made these claims against Parham—or, if he made the claims, if they were true or just sour grapes from another minister disillusioned with the Pentecostal experience.

The clear and detailed charge from B. H. Doss is much harder to dismiss. Doss claims that Parham personally approached him in a sexual way. Why would Doss fabricate such a charge out of thin air? He had been a

---

481. Application Blank for Ordination Certificate, Elias Gerow Birdsall, FPHC.
482. "Rev. E. G. Birdsall Funeral Services to Be Thursday," newsbank.com.

Pentecostal preacher for more than fifty years. Why would he tarnish the movement if the accusations were not true? Why would he tarnish himself? Such accusations can easily be turned against the accuser to discredit their testimony. And would Doss also risk damaging his son's ministry in the Assemblies of God by making false claims?

Doss sounds like a man who kept a dark secret for decades and wanted to relieve himself of the burden by telling someone in authority. He had no apparent animosity toward Parham. He called him "Brother." Whoever read the letter, transcribed it, and filed it did not seem to doubt the story or question its veracity. In court, Doss would be what attorneys call a "credible witness." But a good attorney would want to cross-examine him. Unfortunately, all those involved have been in the grave for decades. The whole truth may never be known, but it smells like smoke.

As early as 1902, the stories of sexual deviancy were already taking a toll on Parham's ministry. In his first book, Parham wrote about David, his sin, his repentance, and his forgiveness. He suggested that if David had been alive in their day, the church would not have forgiven him or given him a chance to reform. Instead, the evangelist suggested they would have followed him around and spread rumors.[483]

Clearly, Parham was taking a not-too-subtle swipe at his own accusers. By now, he had already developed a strategy that had worked well for his supporters for many years. He would confess, deny, and deflect. First, he would confess to some usually vague charge. Next, he would adamantly declare he hadn't done it. Finally, he would throw all the blame to his accusers. Watch for the pattern.

Could it also be that he was comparing himself to David? David was a godly man who fell into serious sin, repented, and was forgiven. Was Parham trying to clear himself by giving a veiled confession and testimony of forgiveness? We may never know.

As the years passed, the accusations increased. Like a snowball rolling down a hillside, the accumulation of gossip gained both volume and momentum. In August 1906, Parham preached in League City, Texas. Details are sketchy, but, once again, he was accused of immoral acts. The

---

483. C. Parham, *Kol Kare Bomidbar*, 58.

accuser is not named except for his initials: S. N. H. For the workers in Texas, this was the proverbial straw that broke the camel's back.[484]

The magnitude of the charges and their toll on the integrity of the movement weighed heavily on Parham's chain of command. The evangelist had chosen Warren F. Carothers of Houston to oversee the work in Texas, and Carothers was pressuring Parham for answers. Unlike some of Parham's other accusers, Carothers had the prestige and the platform to take Parham to task. Before joining the Pentecostal movement, he had been a licensed lay minister with the Methodist Church. Carothers had also been a member of the Houston Bar Association and the Texas Bar Association for more than fifty years. He was a United States Commissioner, a founder of the Houston Real Estate Board, and an amateur astronomer with an observatory in Houston. Carothers was no pushover.

By late fall, Parham had moved on from Texas to California. Yet California was not far enough away for Parham to escape Carothers' demands for accountability. Apparently, an incident on the West Coast led to more charges against Parham. Carothers described it with these haunting words:

> Later in the winter of 1906 the work in Los Angeles separated from us, under circumstances which the present writer believes justified them, but about which it would be too painful to write.[485]

The following year, Carothers wrote about the same incident:

> The Los Angeles revival was a part of the original movement until the brethren there felt justified in separating from the old movement.... They discovered before we did that the man we all supposed to be an Apostle raised up to lead the work of restoration manifestly in progress was not an Apostle, and we never blamed them for pulling off.[486]

Both of these accounts are quite ambiguous as to the problem. One could deduct that the issue was simply the disagreement over Seymour's

---

484. "Parham Is Rallying Forces."
485. Warren F. Carothers, "History of the Movement," *TAF* (Houston, TX), October 1908, 1, FPHC.
486. Warren F. Carothers, "Church Government" (Houston, TX: n.p., 1909), 62, FPHC.

leadership, but there is more here than a power struggle. More than twenty years after the incident, Carothers wrote with a bit more specificity:

> In the fall of 1907 [the schism was actually in 1906] complaints of a serious nature were lodged with Brother Seymour against one of our older leaders then sojourning there and the latter resisting Brother Seymour's scriptural procedure, Brother Seymour assumed that we of the older part of the movement would take the part of the rebel and so withdrew his work from us.[487]

Klaas Brower, a resident of Los Angeles, said the accusation was a "vile life."[488] He also lamented that "if Brother Parham had really committed the sin of which they accused him, was he not to be pitied?" Brower said Seymour spread "all kinds of evil reports" about Parham. He confronted Seymour and asked him if he believed Parham lived an impure life and if he had proof of the same. According to Brower, Seymour answered "O! No!" Notwithstanding, accusations were leveled against the evangelist by the group in Los Angeles.[489]

On November 25, 1906, Carothers sent a telegram from Houston to confront Parham:

> In view of the S. N. H. experience at League City and older cases same nature, you ought to retire to ministry of prayer. Combination of cases known only to me, so retirement wipes out stain. Alternative—an inevitable hopeless failure of world prospect (That is of the Zion movement uniting with the Apostolic Faith movement).[490]

If Parham was guilty, he could not have received a better offer. If Parham would only resign from public ministry, Carothers pledged to keep the charges private. The accused could step down with his reputation

---

487. Warren F. Carothers, *The Church Jesus Promised to Build* (Houston, TX: n.p., 1928), 36.
488. Little is known about Brower. Sarah Parham referred to him as a godly man. He knew both Parham and Seymour and took Parham's side after the rift between them. S. Parham, *Life of Charles F. Parham*, 162–63.
489. Klaas Brower, "Origin of the Apostolic Faith Movement on the Pacific Coast," *TAFGC*, May 1921, 6.
490. "Parham Is Rallying Forces."

intact. Few denominations, and probably no Pentecostal ones, would make such a generous offer to a fallen minister. Parham must have realized Carothers' offer was in his best interest. He waited only two days to respond by telegram:

> Owing to the fact that my position projector of Apostolic movement is misunderstood, many rumors afloat, I resign from such office to devote myself to private ministry and prayer. Letter of explanation follows.[491]

The beleaguered evangelist said he intended his reply to be private, but Carothers circulated it widely among the Apostolic Faith in Texas, angering Parham and causing a stir among the ministers. Parham then released an official statement on his resignation:

> In resigning my position as projector of the Apostolic Faith movement, I simply followed a well considered plan of mine, made years ago, never to receive honor of men, or to establish a new church. I was called a pope, a Dowie, etc., and everywhere looked upon as a leader or would be leader and proselyter. These designations have always been an abomination to me, and since God has given almost universal light to the world on Pentecost there is no further need of my holding the official leadership of the Apostolic Faith movement, which was only a cart in which we pushed the gifts along. Now that they are generally accepted, I simply take my place among my brethren to push this gospel of the kingdom as a witness to all nations.
>
> I shall still remain the same to my brethren in assistance, advice, and in donating to them my extra cash as when I bore the meaningless title of projector.
>
> Yours sincerely,
> C. F. Parham[492]

Parham was obviously attempting to take cover by resigning as the "projector" of the movement. It is also obvious it was only a ploy to distract

---

491. "Parham Is Rallying Forces."
492. "Why Parham Resigned," *THP*, February 19, 1907, 5, newspapers.com.

his opponents and garner sympathy among his supporters. He never surrendered any authority and continued to use the title of "projector" as late as 1926.[493]

The conflict intensified when Parham "persisted in preaching and teaching in the name of the Apostolic Faith movement." Church leaders in Texas demanded he appear before a committee of ministers and explain his behavior.[494]

To try to regain his base of support, Parham wrote a series of letters to Howard Goss, another leader in the Texas Apostolic Faith. Parham explained to Goss why he had "resigned": "I was tired of the name and everywhere I went they yelled Dowie or Pope and said I wanted to rule and proselyte from other movements and I saw I could not unify the world and I did not want to be a leader only just a common preacher." Parham blasted Carothers, accusing him of having "the big head." He claimed the Houstonian had heard some slander and was "trying to get all the movement to follow him in revolt." Parham said Carothers was a failure, foolish, bitter, and backslidden. Leaning heavily on Goss's presumed sympathy, Parham said he was "sad and lonely." "I mean to be true to God," Parham wrote, "my enemies seek my ruin but I am clean before God and know the power of His cleansing blood." Although less than ten years Goss's senior, Parham signed the letter "your Daddy."[495]

In a second letter, Parham told Goss that the "Devil's vile accusations and suspicions" had drawn him closer to God. He stated that Goss knew him well enough to know that he was not "guilty of any sin."

Parham also continued his attacks on Carothers, saying that a "Dowie's spirit" had entered him. He called him an instrument of the devil. In an interesting twist, Parham quoted Carothers as saying he had "done all in his power in meekness to restore me." If Parham was guiltless, why would he need restoration? Parham responded by calling Carothers a vicious, vile, overbearing liar. The evangelist said Carothers had offered him no kindness, not even an offer to pray for him. He also said Carothers was too self-righteous "to extend the hand in even pity."

493. "Divine Healing," *TAF*, March 1926, 2, originalapostolicfaith.org.
494. "Parham Is Rallying Forces."
495. Charles F. Parham, letter to Howard Goss, January 31, 1907, CFSOP.

In the most confusing or seemingly contradictory paragraph of the handwritten note, Parham says:

> My life has been searched as with a microscope and this is what I am accused of, but as I view what God has already done for one who was so vile as I, I feel to trust the power of the blood of Jesus to finish the job. I was a helpless degenerate mind, body and soul, no moral character. What there is of me God hath wrought it. These years he has used this poor broken vessel to carry water and revive his drooping lilies. I have his approval even if self seeking men cry crucify.[496]

Parham's pleas did not satisfy Goss, Carothers, or the other Texas leaders. An ecclesiastical trial was called, and Parham was asked to appear in Orchard, Texas, on April 6, 1907, to answer the charges against him. Parham refused to appear, and the trial proceeded without him. J. Charles Dowling, a member of the Brunner congregation, presided as a trial judge. Dowling was a bakery owner and real estate agent in Houston. He had previously pastored congregations of the "Christian church" in Idaho and Washington but had left formal denominationalism after being healed of consumption in 1901.[497]

Charges were read and testimony was taken. The committee found Parham guilty in absentia and released the following statement:

> At a meeting of the brethren representing the missions of the State of Texas of the Apostolic Faith movement it was found upon the evidence produced that Charles F. Parham is guilty of conduct not becoming to a minister of the cause of Jesus the Christ, and upon the evidence so produced was declared out of divine order in accordance with First Cor. Fifth chapter. That the various missions throughout the State be requested to refrain from permitting him to hold religious meetings or in any way represent the Apostolic movement.

496. Charles F. Parham, letter to Howard Goss, February 13, 1907, CFSOP.
497. "Help Wanted—Female," *THP*, October 2, 1909, 12; "For Sale," *THP*, September 30, 1906, 46; "Didn't Like Some of the Twelve Articles," *Spokane Chronicle*, March 25, 1901, 6; "Personal and Local," *The Caldwell Tribune* (Idaho), August 15, 1896, 3, newspapers.com.

That Charles F. Parham be requested to retire from any active participation in the Apostolic Faith movement, and seek the face of the Lord in the quiet of his home.

The action was signed by the following men:

J. C. Dowling, chairman; J. M. Gates; John C. Lessier; D. A. Horn; Lara Nelson; H. A. Goss; W. A. McMillion; T. W. Reeves; M. E. Layne.[498]

As was Parham's custom, he refused to acquiesce. He returned to Texas and began to rally the troops. Supporters gave him a platform, and he started an extended meeting in Alvin. As mentioned in a previous chapter, some of his defenders naively claimed that Parham was a prophet and that "he cannot sin." They warned his adversaries that they "would bring some terrible judgment upon themselves by opposing him."[499]

J. C. Dowling, who chaired the committee, had a different tone:

> We bear no malice toward Brother Parham. It is simply to protect the movement from degeneracy through degenerate practices of those representing it that we have been compelled to do what we have done. It was no hearsay evidence upon which we took the action. We had clear cut testimony, proving beyond the shadow of a doubt. He absolutely refused to come before the committee. He would answer none of the charges made, saying that he didn't propose to be tried by anybody.
>
> And in addition to the first hand testimony we had letters in which the accused clearly admitted the charges. There was no question of the validity of the charges, there was no question in our minds, and when he absolutely refused to offer any defense or appear before the committee at all, we could not do other than what we did.[500]

In response, Parham sent out a circular letter to all the ministers in Texas. Typical of the evangelist, he assured the brethren that he was not in

498. "Parham Is Rallying Forces."
499. "Parham Is Rallying Forces"; "The Apostolic Meetings," *The Alvin Sun*, May 3, 1907, 4, texashistory.unt.edu.
500. "Parham Is Rallying Forces."

"anyway [sic] making a fight," while declaring war against his antagonists. Parham called for a convention in Katy, Texas, for the last week of May. He said he would call the assembly to "restore order, and to unify the work, and once more establish it on the original principles, free from all rules, ecclesiasticism, systems &c. and to bring it again to the simple teachings of the Apostolic Faith."[501]

Sarah Parham further established the evangelist's authority over the movement in a letter to *The Gospel of the Kingdom* published in Alvin, Texas:

> We have always strived to practice the scripture which says: "resist not evil" and still intend to do so, but hearing that some have misunderstood Mr. Parham's notice resigning as Projector I feel you have a right to know the position we take in regard to the work.
>
> Though Mr. Parham does not assume the title of "projector" and we withdraw from those who are now trying to organize his [sic] work for God, he yet remains a shepherd for the sheep God has given him. I want you to understand, that Mr. Parham's mission, and life work was given to him from God years ago, and cannot be taken away from him by men, nor altered by their opinions or ideas.[502]

It was now abundantly clear that Parham's telegram to Carothers was a sham. He would repent of nothing, apologize for nothing, and resign from nothing. In the *Apostolic Faith*, he wrote:

> In olden times religious differences were settled by men killing their opponents. The law prevents that now. They only kill the character, which is far more dastardly. Religious leaders and sectarians now use but one weapon—*scandal* [italics in the original].
>
> Trials and troubles well-nigh overwhelm us until we find our heirship in Jesus, the Christ; then in times of storm we can take a rapture and rest in the sunshine of heavenly places till the clouds have flown. Glory to God![503]

---

501. Charles F. Parham, letter to workers and missions of the state of Texas, May 15, 1907, CFSOP.

502. "Aug. 10th, '07."

503. *TAF*, April 1907, 9, AFBC.

If Parham thought this would be the end of the matter, he did not have long to wait to find out that he was very wrong. The worst scandal of his life and his greatest trouble was just around the corner.

On July 19, 1907, Parham was arrested in San Antonio, Texas, and charged with sodomy. Nothing in his life, his family, or his ministry would ever be the same.

Parham had conducted several successful meetings in South Texas, and San Antonio would have been ripe for a Pentecostal revival. With a population approaching ninety thousand, San Antonio was the largest city in the state.

Parham had been invited to San Antonio by a congregation of the Apostolic Faith led by former Zionist followers of John Alexander Dowie. The response to the Apostolic Faith message was good, and Parham was building a congregation. However, he also had his detractors. Rev. Lemuel C. Hall and his wife, Mary McGee Hall, were leaders of the Apostolic work in San Antonio but had agreed to turn over the ministry to Parham when he arrived. The couple became the evangelist's worst nightmare.[504]

The Halls were highly respected across a number of faith groups. They were both ministers with the Methodist Church and had served as pastors and evangelists across the South. Mary was known as a "gifted woman" and was reported to have had "no superior as a public speaker, among her sex."[505] Hall was called "the prince of preachers." He had "no equal or peer."[506] Hall came from a distinguished family. His father was a physician from a line of physicians. On his mother's side of the family were a governor and a senator. Hall had been a cadet at West Point and a law student before a spiritual experience changed the course of his life. He then attended Asbury and Vanderbilt.

The Halls launched a church in St. Louis, Missouri, and it was there they were introduced to the ministry of John Alexander Dowie. Both were baptized and installed as pastors of the Christian Catholic Church in St. Louis. From St. Louis they served a short term in Chicago and then

---

504. "Sensation at San Antonio," 14; "Evangelist Denies Charge but Pleads on His Knees for Mercy," SAG, July 19, 1907, 1; "Voliva Split Hits Preacher," San Antonio Light, July 24, 1907, 2, newspapers.com.
505. Beverley Carradine, "Dr. Carradine's Letter," TPH, May 25, 1898, 5, newspapers.com.
506. Gardiner, Out of Zion, 8.

transferred to San Antonio to oversee the Zion work there.[507] Their work was so outstanding that Dowie stopped in Texas to visit them.[508]

Among their friends in the Zionist organization was D. C. O. Opperman. Opperman had embraced the Pentecostal message after hearing Parham preach in Houston. He subsequently came to San Antonio to visit his friends and to introduce them to the baptism in the Holy Spirit. Lemuel Hall received the baptism in the Holy Spirit, and the Zionist work became an Apostolic work.[509]

The Halls were solid, trustworthy, and intelligent people. Charles Parham would try to paint them otherwise.

Parham had been in San Antonio off and on for most of a year and had taken residence in San Antonio at a boardinghouse. Parham's family was not traveling with him, and he was rooming with a young man named J. J. Jourdan.

Jourdan was a twenty-two-year-old whom Parham had asked to accompany him and sing hymns. Parham described him as "angel voiced." Details about Jourdan's life are scarce.[510] He was of Jewish ancestry, called New York his home, and seemed to move about a great deal.[511] In May, Jourdan had been accused of stealing from a businessman in San Antonio. The businessman, C. J. Sedlmayer, had taken Jourdan under his wing and had been training him as a fountain pen salesman for the Barnett Pen Company. The two boarded together, and when Sedlmayer awoke one morning, Jourdan and seventy-five dollars from Sedlmayer's coat pocket were gone. The businessman filed charges against Jourdan, who was subsequently arrested in Dallas by the Fort Worth Police Department.

Jourdan did not deny taking the money but argued that it was the financial fruit of his business partnership with Sedlmayer. His only offense, he stated, had been leaving in such a hurry and not hanging a "23" on the door.

---

507. Gardiner, 161–162; "Dowieites Are Installed," *The Republic*, September 9, 1901, 9.
508. "Life of Misery," *GDN*, April 9, 1906, texashistory.unt.edu.
509. Gardiner, *Out of Zion*, 140–142.
510. This author has spent hours searching census records trying to locate Jourdan's name without success. His name is also variously spelled Jourdain and Jordan. It is quite possible that Jourdan does not show up in the census because "J. J. Jourdan" was only a stage name.
511. "St. Voliva Springs a Sensation."

At the time he was apprehended, Jourdan had only ten dollars left of the money because he had bought new clothes.[512]

Acting was Jourdan's primary profession. In 1904, he had been in a play on Broadway. At the time of his arrest, he had been engaged in more of a vaudevillian-style act. Jourdan was a female impersonator. It was reported that he was "good" at it.[513]

Was Jourdan a homosexual? That may never be known. At that time in American history, enough female impersonators were gay that their performances eventually became illegal in many cities. Although this provides no proof of Jourdan's sexual orientation, he had been trying to arrange "a date" with a lady when he was arrested.[514]

Considering the rumors that continually followed Parham's life, most men wishing to maintain their respectability would not have been foolish enough to room with a person of Jourdan's vocation and reputation. Even if the young man had had a dramatic conversion, considering the awful charges recently leveled against Parham, wouldn't discretion have demanded a certain distancing from Jourdan?

Parham rented the Majestic Theater in late June. His meetings received favorable press coverage and had "many indications of spiritual awakening." Parham announced his sermon titles as "Israel, or Are We Descended from Abraham?" "Pentecost and the Gift of Speaking in Unknown Tongues," and "The Soon Coming of Christ." Parham offered free admission and took no offerings.[515]

The revival continued for several weeks. Parham had calls for meetings in other cities and intended to close the services on July 14, but because of "the interest manifest" in San Antonio, he decided to stay through Sunday, July 21. That was among the worst decisions of Parham's life.

512. "Says Roommate Took His Money," *SAG*, May 21, 1907, 10, newspaperarchive.com; "Jourdan Here Denies Guilt," *SAL*, May 24, 1907, 12, newspaperarchive.com; "$60 Gone: Want a New Yorker," *SAL*, May 21, 1907, 2, newspaperarchive.com. To hang a "23" on the door was a popular slang term related to "23 Skidoo." It meant to "run off in a hurry" and had its origins on 23rd Street in New York City. The odd shape of a ventilation grate would cause a draft that lifted women's dresses. Men would gather to catch a peek. It is not known if Jourdan was making a similar veiled sexual reference.
513. "Jourdan Here Denies Guilt."
514. "Traced Over the Phone," *SAG*, May 24, 1907, 10, texashistory.unt.edu.
515. "Revival Gathers Interest," *SAL*, June 29, 1907, 3, newpaperarchive.org.

On Thursday, July 18, the evangelist had a visit from Charles F. Stevens, a city constable, and unspeakable charges were leveled against him. When first approached by the authorities with the accusations, Parham signed a confession written by District Attorney I. C. Baker with the understanding that he would be allowed to quietly leave San Antonio without facing charges. The confession is purported to have read:

> I hereby confess my guilt in the commission of the crime of Sodomy with one J. J. Jourdan, in San Antonio, Texas, on the 18th day of July, 1907.[516]

Official copies of Parham's confession are not known to exist. In his ongoing smear campaign against Parham, Wilbur Voliva claimed to have a copy and tried to make it widely available. Voliva also published an affidavit signed by District Attorney Baker attesting to the accuracy of the confession:

> I hereby certify that the above and forgoing is a true correct copy of the confession made to me (and written by me) by Chas. F. Parham, in San Antonio, Texas, on the 18th day of July, 1907.[517]

At the time, Parham claimed the confession was "wrung" from him by force. It was not until eight years after the incident that he shared what he said were the awful details about his ordeal:

> So one day an officer said to me you are wanted to explain certain things over here so I went with him into a room in some city buildiding [sic] when I got in there they rpoduced [sic] for me to sign [sic] said that they had all the evidence they needed and that if I signed the confeession [sic] I would get off light [sic] I gaid [sic] no never [sic] then there came in three rough necks from [sic] side room who rpoceeded [sic] to beat me up in a most terrible third degree [sic] every once in a while they would say sign sign and we will quite [sic] I refused [sic] I said you can KILL me but Ill [sic] not sign [sic] when I was hurled into a corner nearly dead they then threw me into a chair and one with a gun another with fist doubled

516. "Local Items," *ZCH*, December 16, 1908, 3, newspapers.com.
517. "Local Items."

up threatened me if I hindred [sic] them they would use one or the other [sic] almost fainting a third person put a pen in my hand and with his hand traced my name on the paper and then official wrote something more. [518]

Parham then said his torturer called in three "Holy Roller preachers" that had plotted against him, and the preachers paid money to the law officer (apparently District Attorney Baker) for exacting a confession from him.[519]

As incredible as it may seem, it's possible that everything written in this account happened exactly as Parham told it. There is no way to know. It does seem quite suspicious that Parham would not have shared such a flagrant violation of his rights at the time of his arrest instead of years later. If he had received a beating as severe as he had described in his accounting of the incident, he most certainly would have had physical evidence of it. Considering Parham's passion for publicity and affirmation, it seems he would have been quick to show his bruises—if not to the press, then certainly to his faithful supporters. Would he not have been outraged? Wouldn't anyone have been? Instead, the morning after the confession was supposedly "wrung" from him, Parham was teaching a group of children at the Majestic.

To find Parham's story credible, one must believe that clergymen of Parham's own organization held him in such contempt that they paid a district attorney to beat him into a false confession. One would also have to believe that the DA would risk his career to participate in such an egregious abuse of Parham's civil rights. Baker was a native of San Antonio. He had practiced law there since 1899 and had been elected district attorney in 1904. He served four consecutive terms.[520] The newspaper described him as "the popular district attorney."[521] Would a highly respected public

---

518. Charles F. Parham, "Charles F. to Dear Ones All," digitalshowcase.oru.edu. This is from a typed letter on Parham's letterhead and bearing his signature. The date is February 7 without a year. The letter was sent to Pauline Parham by Homer Coberly. He says he received the letter from Parham in 1915.

519. C. Parham, "Charles F. to Dear Ones All."

520. "Body of I. C. Baker Found in Jail Cell," SAL, January 14, 1915, 2, newspaperarchive.com.

521. "District Attorney Baker Back Ready for Work," SAL, January 6, 1906, 11, newspaperarchive.com.

official risk the sullying of his reputation in his hometown to take a bribe and frame an itinerant preacher? Parham's faithful followers believed it. Maybe they were right.

The next morning, an eyewitness (perhaps the landlady who testified against Parham) accused Parham of committing unnatural acts with Jourdan.[522] The Halls and other members of the congregation that had invited Parham to the city brought the charges, and they were well prepared. They presented Constable Stevens with letters from other cities where Parham had recently preached and where similar charges had been leveled against him. They also had a letter from Ed Neer from Colorado Springs, Colorado, bringing charges against Parham.

Additionally, the constable was shown letters that claimed Parham had been accused of the same offense in Waco, Texas; League City, Texas; and Orchard, Texas. Along with the letter from Orchard was a certified copy of a confession Parham had given when leaving the city:

> I am a helpless degenerate physically. I will swear, however, that I never committed this crime intentionally. What I might have done in my sleep I can not say, but it was never intended on my part.

Considering the seriousness of the charges and the "mass of evidence" against Parham, the constable had no choice but to secure an arrest warrant. Justice of the Peace Ben S. Fisk quickly issued the warrant.[523]

Parham's request to "flee" the city was denied. As mentioned previously, the evangelist was teaching a Bible class to children that morning at the Majestic Theater, and Stevens disrupted the service and took him into custody.[524]

---

522. "In Religion's Name!" *CDJ*, September 23, 1907, 3, newspapers.com. This article says the complaint came from "a small boy." This is the only time the author has seen this, and the veracity of the statement is questioned. Danny Aylor, a grandson of H. H. Aylor, says there was an oral rumor that a child saw the two men through a keyhole. There is nothing to substantiate this claim. Aylor is a strong Parham defender and believes all the charges were trumped up by Voliva.

523. "Evangelist Is Arrested," *SAL*, July 19, 1907, 1, newspaperarchive.com.

524. "Sensation at San Antonio," 14. The article only refers to the constable as "Constable Stevens," but his name is Charles F. Stevens. "Attempt Made by Firing from Ambush to Murder Stevens," *SAG*, September 30, 1907, 1, newspaperarchive.com.

In his defense, Parham said, "This is a plot to drive me from my work. My enemies have pursued me from city to city and they are aided by the devil." When confronted by the evidence, the evangelist said, "I am the victim of a nervous disaster and my actions have been misunderstood."[525]

Following their official arrest, Parham and Jourdan were both given a bond of one thousand dollars. Today, that would be a sum of about thirty thousand dollars.[526] Since neither had the money, both were booked into the local county jail. All services at the Majestic Theater were canceled.[527]

While vigorously defending himself against the charges, Parham claimed, "I am a believer in the doctrine of non-resistance. I preach non-resistance to my people. These charges are not true, although my actions, due to a nervous disorder, may have given some people a mistaken impression. I will not fight this case. Even if they kill me, I will not resist."[528]

When Parham realized his pleas were not producing the desired results, he became quite animated. He fell to his knees and begged that the charges would be "kept quiet" and not published in the local papers. Unfortunately for Parham, that request was also denied. The incident became front-page news in San Antonio and spread across the nation.

When Parham and J. J. Jourdan faced Judge Fisk, Jourdan refused to make a statement. Parham also forfeited his right to make a statement but continually repeated, "I am not guilty of intentional crime."[529]

Parham spent several days in the county lockup but was released by Sheriff John W. Tobin on the evening of July 22 when two businessmen from Houston, F. Colton and J. Ed Cabaniss, paid his bail. Judge Fisk was not satisfied with the arrangement, and Parham was re-arrested the morning of July 23 and held in the sheriff's private office until the security of the bond was confirmed shortly after noon.[530]

525. "Evangelist Denies Charges but Pleads on His Knees for Mercy," *SAG*, July 19, 1907, 1, newspapserarchive.com.

526. https://www.in2013dollars.com/us/inflation/1907?amount=1000 (May 3, 2022).

527. "Meetings Halt at Majestic," *SAL*, July 20, 1907, 8, texashistory.unt.edu.

528. "Evangelist Denies Charges but Pleads on His Knees for Mercy."

529. "Meetings Halt at Majestic"; "Justice Ben Fisk's Court," *SAE*, July 20, 1907, 12, texashistory.unt.edu.

530. "Parham Free Again; Preaches," *SAG*, July 23, 1907, 7, newspaperarchive.com.

Jourdan remained incarcerated until mid-August when a friend of Parham paid his bond.[531] There is no information available on the actor after his release.

Parham announced that the charges against him were "trumped up" and that services would resume immediately.[532] The same day he was released, he was back at the Majestic Theater preaching to his flock. Mary McGee Hall showed up and tried to start an argument with Cabaniss, who said he intended to defend Parham and rebuff the charges against him. Hall then tried to file a complaint against Cabaniss with the county court. Because there was no actual violation of the law, County Attorney Tom Newton refused to hear the complaint.

Parham's assistant W. R. Quinton led a chorus of girls and young women in singing hymns on the street in front of the theater while Parham stayed inside. Because of threats of bodily harm to the evangelist, a large contingency of policemen and detectives guarded the theater. The lawmen were led by Assistant City Marshall McCabe.

Two men entered the building with buggy whips and sat near the exit doors. Word spread through the congregation that they intended to horse-whip the preacher when he made his exit. Parham told the congregants, "I am guiltless of this charge. My enemies here are seeking to drive me from my work, but I will not surrender. I hold no bitterness, however, against anybody." Parham and his coworkers then escaped a trouncing by taking the back exit.

News of Parham's release spread through the city, and a larger, angrier crowd gathered outside the Majestic that evening. There were more whips and more threats of violence. The "presence of a large force of policemen" kept the hostile crowd at bay.[533]

By this time, Parham had changed his tune, saying through intimate friends that he would fight the charges to the "last ditch." He boasted he

531. "Rev. Parham Still in Jail," *SAL*, July 21, 1907, 2; "Parham Released," *SAL*, July 24, 1907, 12, texashistory.unt.edu; "Offer Bail for Parham's Friend," *SAG*, August 10, 1907, 10, newspaperarchive.com.

532. "Preacher Is Out of Jail," *SAL*, July 23, 1907, 7.

533. "Police Save Parham from Horsewhipping," *SAG*, July 24, 1907, 1, newspaperarchive. com.

would not leave the city and avoid prosecution even though that option didn't seem to be available at the time.[534]

Fallout from the arrest forced Parham to leave the Majestic and move his meetings into a tent on the corner of Commerce and Olive streets. In late July, only days after his arrest, Parham announced he would be building a permanent church edifice on the property occupied by the tent. San Antonio, he said, would be the world headquarters for the Apostolic Faith. In his embarrassingly grandiose style, Parham reported he would build a printing plant, a Bible school, and a "temple of healing." The evangelist boasted, "They can throw me in a dungeon cell, but they can not stop my work. The lies and the scandal have only made my congregation stronger. We have lost a half dozen venomous backbiters from our midst, but it was not a loss but a gain, and for every one we have lost we have gained two." Parham added, "The adherents in this city are now thoroughly united and great results are anticipated. My recent trouble has made many friends for me and my enemies have failed in their attempt to blast my character."[535]

Hardly. Joseph Atkinson, a Parham loyalist in charge of the tent meetings, saw it differently. He lamented, "Much as I regret to say so this trouble has caused a split among the ranks of the Apostolic Faith in San Antonio, but I trust it will offer no serious bar to the advance of the faith."[536]

Parham's trial was set for the October docket of the district court. For reasons unknown today, his case never went to trial. Perhaps the grand jury failed to indict.[537] Parham might have benefited from "unusually heavy civil dockets" and a high-profile murder case scheduled for hearings.[538]

Parham was in San Antonio the week of the scheduled trial.[539] According to his wife, the evangelist was told by the city attorney that "he

534. "Parham a Devil Worshipper?" *ZCH*, September 6, 1907, 1, newspapers.com.
535. "Parham Announces Plans for Church," *SAG*, August 7, 1907, 5, newspaperarchive. com; "Hold Tent Meetings Every Day," *SAL*, August 15, 1907, texashistory.unt.edu; "San Antonio the Capital of Parham's Spiritual Kingdom," *SAG*, July 31, 1907, newspaperarchive. com.
536. "Voliva Split Hits Preacher."
537. "In the Churches," *GDN*, October 7, 1907, 5, newspaperarchive.com.
538. "All Courts Open for October Term This Morning," *SAE*, October 5, 1908, 10, texashistory.unt.edu.
539. "In the Churches"; "Parham Denies Chicago Story," *GDN*, October 7, 1907, 5, newspaperarchive.com.

would not have to appear." The official had said he "was satisfied it was all spite work." According to Sarah Parham's report, she and her husband showed up in court on the day of the "indictment," but "the case was never called." Again, quoting Mrs. Parham, the prosecuting attorney said there was "absolutely no evidence which merited any legal recognition."[540]

Perhaps this is absolutely the way it transpired. If so, it would be a complete reversal from the first hearing before Judge Fisk. If there was another side to the story, it will never be known. There are no records about the case in San Antonio.

Parham dismissed the charges, saying the matter had "ended in smoke." He boasted, "Not even an indictment was returned."[541] Parham must have known that the standard for evidence required for a conviction in a court of law is much greater than what is needed for conviction in the court of public opinion.

Within a short time, Parham had left San Antonio for greener pastures. Mary McGee Hall claimed it was because "public sentiment" against him was so strong. Hall said, "No more guilty wretch ever cursed a city with his presence than this ungainly bird of an ill omen."[542] Another person said the public opposition against him was "bitter."[543]

No church was built. No headquarters were established. There was no Bible school and no healing temple. Perhaps Parham had reached an agreement to "flee" the city and avoid jail time. Perhaps he was fully vindicated.[544] Regardless, the fallout from the events in the Alamo City haunted him for the rest of his life. At the time of the arrest, he said, "I am innocent of this charge and expect to prove my innocence to the court."[545] If he was as truly innocent as he claimed, he would have been much better served by insisting on a trial. Maybe that was not possible, but facing a jury of his

---

540. S. Parham, *Life of Charles F. Parham*, 198.
541. "Parham Says the Charges Are False."
542. "Parham a Devil Worshipper?"
543. "Local Items," *ZCH*, August 30, 1907, 3, newspaperarchive.com.
544. Parham's name disappeared from the newspapers in San Antonio. This author has written every legal authority in San Antonio numerous times requesting any official records of the arrest or trial. It is clear that none exists. Unless further information surfaces, it is reasonable to believe that the charges were dropped, quite possibly with an agreement from Parham to leave the city. Parham was represented by C. A. Davis, a local attorney.
545. "Parham Free."

peers and receiving a "not guilty" verdict would have saved him countless heartaches. Without a jury verdict, the verdict of history has not been kind.

At the time, Parham blamed his arrest and all the resulting fallout on a smear campaign by Wilbur Voliva. Many of his faithful defenders still do. It could be true. Voliva certainly seemed like someone who would do exactly that. He and Parham were "bitter enemies." One paper reported that the news of Parham's downfall was "received with rejoicing" among Voliva's followers in Zion City.[546]

Voliva printed a pamphlet with news of Parham's arrest and circulated it widely. Because Voliva used the United States Post Office to spread the scandal, Parham's followers threatened Voliva with prosecution. Postal Inspector James E. Stuart submitted the complaint to the United States district attorney, who found no reason to press charges. If Voliva's allegations were the only side of the story, Parham's innocence might seem obvious. Unfortunately, they weren't.[547]

First, it was not Voliva or his group who brought the charges. The charges came from the Halls, former Zionists who had adopted the Pentecostal doctrine and were leading an Apostolic Faith congregation in San Antonio. It is likely that the Halls would have been as despised by Voliva as they were by Parham. This couple had had enough confidence in Parham to invite him to preach after the church leadership in Texas had defrocked him. They were not his enemies.

Years later, Parham said his arrest was part of a plot by nine "Holy Roller" preachers in the Pentecostal movement who met in secret and vowed to get rid of him by "fair or foul means even if it took death." He said they moved against him in San Antonio because the mayor was Roman Catholic and "part Negro Mexican and white" and fought against him. He also claimed they paid money to an official to get a confession from him. Purportedly, one of the backstabbers confessed this on his deathbed. Parham does not supply the name of the dying conspirator or any of his collaborators.[548] It seems quite possible that he is talking about the nine

---

546. "Voliva Takes Up Parham Fight," *SAG*, August 5, 1906, 2, newspaperarchive.com.
547. "May Oust Voliva for Making Charge," *LCI*, July 27, 1907, 8, newspapers.com; "Voliva May Be Arrested for Misusing the Mails," *The Marion Daily Mirror* (Ohio), July 27, 1907, 4, chroniclingamerica.loc.gov.
548. C. Parham, "Charles F. to Dear Ones All."

men who met in Orchard, tried him in absentia, and disfellowshipped him. Perhaps these men did take a vow to destroy him. Without knowing the identities of the parties involved, and with no one to confirm Parham's account, it all seems quite dubious.

There is also the matter of the letters presented to the constable. Supposedly, there were letters from Waco, League City, and Orchard. Each accused Parham of deviancy in those cities. According to some reports,[549] the letters were published by Voliva. The letters no longer exist, and the specific contents are unknown; however, whatever they said, it was enough to convince the constable and the justice of the peace to issue and execute an arrest warrant for Parham.

Perhaps more damning is the letter from Eddie Neer. Neer had been a student at the Bethel Bible School in Topeka, Kansas, where the revival began. He received the baptism in the Holy Spirit with the evidence of speaking in tongues at Topeka. He married Maude Stanley, an early Pentecostal adherent who also received her baptism in the Spirit at Bethel. All of the Stanley family members were significant leaders in the earliest propagation of the Pentecostal message.[550] None were Zionists or followers of Voliva.

Why would Ed Neer write a letter testifying against Parham if it were not true? Neer was gravely offended by something Parham had previously done. Not only did he send the letter, but, in a day when travel was much more difficult, he offered to make the 850-mile trip from Colorado Springs, Colorado, to testify in person. Neer said, "If this comes to a pinch, I will stand on the witness stand and swear to what I know."[551]

The Neer family's animosity toward Parham must have run deep. Maude wrote a personal account of what happened at the Topeka revival and never mentioned Parham's name.[552]

Neer didn't speak only for himself. He reported that A. E. Gammage of Kansas City and G. L. Stanley of Colorado Springs would corroborate

549. "St. Voliva Springs a Sensation"; "Nameless Crimes in Texas Cause Arrest of Parham Who Makes Confession," *WNS*, July 27, 1907, 1, 5, newspapers.com.
550. Martin, *Topeka Outpouring of 1901*, 36, 41.
551. "Sensation at San Antonio."
552. Martin, *Topeka Outpouring of 1901*, 155–162.

his story. Neer, Gammage, and Stanley are all credible witnesses with no axe to grind against the Pentecostal movement.

Gammage had been a Christian and Missionary Alliance pastor in Kansas City. Early in the 1900s, he encountered Pentecost while serving a Baptist congregation. His introduction to Pentecost was likely through the ministry of Parham, since the evangelist frequently preached in Kansas City. In 1903, Gammage was asked to resign from his church for not preaching "the true Baptist religion." He was teaching divine healing and entire sanctification.[553] The displaced pastor took several members, aligned with the Alliance, and started a new church called Gospel Tabernacle. He served the congregation for many years, built a nice new building, started satellite churches, and established a rescue home for young girls.[554]

George L. Stanley was the youngest member of his family. And he was Neer's brother-in-law. George, too, had been in the Topeka revival, even though he had only been seventeen years old on January 1, 1901, when the Pentecostal movement started, and he would have been in Parham's company.

Do these credible witnesses add weight to the charges? Parham's loyal supporters at the time would have said no. His family and a group of faithful friends stuck with him to the end, ever denying he had a problem.

Henry Tuthill was one of Parham's chief lieutenants in the early days of the Texas work. His response is typical of Parham's supporters:

I was very closely associated with Brother Parham for three years, sleeping with him for weeks and months at a time, with him in the meetings and out of the meetings and with him striving for a standard of perfection in the Christian life, preaching that kind of standard to one and all, everywhere, all the time and taking all the reproaches that so-called Christians wanted to throw at us for preaching perfection in this life, and taking all the scoffing and ridicule that the learned church preachers with D.D. at the end

553. "Baptist Preacher Is Forced to Resign for Advocating Faith Cure," *Indianapolis Journal*, October 27, 1903, 5, newspaperarchive.com.
554. *Kansas City Missouri City Directory* (Kansas City, MO: Hoye Directory Company, 1907), 542; Ulysses Lewis, "Sustentation Fund," *The Christian and Missionary Alliance*, April 23, 1910, 65, cmalliance.org.

of their names could cart around and try to dump on us but Jesus said, "The reproaches of them that reproached thee fell on me," so they did not hurt us. And when I know Brother Parham as well, or did know him so well, it is hard for me to believe the statement of some one who confesses to a vile life as against the statement of one who had hazarded his all, even his life for this gospel and for the power of Pentecost, and healing, and all.[555]

Not everyone saw it that way. Many of Parham's dearest friends and closest associates distanced themselves from him. Again, Howard Goss and Warren Carothers, two of the generals of the Apostolic Faith, had "disfellowshipped" Parham from the movement he had started.[556] They broke all ties with the evangelist and his followers and, a few years later, were leaders in the formation of the Assemblies of God.

Parham continued to blame and attack Carothers for the accusations against him. Finally, the Houston attorney had had enough. He gave Parham an opportunity to clear his name or clear Carothers' name. One of Parham's lieutenants had claimed that the evangelist would be willing to face the charges against him before a committee of Christian men, but it would be too hard to find unprejudiced jurors.

Carothers called his bluff, proposing that just such a meeting could take place at Brunner Tabernacle. He suggested that Parham could present a list of Apostolic Faith ministers that were clearly in his corner. Any who were opposed to Parham would be omitted from the list, and Parham could have full control of the choices. The names of those friendly ministers would be put in a proper receptacle, and twelve names would be drawn to serve as a jury. Parham himself would draw every name. Every juror would be a supporter of Parham. If that did not seem fair enough, Carothers allowed Parham to make any further suggestions to guarantee impartiality. It is hard to imagine how an accused could face a more equitable or unbiased tribunal.

The proposal was personally presented to Parham. He declined the offer, once again refusing to face his accusers. Carothers then published his

---

555. Henry G. Tuthill, "History of Pentecost," *The Faithful Standard*, July 1922, 28.
556. "Reminiscences of an Eyewitness," *TWE*, March 4, 1916, 5, ifphc.org; "Brother Carothers to Enter the General Field Work Again," *TWE*, August 19, 1916, 6, ifphc.org.

proposal and Parham's refusal to appear in the *Houston Post*, to satisfy "all concerned of the character of the accuser."[557]

For years, Parham continued to blame much of his troubles on Carothers. Some of Parham's followers still do. Parham argued that the charges against him were trumped up by Carothers because the latter wanted to organize the movement into a denomination. Although Carothers helped to add some structure to the movement, he was not as ambitious as charged. When the Assemblies of God was formed in 1914, Carothers was among those who called for the meeting. Afterward, he said:

> The report of the convention looks good to me. If it is only allowed to stay on the basis where it has been put, we shall have accomplished that which none before us have done, namely, the securing of Bible Order and promotion of missions without making a new sect or another denomination.[558]

Writing in 1938, Carothers still expressed his total opposition to organization and denominations. He said the devil had a mortgage on every organization of men "because they have invaded his territory by organizing."[559]

Clearly, Carothers was not trying "organize" or start a denomination. He opposed the very idea. He was merely trying to bring order and integrity to an existing movement. For his efforts, he became one of Parham's many scapegoats.

Over the next months and years, thousands left Parham's organization. Pentecostals abandoned him. Some would not even speak his name. At Azusa Street, the worshippers wouldn't even allow a prayer to be offered for Parham.[560] The Apostolic Faith movement, like the man who started it, never recovered. If Parham was guiltless, the campaign against him would be as ugly and malicious as any assault ever launched against a godly man.

After the arrest in San Antonio, it seems there were no new accusations leveled against Parham. Howard Goss said the evangelist's failure was

557. "Investigations," *THP*, May 19, 1908, 11, texashistory.unt.edu.
558. *Word and Witness*, May 20, 1914, 1 (hereafter cited as *WAW*), ifphc.org.
559. Carothers, *Church Jesus Promised to Build*, 18.
560. Brower, "Origin of the Apostolic Faith Movement on the Pacific Coast," 7.

only "a temporary affair," after which Parham "lived an exemplary life as far as I ever heard."[561] In 1912, in a moment of "retrospection," Parham offered up a nonspecific confession:

> I realized and need not be reminded that my past life and conduct has fallen short of that of the Master. Inaccuracies and weaknesses of the flesh and mind have cropped out time and again, but thank God, I feel His approval of my efforts in the main, and am determined, more than ever, to abandon all to him and press to the end.[562]

Maybe it was after this incident in San Antonio that Parham conquered the "one thing." If so, he still continued to scorch those who besmirched his name with "scandalous lies and slanderous reports."[563]

Some people have been tempted to color the entire Pentecostal movement with Parham's failure or supposed failure. For example, R. A. Torrey reportedly said that Pentecostalism was "emphatically not of God, and founded by a sodomite."[564] Such conclusions are grossly unfair and clearly lacking in objectivity. They demonstrate a bias, not toward Parham but toward Pentecostalism as a faith group. It would be no less unfair to say an entire household was immoral because a parent committed some egregious offense. Is a son bad simply because his father was? Of course not. As I have previously stated, early Pentecostals rejected Parham's missteps and rejected sexual sins. There was no widespread endorsement of homosexuality or any other transgression among Pentecostals, let alone practice of the same. Most Pentecostal pioneers were arguably as pure, pious, and passionate about holiness as any people who ever walked on the earth.

The accusations against Parham were real. The evidence is mostly circumstantial. The testimonies are mostly secondhand hearsay. Was Parham sexually drawn to men? His detractors will say yes, while his defenders will emphatically say no. The world may never know.

But is it possible that a man used by God could be guilty of such a grievous transgression? Of course it is. The Bible is filled with flawed men

---

561. Goss, *Winds of God*, 134.
562. "Backward, Forward," *TAF*, December 1912/January 1913, 8, FPHC.
563. "Backward, Forward."
564. This statement is often quoted, but the source is obscure.

who were mightily used by God. The example most often cited is David. In 1 Samuel 13:14, the Scripture calls the sweet singer of Israel a "man after [God's] own heart." Yet, while David was a great king, he was also an adulterer and a murderer.

In two thousand years, the Christian church has had more than its share of leaders with feet of clay. Preachers of the gospel have had drinking problems, financial problems, and lust problems. Yet God used many of these people in extraordinary ways.

God will always answer a prayer for forgiveness. No sin is so hideous or so public that God cannot forgive it, though the person who committed it may well need to face the consequences of their actions. The book of Proverbs says, "For a just man falleth seven times, and riseth up again."[565] Knowing all things, in His wisdom, God chose to put the gift of eternal life, His most valuable treasure, in earthen jars of clay.[566] Clay jars are very fragile. Parham once admitted to Howard Goss that he was a "poor broken vessel."[567] Perhaps, in some way, we all are.

To say this is not in any way a justification for sin. None of the true men and women of God who have fallen into sin would condone their sins. Charles Parham might have denied committing wrongs, but would not condone his own sin. Neither should the church overlook serious wrongs, while also demonstrating the love of God in forgiveness. God seeks a holy and sanctified church and ministers who are above reproach. No minister is used because of their unrighteousness. Some are used in spite of their unrighteousness. Perhaps Parham was one such man. We may never know.

Certain failures are not as awful as others. The charges and accusations against Parham seem particularly revolting. Many failures are not nearly as public as others. Parham's failure was widely made public. The apostle Paul gave his spiritual son Timothy a poignant and relevant description of human failures:

The sins of some are obvious, reaching the place of judgment ahead of them; the sins of others trail behind them.[568]

---

565. Proverbs 24:16.
566. See 2 Corinthians 4:7.
567. Parham to Goss, Feb 13, 1907.
568. First Timothy 5:24 (NIV)

10

LIMPING TO THE FINISH LINE

The most positive thing that can be said about Charles Fox Parham is that he never quit. His shortcomings and stumbles would have finished most men. Yet whether he was driven by a divine call, his own ego, or just plain stubbornness, he refused to surrender until he completed the race.

That, however, does not mean the race was easy. When Jacob wrestled with the Lord at Peniel, the Lord touched his hip and moved the socket out of joint. Jacob rejoiced that he had encountered God and lived to tell about it, but the experience cost him. He walked away with a limp.[569] After the events of 1907, Parham continued his journey, but the experience had crippled him. The days of sprinting were over; the beleaguered evangelist limped to the finish line.

Ignoring those who wanted to remove him from the Apostolic Faith movement, Parham continued to crisscross America preaching the gospel. He preached in small churches and large auditoriums. Of all the negative and unpleasant things that have been said about Parham, no one ever said he was a slacker.

Parham seldom, if ever, traveled alone. He liked to be a leader and liked having a team. Sometimes, there were so many team members

---

569. See Genesis 32:24–32.

accompanying him that they all had to travel in two cars. At other times, it might have been just Parham and a soloist, often a man named Fred Campbell.[570]

Despite the mark on Parham's reputation, many of his meetings were very successful. A number of these meetings stand out as particularly victorious. In the spring of 1914, the evangelist held a revival in Webb City, Missouri, that was deemed "one of the most successful from every standpoint, that he has held during all his years in the full Gospel ministry." God was present "in a marvelous way to save, heal, sanctify, and baptize with the Holy Ghost."[571] One attendee said, "I never saw our town and country so stirred over a meeting. People are coming for miles around for salvation and healing."[572]

Revivals like that one were the bright spots in Parham's life and ministry. But there were also dark days. He could never run fast enough or far enough to escape his past. Pentecostal periodicals denounced him. Articles in *The Bridegroom's Messenger* spoke disparagingly about him, going so far as to say his work was "purely of self and the Devil."[573] The *Word and Witness*, published by E. N. Bell, who would later serve the Assemblies of God as its first general chairman, called Parham's doctrines "damnable heresy."[574] Bell published a scathing notice about Parham:

> Chas. F. Parham, who is claiming to be the head and leader of the Apostolic Faith Movement, has long since been repudiated. He has refused to "hear the church" and we are obeying the command of Christ, the Head of the church by letting him be unto us as a "heathen and a publican." We are sorry it is so, but until he repents and confesses his sins we cannot obey God and do otherwise. Let all Pentecostal and Apostolic Faith people of the churches os [sic] God take notice and be not misled by his claims.[575]

---

570. S. Parham, *Life of Charles F. Parham*, 412.
571. "The State Convention at Temple, Texas," *TAF*, June 1914, 1, originalapostolicfaith.org.
572. "Report from Webb City," *TAF*, April 1914, 1, originalapostolicfaith.org.
573. "Letter from Thomas Junk," *TBM*, July 15, 1909, 1, ifphc.org; "From Bro. Thomas Junk," *TBM*, November 1, 1909, 1, ifphc.org; "Letter from Brother Cashwell," *TBM*, October 1, 1908, 4, ifphc.org.
574. "Revival News in Home Land," *WAW*, November 20, 1913, 3, ifphc.org.
575. "Notice about Parham," *WAW*, October 20, 1912, 3, ifphc.org.

A newspaper in Parham's hometown was even more vicious in its attack. It threatened to print letters accusing him of "a crime we cannot publish." In a malicious swipe at Parham, the editor wrote, "It is bad enough to have to watch our daughters, but when we must watch our sons, it keeps us up too late." If people knew the truth about Parham, the paper wrote, they "would move so fast one could not see his coat tail for dust, even if the roads were muddy."[576]

Well aware of the charges against him, Parham published responses in the *Apostolic Faith*:

> There are those who continually and everlastingly throw mud into the stream of life. If they cannot find enough present day mud, they will hunt way back for ten or twelve years or more, and rake up all the old dry scraps of their memorized mud-holes, and cast it forth at the call of the tempter and plaster a double coat of imagined nastiness on the good name of the victim of their personal spite.[577]

> For years the bitter war was waged. The poignant, peppery, pugnacious, passionate scandal mongers were determined to forever sidetrack the real Apostolic Movement, and bury its founder in oblivion.[578]

Late in 1908, Parham returned to Zion City, where he had held successful meetings. The Full Gospel brethren there were hesitant to embrace him. Upon his arrival, he was not invited to preach or sit on the platform. Although Thomas G. Atteberry told the local pastors "there was nothing any man could do to cause Brother Parham to feel offended," it was obvious that Parham was hurt by the chilly reception. When asked if he expected to take the platform and give a message, Parham replied, "Do you think that I am going to butt in to a meeting such as this, and speak without an invitation? They have invited Bro. [William] Durham to preach, but when I come to the town after being used of God in bringing the message to Zion City, they refuse to invite me." At least one pastor eventually warmed to Parham and asked him to preach and conduct a week of meetings.[579]

---

576. "Heraus Mit Ihm."
577. *TAF*, June 1913, 6, originalapostolicfaith.org.
578. "Greeting," *TAF*, December 1912, 8, FPHC.
579. Thomas G. Atteberry, letter to Marie Burgess, December 12, 1908, AFBC.

Not surprisingly, considering the pressure he was under, Parham suffered some serious physical problems. In March 1909, the Baxter Springs newspaper reported, "C. F. Parham is ill in this city."[580] Physical challenges, which had been a part of his life since childhood, would continue to plague him. Some years later, he suffered much when he injured his back trying to separate two men who were fighting.[581]

A year earlier, when it hadn't seemed as if things could get any worse, five of the Apostolic Faith adherents were arrested for murder in Zion City. An elderly woman, Letitia Greenhaulgh, had died while the "Parhamites" prayed for her. Apparently the sixty-four-year-old woman was an invalid and had suffered from rheumatism and other maladies for twenty years. The faithful concluded that her illnesses were caused by demons, and they believed they could cure her by prayer. The Apostolic group, including Greenhaulgh's son and daughter, twisted on her neck and crooked limbs, trying to exorcise the devils. When the poor woman would cry in agony as they broke her fragile bones, they imagined it was demons manifesting from within her, and shouted in triumph. When her cries for mercy continued, one man put his hand over her mouth to muffle her screams while he sang hymns. Finally, the victim died at their hands. Not to be defeated, the five then began attempts to raise her from the dead.

Zion City, already unhappy with Parham's proselytizing, was so aroused over the incident that a mob gathered at the jail wanting to lynch the perpetrators. The more that information was released to the public, the worse the anger became. After performing an autopsy, the coroner presented broken, shattered bones he had removed from the woman's remains. Hardly one large bone in her body was unbroken, the medical examiner reported.

The coroner's jury confirmed Greenhaulgh's death was "by violence" and called for a trial of all involved. They also found Parham culpable, although he was not charged with a crime.[582]

---

580. *Baxter Springs Daily Enterprise*, March 18, 1909, 1, newspapers.com.

581. *TAF*, October 1916, 9, FPHC.

582. Harold Mitchell, the main instigator of the matter, was found guilty of manslaughter. He spent several months in jail, after which the verdict was overturned, and he was given a new trial. The trial was delayed for almost two years. It is not clear if he was found not guilty or if the case never went back to trial. In any event, he was never convicted and was allowed to become a US citizen in 1910. Mitchell's wife was also charged but not convicted. No one else involved was charged or tried. "'Guilty' Says Jury of Mitchell," *WNS*, November 15, 1907, 1, newspapers.com; "Thrill a Minute at Court Term for October," *WNS*, September 28, 1909, 1, newspapers.com; "Mitchell Gets Papers: Now Citizen," *WNS*, Dec 6 1910, 1, newspapers.com.

And we find that certain practices are being carried on in Zion City under the leadership of one Parham, which are both disgraceful and dangerous to society, and we believe that these practices should be thoroughly investigated by the proper authorities.

Tar and feathers were prepared for Parham if and when he returned to Zion. Followers of Voliva promised to run him out of town on a rail. Parham's followers armed themselves with rifles and shotguns in a promise to protect him.

News of this travesty quickly spread from New York to Los Angeles as dozens of papers carried the story under bold headlines. Every account linked Parham to the action of his followers. Once again, he was in the middle of a scandal. Parham refused to take any responsibility for the grievous incident, saying that "his teachings did not prescribe torture as treatment for the sick." He made excuses for the foolish acts of the zealots, saying his followers "rubbed the limbs of the woman too hard."[583]

Just over a month later, a similar tragedy struck Parham's hometown of Baxter Springs. A nine-year-old child, Nettie Smith, died after her father, a follower of Parham, refused medical treatment for her. Local physicians said the child easily would have recovered with proper medical attention. This heartbreaking incident did not get national publicity, but it aroused the community "as never before." A Topeka newspaper reported that "several deaths, particularly of children, are charged directly to the operation of the doctrine of Parham." "Parhamism is being roundly scored at every turn," they said.[584] Another paper stated it was "a lucky circumstance" that Parham was out of town at the time.[585]

---

583. "Is Hypnotism Secret of Power for Mitchell?" *WNS*, September 21, 1907, newspapers. com; "Parham Not Responsible," *The Boston Globe*, September 21, 1907, 2, newspapers. com; "Followers of Charles F. Parham, Formerly of Topeka Accused of Torturing Aged Woman to Death," *TC*, September 21, 1907, 1–2, newspapers.com; "'Strangler' Mitchell Shows How He Mistreated Woman Victim," *WNS*, September 21, 1907, 1, 4, newspapers. com; "Mob Storms Jail?" *WNS*, September 21, 1907, 1, newspapers.com; "Desert Torturer," *Daily Republican Democrat* (Mount Carmel, IL), September 24, 1907, 4, newspapers.com; "Five Torturers of Aged Woman Held by Jury," *The Inter Ocean* (Chicago, IL), September 22, 1907, 4, newspapers.com; "Repudiates Torture of Women by Followers," *Evening Star* (Newark, NJ), September 21, 1907, 11, chroniclingamerica.loc.gov; "Parham Denies Story."
584. "Parhamism Blamed for Child's Death," *TC*, October 29, 1907, 3, newspapers.com.
585. "Parhamism's Fatal Result," *The Inola Daily Index* (Kansas), November 4, 1907, 7, newspapers.com.

In addition to his evangelistic meetings, Parham continued his involvement in other activities. Caring for the poor and oppressed was always part of his ministry. The Bethel Healing Home often fed the unfortunates of the city. And, stinging from the troubles in Texas, Parham reached out to the downtrodden in Los Angeles. In 1908, he started a daily outreach that fed soup and bread to more than a hundred hungry men on the streets of the city.[586]

He also organized a group to demand that city and county officials immediately release all persons incarcerated for vagrancy. He said the City of Angels was guilty of arresting unemployed men and housing them in a jail so crowded it was "unfit for the stabling of beasts." He further demanded that the city provide immediate provisions and a job for every man out of work.[587] Parham did not explain where the city would get the resources to meet his demands, but he did get his name back in the newspapers. One can only imagine the city's response to the grandiose demands of a pompous interloper from Kansas, but Parham did not wait around to see. In a couple of weeks, he had left the city to crusade for another cause in another place.

After many years of moving from place to place and from one rental property to another, the Parham family purchased a permanent home in 1910. Supporters in Texas had tried to get the family to move to the Lone Star State, but when the Parhams' friends in Kansas got a whiff of this, they rallied and helped to find a place in Baxter Springs. The Parham "house" was a seventeen-room brick building that had been a brewery prior to Prohibition.

The building occupied a full city block, and the outside space allowed the Parhams to have pets, a cow, chickens, and a garden. Sarah said she never expected to have a home "in this life."[588]

The building had a large room to accommodate a print shop and lots of extra space to entertain guests. Francis Rolland Romack, a single man in

---

586. "Many Hungry Given Food," *LAH*, February 18, 1908, 9, newspapers.com.

587. "Demands Prisoners Be Given Liberty," *LAH*, February 2, 1908, 4, newspapers.com.

588. S. Parham, *Life of Charles F. Parham*, 235–236; "Bible School Will Be Held at Baxter," *Joplin Globe* (Missouri), December 20, 1936, 20 (hereafter cited as *JG*), newspaperarchive.com; "See-Kan RC&D Group Plans to Develop Park, Museum," *JG*, August 29, 1974, 6, newspaperarchive.com.

his early twenties, moved from Katy, Texas, to join the Parhams in Baxter Springs, and he "consecrated his life" to printing the paper.[589]

In an effort to raise funds to remodel and equip the print shop, Parham advertised some old coins for sale. He announced that one of the treasures had been "coined by King Solomon" and was worth thousands of dollars. Actually, the first coins in the Holy Land were issued several hundred years after the death of Solomon. It seems the evangelist was too easily duped.[590]

Whenever possible, Parham published the *Apostolic Faith* newspaper on a monthly basis. The paper contained sermons, glowing reports of his ministry, letters from supporters, and Parham's ramblings on various subjects. But the paper also had a darker side. For years, almost every issue contained bitter criticism of almost everyone but Parham. William Seymour and the Azusa Street Mission were the subject of many attacks, but they were not alone. In just one article, he blasted Seymour, Warren F. Carothers, G. F. Fink, Levi Lupton, William Piper, Elmer Fisher, and William Durham. He claimed to have successfully prophesied the failure or even death of each and seemed quite pleased by their misfortunes.[591] Having a remarkable way with words, he castigated his opponents, calling them "driveling, spiritual idiots" and even worse.[592]

Parham consistently attacked almost everyone who was not a loyal soldier in lockstep with his Apostolic Faith army. Here is just one example of the type of rhetoric that appeared in many periodicals:

Two-thirds of the so called baptisms are only a worked up animal spiritism with chattering and jabbering and no language at all…

One is driven to distraction in some Missions by the emitting of all kinds of animal sounds, from the cackling of hens to the shrill cry of the panther, in fact everything that proves a state of animalism and developing of spiritistic mediums, rather than the power of the Holy Spirit.[593]

589. "Regarding the Paper," *TAF*, February 1929, 7, originalapostolicfaith.org.
590. *TAF*, December 1912, 7, FTSL; "Coins," *TAF*, September 1913, 8, AFBC; "Special Notice," *TAF*, January 1913, FPHC.
591. "Leadership," *TAF*, June 1912, 5–7, originalapostolicfaith.org.
592. *TAF*, November 1912, 7, FTSL.
593. "A Happy New Year to All," *TAF*, January 1912, 6, originalapostolicfaith.org.

In 1916, Parham changed the name of his periodical from *The Apostolic Faith* to *The Everlasting Gospel* and published several issues under the new banner.[594] When Rolland Romack was drafted in 1917, the *Apostolic Faith* presses went silent for almost ten years. Corporal Romack's death on the battlefields of France on September 12, 1918, was a serious blow to Parham and his dreams of continuing the publication after the war.[595] Only after an almost decade-long pause did Parham restart the paper in 1925, returning to the original name. Parham claimed he had published the *Apostolic Faith* since 1897,[596] although the actual inauguration date was 1899.

Parham continued to experience setbacks. As fledging Pentecostal denominations became more structured, and others began to organize, Parham's leadership over the movement was fading further. He wrote:

> While there are camp meetings held all over the world, I wish to say right here, and that without prejudice this is the only place that the full Pentecostal Gospel teaching of the Latter Rain, which first fell in Topeka, Kansas, Jan 1, 1901, is taught and practiced in all its fullness.[597]

One of the saddest episodes of Parham's life took place in December 1908. For more than a decade, the evangelist had spoken of going to the Holy Land. In the fall of 1908, he announced he would be leaving "to spend an indefinite time searching for sacred relics."[598] He journeyed to New York with plans to leave for Palestine the first of January 1909.

According to Parham, before he could buy his ticket, he was robbed three times in just over twenty-four hours. First Parham said he had invited a needy man to his room to give him some articles of clothing. The act of kindness was repaid with theft and injury. The man knocked the preacher down, beat him, and robbed him of "what he could lay his hands on."

The next day, while Parham was preaching, someone broke into his room, pried his trunk open, and stole his personal papers and seven

---

594. A few issues of *The Everlasting Gospel* are located at FTSL, AFBC, and FPHC.
595. findagrave.com.
596. *TAF* January–February 1925, 1, AFBC.
597. *TAF*, October 1913, FPHC.
598. "Kansas Notes," *The Evening Herald* (Ottawa, KS), September 21, 1908, 2, newspapers. com.

hundred dollars he had reserved for his trip to the Holy Land. That night, on his way to church services, he was approached from behind, knocked unconscious, and dragged into a dark sideway. His assailant took his watch, his overcoat, and more of his personal items.[599]

The bruised and battered pilgrim borrowed money from a friendly New Yorker and returned to Kansas.[600] Although the story seemed quite suspicious to Parham's doubters, it satisfied his faithful followers.

In 1914, Parham published his second book, *The Everlasting Gospel*. This volume contains more of Parham's sermons and unique doctrines, but it has a darker, more foreboding tone. He warned of a "gathering storm." Much of the book is prophetic, dealing with apocalyptic events on the horizon. He downplayed the League of Nations as illegitimate and foretold the destruction of America. As war clouds were gathering, he called for the nations of Europe to "seek the will and purpose of the Almighty."[601]

Parham seemed the most engaged when he had a battle to fight, whether it was with a man, a method, or a message. William H. Durham became his public enemy number one. Durham was a Baptist pastor at the North Avenue Mission in Chicago. When Durham first heard of the Pentecostal outpouring, he was skeptical. However, once he saw the Holy Spirit at work in fellow Chicagoan John Sinclair's church, he became hungry for the experience.

Like so many others, Durham made his way to the Apostolic Faith Mission at 312 Azusa Street in Los Angeles. He received the baptism in the Holy Spirit at the mission on March 2, 1907. Bishop Seymour prophesied over Durham, "Wherever this man preaches the Holy Spirit will come down on the people."[602] Seymour was right.

A great revival broke out in Durham's Chicago church. From 1908 to 1910, over eight hundred new converts were baptized. At times, as many

599. "Was Robbed Three Times," *WNS*, January 9, 1909, 1, newspapers.com; "Discredit Charles Parham," *WNS*, January 16, 1909, 1, newspapers.com.
600. S. Parham, *Life of Charles F. Parham*, 208.
601. C. Parham, *Everlasting Gospel*, 77. The foreword to the book, written by Robert Parham, says it was written in 1911 and that it had been reprinted in its "original form," but it contains a sermon preached on November 31, 1913. If it can be shown that the sermon was added in a later edition, the author stands corrected on the original date of publication.
602. William Durham, "Personal Testimony of Pastor Durham," *The Pentecostal Testimony*, n.d., 7, FPHC. Only pages 5–12 are known to exist.

as twenty-five preachers would be in the altars at North Avenue seeking the Holy Spirit baptism. One year, four hundred people received the Holy Spirit. Among those filled was E. N. Bell, who, as stated before, became the first general chairman of the Assemblies of God. Robert and Aimee Semple traveled with Durham before going to China. Durham was the rising star in the Pentecostal galaxy.[603]

However, there was one problem. Durham did not embrace the Wesleyan view of sanctification as taught by Parham, Seymour, and most early Pentecostals. He was quite vocal about it, both in his sermons and in a periodical he published, *The Pentecostal Testimony*. Durham taught that when an individual was saved, they were immediately sanctified, but, as they walked with God and drew closer to Him, sanctification grew like fruit in their daily lives. In other words, at salvation, the believer was sanctified, but, day by day, they were *being* sanctified. He totally rejected the notion of a second work of grace that involved becoming "fully sanctified." He called his view "The Finished Work of Calvary."

When Durham preached the finished-work message at Azusa Street, Seymour locked him out of the building.[604] Parham was even more agitated than Seymour was. He declared all-out war against Durham, regularly lambasting him in the *Apostolic Faith*. He called him "the most bold, brazen opponent of a second work of grace...."[605]

Parham said the "new doctrine, and yet an old one" originated because a "new hobby was needed." He said "fanatics had worn the hair, main and tail off their counterfeit tongue hobby and needed a new steed to attract attention."[606]

Accusing Durham of a "sifting wind of doctrine," he said, "With that wind went the biggest mess of chaff, rubbish and accretion of free-loveism

603. William H. Durham, "An Exhortation," *TPH*, September 15, 1922, 1, ifphc.org; Nichol, *Pentecostals*, 24; C. M. Robeck Jr., "Aimee Semple McPherson," in *Dictionary of Pentecostal and Charismatic Movements*, ed. Stanley M. Burgess and Gary B. McGee (Grand Rapids, MI: Zondervan, 1988), 569; Wayne E. Warner, "Eudorus N. Bell," in *Dictionary of Pentecostal and Charismatic Movements*, 53; Richard M. Riss, "William H. Durham," in *Dictionary of Pentecostal and Charismatic Movements*, 255–256.
604. Ian McRobert, *The Black Roots and White Racism of Early Pentecostalism in the U.S.A.* (New York: St. Martin's Press, 1988), 63.
605. "Camp Meeting Snap Shots," *TAF*, September 1912, 9–10, originalapostolicfaith.org.
606. "A Happy New Year to All," 7.

and affinity fools ever gathered by the momentum of any religious movement. The seceders are now the laughing stock of the world."[607]

In the June 1912 issue of the *Apostolic Faith*, Parham said Durham was "riding blindly to his fall." He later stated that Durham had taught "damnable heresy" and "committed the sin unto death." Parham predicted that Durham would be destroyed in six months. He said he cried in travail, "Oh, God, judge between righteousness and sin, truth and error, even if it takes life; if this man's doctrine is true, let my life go out to prove it, but if our teaching on a definite grace of sanctification is true, let his life pay the forfeit."[608]

It is hard to imagine how any man of God could pray such a vindictive prayer. It is more difficult to imagine that they could find pleasure in publicizing it.

Unfortunately, Durham contracted a severe head cold that turned into pneumonia, and he died in the summer of 1912 at the age of thirty-nine.[609] Parham felt totally vindicated. He said, "How signally God has answered."[610] Small man that he was, he celebrated Durham's premature death by saying, "God delivered Durham over to death" and that his death was "evidence of divine approval."[611] As difficult as it is to comprehend, Parham was so narcissistic that he sincerely believed God would kill another of His faithful ministers just to prove that Parham was doctrinally correct. Lest anyone else should challenge Parham's theology, he warned, "The religion that killed Ananias and Sapphira is here."[612]

Over one hundred years after his death, Durham's doctrine of the finished work of the cross has become the standard for a vast majority of Pentecostals and charismatics. Even those who still hold to crisis sanctification as a doctrine seldom practice it. Durham died, but his message outlived Parham's attempts to squelch it.

Regardless of the odds against him, Parham continued to dream big. As described in an earlier chapter, he envisioned large meetings that never

---

607. *TAF*, September 1913, 8, FTSL.
608. "Durham Is Dead," *TAF*, September 1913, 10–11, FTSL.
609. Riss, "William H. Durham," 256.
610. "Durham Is Dead."
611. "Camp Meeting Snap Shots," *TAF*, September 1912, 9, originalapostolicfaith.org; *TAF*, Camp Meeting Special edition, August 1912, 11, originalapostolicfaith.org.
612. "Durham Is Dead."

materialized. He hoped to raise a million dollars and five hundred workers to evangelize at the World's Fair in San Francisco in 1915. He claimed that it would "perhaps be the last great battle before the Lord comes." The evangelist even asked his supporters to sell property to support the campaign.[613] But like so many of his grandiose dreams, the great outreach never happened. Parham also wanted to visit England, South Africa, and Australia. He said he had "a great burden" on his heart for these places, but his feet never touched their soil.[614]

In 1923, Charles Parham turned fifty years of age. In his photographs, he looks older than fifty. Years of travel and trials had taken a toll on him. Always a small man, he looked even smaller as he aged. A receding hairline accentuated his enlarged forehead. He was no longer the young visionary from Topeka.

His appearance is not all that had changed. Age had mellowed him. That is not to say he had totally changed. Oh, no, the real Charles Parham was still there, just less so. In the *Apostolic Faith*, he began to laud preachers like Aimee Semple McPherson, Raymond Richey, and Smith Wigglesworth. [615] A decade earlier, he would have had only the harshest criticism for these preachers who didn't teach entire sanctification. Another dramatic shift came when Parham's *Apostolic Faith* began to publish articles by Assemblies of God ministers such as Robert Brown and Stanley Frodsham.[616]

Doors opened for Parham to preach in Assemblies of God churches. He enjoyed the fact that a church in New York was "one of the largest Pentecostal churches in the world" and made sure to note that it was a product of his ministry.[617] Not many years earlier, he had printed an article that said Pentecostal assemblies "originated in a negro mission in Los Angeles, Calif., and is a cross between the old fashioned negro worship of the south

---

613. "World's Meet at San Francisco," *TAF*, June 1914, 9–10, originalapostolicfaith.org.

614. "Alma, Michigan," *TAF*, January 1927, 7, originalapostolicfaith.org.

615. Charles Parham, "Prophecy," *TAF*, October 1925, 5, originalapostolicfaith. org; "An Account of Brother Smith Wigglesworth's Meeting," *TAF*, January 1927, 7, originalapostolicfaith.org.

616. Robert Brown, "The New Birth," *TAF*, March 1928, 17, HLFTS; Stanley Frodsham, "Try the Spirits," *TAF*, September 1928, 9, FPHC.

617. "Leaves by the Wayside," *TAF*, March 1927, 7; S. Parham, *Life of Charles F. Parham*, 338–39.

and holy-rollerism. Three-fourths of their so-called speaking in tongues is only a chatter and jabber and they have no Pentecostal power at all."[618]

In a particularly amicable article, he even spoke kindly about Azusa Street for perhaps the first time. He said, "Pentecost was clearly taught by all the preachers at Azusa and those that went out from there to all the world." He qualified the comments by saying, "Except for the many spiritualistic hypnotic and old fashioned negro contortions." However, the change in tone is still remarkable.[619] Fifteen years earlier, he had a much different description of those who went out from Azusa:

> Seymour, drunken with power and swollen to bursting, sent forth a hundred or more of this kind of workers to fill the earth with the worst prostitution of Christianity I ever witnessed; in shame we have had to hang our heads, as fanatics and fools have returned from foreign fields in disgrace and shame, with only a monkey chattering; bringing a just criticism and condemnation from the Christian press and public.[620]

Why such an obvious change of heart? Time had softened Parham's rhetoric. He also seems to have had a fear that history would pass him by. Parham had been marginalized by the Pentecostal church, while the revival at Azusa Street had been celebrated. He wanted the world to know the role he had played in the Azusa revival. He reminded his readers:

> This culminated in a Bible School where J. W. Seymore [sic] (colored) attended three months then we paid his way to Los Angeles. [sic] where in 1906 the Pentecostal Power fell at Azusa Street.... The truths taught at Azusa and printed in the paper that went out from there were taken bodily from my books and writings.[621]

It would be difficult to claim ownership of the Azusa Street revival and, at the same time, denounce it as a kind of hypnotic fanaticism, which

618. "Editorial," *TAF*, September 1914, 9, originalapostolicfaith.org.
619. "The Twenty Sixth Anniversary of the Outpouring of the Pentecostal or Latter Rain...," 6.
620. "Leadership," 10.
621. "The Twenty Sixth Anniversary of the Outpouring of the Pentecostal or Latter Rain...," 4.

Parham had done for years. By this time, it was convenient, even beneficial, for Parham to modify his views of the California revival and magnify his connection to it.

In his fifties, Parham seemed to be more at peace with himself and with others. He was still a fighter, but not the ugly street fighter he had been most of his life. He seemed to relish his role as the founder of Pentecostalism. Rather than claim that three-fourths of Pentecostals were fakes, as he used to, he enjoyed boasting of the success of the movement.

Of course, it probably goes without saying that he *always* emphasized his role as the originator. In a 1925 sermon, he said:

> The world is astounded at the most phenomenal [sic] movement in religious history known by various names, and being conducted by various leaders and organizations. Such as Apostolic, Pentecostal or Full Gospel. Which in 25 years has girthed the world and won to its standards ten million of people, great and small, learned and ignorant, and thousands of preachers who are today permeating every quarter of the world, carrying the restored gospel into isolated districts, villages, towns and cities. Holding services in the open air, in cottages, small halls, rickety store buildings, tents, school houses, theaters, auditoriums and manificent [sic] temples costing over a million dollars.[622]

Early in his ministry, Parham had wanted to be the leader of the pack. Despite his claims to the contrary, he had wanted to be up front and up first. In middle age, he was content to take a middle seat, as long as everyone was aware that he had once been the driver. He knew that other movements had passed the Apostolic Faith in effective outreach. He was satisfied to say the Apostolic Faith was simply the "apple cart to push the truth of Pentecost along in until it became a world wide blessing." He admitted it had "fulfilled its mission, and now fades in the light of recognition of a general world wide fellowship in extending the hands of love to all Full Gospel Movements and Churches."[623] Those words mark a seismic shift in Parham's demeanor.

---

622. "The Coming of the Lord," *TAF*, January 1926, 4–5, originalapostolicfaith.org.
623. "Editorial," *TAF*, July 1925, 8, originalapostolicfaith.org.

Parham received a letter from John G. Lake in March 1927. Lake and Parham had been friends since the earliest days of Parham's ministry in Zion City. Lake pontificated about a host of things, including telling Parham he was too fat and ate too much for a man of his age. In what seemed like a prophecy, he warned him that he might be damaging his heart. Lake, too, was facing his own mortality. The aging missionary said that Parham, he, and hundreds of other "original missionaries" were rapidly slipping toward the graveyard. He confessed, "We are shouting loudly about living until Jesus comes, but one by one our toes are preparing to be grass root extensions."

He rebuked Parham for not taking a bolder leadership position, saying, "Personally, I have never felt that you occupied the place in the movement that God intended you to occupy, and that your effort to sort of father the movement in some respects has been rather an effort to keep from being submerged, rather than to lead the hosts of God." Lake wanted Parham to step up with a new vision for the future at the same time Parham was quite content to step downward and celebrate the past.

Despite the overall tone of the communication, Parham must have been encouraged that Lake said, "...the truth of the origin of the Pentecostal movement, and its origin in your school at Topeka, and the fact that you formulated the first Pentecostal message to the world is growing and is daily becoming a better known fact." Lake added, "I will never forget the man who brought the glorious message of Pentecost and all that it has meant of both hell and heaven in my life."[624]

Even though Parham realized his role had been diminished, the evangelist never slowed down. He traveled coast-to-coast in a Ford automobile, preaching wherever doors were opened to him. He would be gone from his home and family for as long as six months at a time.[625] Many of his meetings were quite significant and well-received, often lasting for weeks.

On other occasions, he faced severe persecution. In Katy, Texas, there were various threats against his life, and he was escorted to his meetings by

624. John G. Lake, letter to Charles H. [sic] Parham, March 24, 1927, FPHC. It is worth noting that John G. Lake is one of the patron saints of the Word of Faith movement because of his incredible faith, but in this letter, Lake laments the fact he had been sick for three years and was in financial distress.
625. "Rev. C. F. Parham Back from California," *The Joplin News Herald*, June 6, 1912, 2, newspaperarchive.com.

the local police.[626] In Colby, Kansas, people pelted him with eggs. Parham saved enough unbroken eggs to make noodles for the next day's meal.[627] Buildings were locked against him.[628] Nothing stopped him.

In the *Apostolic Faith*, Parham revisited the story of David and repeated some of what he had written twenty-five years earlier:

> Even a brother who is guilty of an offense is not to be cut off from our affections, though we go to him personally, or send two or three of the brethren [sic], or call him before the church; yet we are not to ostracize him, but treat him with the same love as we would a sinner, with such love as God manifested when He gave His only begotten Son; if necessary laying our own lives down for them.
>
> David was a man after God's own heart, yet fell into a grevious [sic] sin, which after sincere repentance, God forgave him; yet if David had been a member of some modern churches of so called holiness movement though God did forgive him, his brethren [sic] would not, or have ever given him a chance to reform, but would have followed him from city to city, becoming the peddlers of foulest scandal; while at the same time making a virtuous attempt in the salvation of other fallen creatures. How much easier it would be to give a loving hand to the one who has taken but a step from the path of rectitude, than it is to kick him down and reach over into the mirky depths in a pharisacial [sic] attempt to draw one wreaking with corruption from the mire beneath.[629]

Decades of rumors and scandals had worn him down physically and emotionally, and the defamed evangelist wanted to spend his golden years at peace with God, himself, and the church.

Sarah Parham, too, must have been worn down by the years of accusations and persecution. She had always been a selfless defender of her husband, but, no doubt, she would have changed some things if she could have. In 1926, she composed these haunting thoughts:

626. "The Southern Trip," *TAF*, August 1926, 5, originalapostolicfaith.org; "Last Word," *TAF*, August 1926, 8.

627. S. Parham, *Life of Charles F. Parham*, 270–71; originalapostolicfaith.org;

628. "Apostolic Faith," *TAF*, October 1912, 6, originalapostolicfaith.org.

629. "Forsaking All and All Things in Common," *TAF*, May 1926, 4, https://digitalshowcase.oru.edu.

As we read these scriptures [1 Corinthians 6:2; Hebrews 3:15; 4:7], we see that they are for the present, not for tomorrow, yesterday has gone into the past. Has returned to God who gave it to us. We can thank God for the blessings of the past and ask Him to let His precious blood cover our failures and mistakes, but we can't change our yesterday's [sic] or live them over.[630]

However, there were also some days of great joy. A highlight of Parham's years was an annual national camp meeting held in Baxter Springs, which was scheduled to coincide with the evangelist's birthday. It was a remarkable event with thousands in attendance. In the tradition of old-fashioned camp meetings, people would bring tents and stay on the grounds. Local politicians would make appearances and give their blessings. Music was provided by a twenty-piece orchestra, a one-hundred-member choir, and various quartets, duets, and soloists from around the nation. There were always testimonies of healings and sermons, during which Parham would rehearse the trials and troubles he had faced while spreading the gospel across the nation. For a few weeks each summer, Parham and his family could relive the glory days. After the 1927 camp (which had more than 5,000 in attendance), Parham's *Apostolic Faith* reported "not a word of criticism or scandal escaped any one's lips."[631] It must have been like heaven for him.

Late in 1927, Parham realized the dream of his lifetime. He boarded the steamer *Carinthia* in New York and headed for the Holy Land. He had a marvelous time, spending four months in the land of the Bible. Gone were the dreams of finding the ark of the covenant. The evangelist was content to see the biblical sites and purchase photographic slides to use in his meetings in the United States. Although the trip was extremely important to him, and he enjoyed it thoroughly, he was saddened by the fact there were few opportunities to minister there. He called Jerusalem "the greatest place for petrified religion in the world."[632]

630. "Now," *TAF*, September 1926, 8, originalapostolicfaith.org.
631. There were reports of the camp meeting every year in *TAF*. Cited are these examples: "Parham Revival Starts with Great Promise," *TAF*, August 1927, 2, originalapostolicfaith. org; "The Last Word," *TAF*, August 1927, 2, originalapostolicfaith.org; "National Camp Meeting Closes with Large Crowd," *TAF*, August 1927, 21–22, originalapostolicfaith.org.
632. S. Parham, *Life of Charles F. Parham*, 372.

Unfortunately, Parham was ill much of the time he was in Palestine.[633] The fatigue from travel, the foreign foods and climate, and the years of stress all may have weakened the worn-out pilgrim. Parham called the Christian and Missionary Alliance Church in Jerusalem. Two men came to pray for him, and God touched him. He was much encouraged to learn that one of the men was a convert of F. F. Bosworth, one of Parham's disciples in Zion City. He told Parham he was his "grandson in the gospel." Parham felt his labors had not been in vain. [634]

A five-volume history of the state of Kansas was published in 1928. The work contained a most laudatory biography of Parham, which reads like a press release the evangelist would have written. There is no hint of scandal or controversy, just a glowing sketch of his life and work. Parham was so impressed with the essay that he reprinted it in the *Apostolic Faith*.[635]

That year, hundreds gathered in Baxter Springs to celebrate Parham's fifty-fifth birthday. Greetings, presents, and offerings "came from a host of people who had been benefited by his ministry." He received seventy-five dollars' worth of song books, a rocking chair, and "a shower of kerchief's [*sic*], neckties and socks." The best present for a traveling preacher was a new Ford coupe. Parham joked that he might "just have two birthdays a year instead of one." The event was described as "a great day of comfort, gladness and cheer to the one who has fought for many years in the front of the battle."[636] Life was finally good for Charles Parham.

After his return from Palestine, Parham resumed his relentless schedule of meetings, proudly lecturing with the slides he had brought home from the Holy Land. Yet he was obviously road weary. As 1928 dragged on, he began to talk of another visit to the Holy Land. During the summer camp meeting, he had told a friend he felt his work was nearly accomplished. He joked with some people that he knew he was not old, but he had put in enough miles that he felt he had spent seventy-five years in the ministry.[637]

In December, Parham wrote his son Philip and said, "I am living on the edge of Glory Land these days and it's all so real on the other side of

633. S. Parham, 382.
634. S Parham, 190.
635. "A History of Kansas Just Published in Five Volumes."
636. "The Birthday Meeting," *TAF*, June 1928, 16, originalapostolicfaith.org.
637. S. Parham, *Life of Charles F. Parham*, 405, 413.

the curtain that I feel I might be tempted to cross over." He told him "I can scarcely stay here.… Some day I may slip over."[638]

Parham spent most winters in Texas or California. For many years, he had not been with his wife or family on Christmas. He made an exception in 1928 and promised he would be home for the holidays. He not only celebrated the Lord's birth with his family, but he also led a watch-night service in Baxter Springs. It was the twenty-seventh anniversary of the out-pouring in Topeka.[639] Parham talked about his memories of being onboard the ship headed to Palestine, and he repeated his comment that "he would soon slip away" but would be watching for the rest of his friends and family to come.[640]

Parham left for his last earthy journey on the second day of January 1929. He was scheduled to preach and present his slides in several churches in Texas and then travel on to Arizona and California.[641] The weary traveler was too physically weak for the trip, but, throughout his ministry, he had insisted that he never miss a commitment.

On Saturday evening, January 5, he collapsed while speaking in Temple, Texas. When his faithful wife, Sarah, rushed to Texas to be at his side, she found a very sick companion. Parham's heart was failing, and he was unable to eat. Soon, Sarah was joined by two of their sons. Together, they managed to get the ailing preacher on a train back to Kansas. Parham was attended by a nurse and by his family. He refused a physician or any medicines.

During the evening of January 28, Parham sang part of the old hymn "Power in the Blood." When he was too weak to finish, he asked his family to sing it:

Would you be free from the burden of sin?
There's pow'r in the blood, pow'r in the blood;
Would you o'er evil a victory win?
There's wonderful pow'r in the blood.

638. S. Parham, 406–407.
639. "Last Word," TAF, December 1928, 20, originalapostolicfaith.org.
640. "In Loving Remembrance," 3.
641. "Baxter Springs," Miami News Record (Oklahoma), January 6, 1929, 13, newspaperarchive.com.

It was his last song. The next day, Charles Parham died. His death certificate said he died of an "over-taxed" heart. He had finished his journey. His faithful wife reported he died with a smile on his face. He finished well.[642]

Parham's funeral was held in the Baxter Theater, the largest building in the city. Even in a Kansas blizzard, twenty-five hundred people attended the funeral services. Almost half of those were unable to get in the overflowing building and stood outside in the cold. It took an hour for the throng of mourners to pass the casket for a last glimpse of the controversial but beloved preacher.[643]

After Parham's passing, his widow and family received glowing tributes about him from all around the world. Perhaps the greatest tribute to his life was the fact that all of his family and all of their companions "stood for the faith that he preached."[644]

His family was not alone in standing for the faith. Parham had touched thousands of lives with the gospel. He had changed history in ways that few men have ever done.

LEGACY

What is Charles Fox Parham's legacy? As I have expressed throughout this book, it is hard for many people to see the good that he did. His personal failures are so great that they get in the way. This book has illuminated many of them. His misjudgments, transgressions, and egotism clearly hurt other people in a number of ways, and this reality should be fully acknowledged.

Yet, he did do good—lots of good. He developed, or at the very least elucidated, the most fundamental tenet of Pentecostal theology. From the framework he laid in Topeka, Pentecostalism has grown to become one of

---

642. S. Parham, *Life of Charles F. Parham*, 409–413; "Rev. Parham, Evangelist, Seriously Ill in Texas," *JG*, January 9, 1929, 2, newspaperachives.com; "Rev. Parham Unimproved," *JG*, January 15, 1929, 13, newspaperachives.com; "Charles F. Parham, Evangelist, Dies," *JG*, January 30, 1929, 2, newspaperachives.com; "Parham Funeral Will Be Conducted Today," *JG*, February 3, 1929, 2, newspaperachives.com; "In Loving Remembrance"; Lewis E. Jones, "There's Power in the Blood," 1899.
643. S. Parham, *Life of Charles F. Parham*, 415. From a report in the *Baxter Citizen*.
644. "His Works Do Follow Him," *TAF*, February 1929, 20, originalapostolicfaith.org.

the strongest religious movements in human history. Some might argue that if Parham had not rediscovered this glorious truth, someone else would have. But someone else didn't—Parham did. Millions of people who have enjoyed the blessings of a Spirit-filled life should feel a sense of gratitude toward Charles F. Parham for reintroducing God's gift to the church.

Late in Parham's life, a newspaper in Spokane, Washington, attested to his legacy:

> Few men have lived to see the fruitation [sic] of their life's work as has Mr. Parham, all Apostolic missions, Pentecostal missions and Assemblies of God, have their beginning, (directly or indirectly) from Parham's Bible School in Topeka, Kansas.[645]

But Parham did more than just start a movement. He touched individual lives in a very positive way. He personally impacted countless multitudes. Thousands of people were physically healed in direct answer to his prayers. The relief from sickness and suffering cannot be adequately measured. This is not an unsubstantiated claim; neither is it quackery. The testimonies remain to this day. God used this man as an instrument of healing. No failing he ever had in his life will change that fact.

More important than physical healings, however, is that thousands were saved in his meetings. Thousands of people will be in heaven because Charles Parham told them about Jesus Christ, the Savior of the world. Only eternity will tell how many. Additionally, a number of the men and women who were saved in Parham's meetings were used to preach the gospel to hundreds and thousands. Gordon Lindsay, founder of Christ For The Nations, was saved in one of Parham's meetings.[646] Lindsay preached to thousands, but the school he built has trained even more thousands to preach to tens of thousands. Charles Parham had a hand in that. He will be rewarded for it.

It is certain that the preacher from Kansas did at least one other thing right. As a young boy, he trusted Jesus Christ as his Savior and Lord. With all his weaknesses and shortcomings, he never turned away from that decision. God is a good God and gracious to forgive. The work of Christ on the

---

645. S. Parham, *Life of Charles F. Parham*, 317. Sarah quotes from a newspaper article.
646. Gordon Lindsay, *The Gordon Lindsay Story* (Dallas, TX: Voice of Healing, 1964), 56–57.

cross purchased a home in heaven for Parham and every other man and woman of Adam's race who has trusted Him for their salvation.

Parham described this wonderful hope in one of his sermons:

> There is also a future. Our bodies are healed as well as our souls saved, we can live a beautiful life here, but when the battle over, when the soldiers of the cross have fought their last battle, we will rest through all eternity. When we have fought the last battle here, prayed our last prayer and sung our last song, there is laid up for us a crown of rejoicing in the pearly city, which descends with God from heaven, and then shall the hosts of God review the army. Heroes of the cross are going to follow the Lamb of God, the King of Kings, through the streets of gold to the throne of God where He sits in His glory. There where Christ the Son of God, lays His crown at His feet, places the scepter in His hand, and lovingly turns about and says to the Father, "These are the trophies of my life, the purchase of my blood."
>
> Oh! How we will worship Him!... As I close my eyes I can almost hear them sing "Redeemed, Redeemed, Redeemed, out of every kindred and people and tongue and nation, by the blood of the Lamb! Hallelujah! and the people said, Amen."[647]

History has judged Charles Fox Parham quite harshly. Perhaps, rightly so. Perhaps not. Only God is the ultimate Judge. I pray that heaven will be kinder to this unlikely but undeniable father of modern Pentecostalism.

> God shall wipe away all tears from their eyes;...neither shall there be any more pain: for the former things are passed away.[648]

---

647. Charles F. Parham, "We Have Found Him" in *Selected Sermons by the Late Charles F. Parham and Sarah E. Parham*, comp. Robert Parham (Baxter Springs, KS: Apostolic Faith, 1941), 7–8.

648. Revelation 21:4.

ABOUT THE AUTHOR

D r. Larry Martin has given more than fifty years to gospel ministry, serving almost twenty-five years pastoring churches in Oklahoma, Texas, Florida, and Tennessee. While still in his teens, Martin launched his ministry career as a traveling evangelist. He returned to evangelism in 1997 and has continued in that work for most of the last twenty years through his ministry, River of Revival Ministries.

Dr. Martin has traveled in seventy countries, teaching in Bible schools, preaching in mission churches, and leading mass evangelism crusades where as many as 40,000 have professed Christ in one event. From 2001–2004, Martin served Brownsville Revival School of Ministry in Pensacola, Florida, as academic dean. He taught a number of courses in the college and was a regular speaker at the Brownsville Assembly of God Church. He served as president of Messenger College in Joplin, Missouri.

Considered by many to be an authority on the origins of the Pentecostal movement and especially the revival at Azusa Street, Martin is the editor of the twelve-volume Complete Azusa Street Library and the author of *The Life and Ministry of William J. Seymour* in that series. He is also the author of *In the Beginning, We've Come This Far by Faith,* and *Kansas City, Here We Come,* histories of early Pentecostals and the Pentecostal Church of God; and *The Topeka Outpouring of 1901.* Among his other books are *For Sale: The Soul of a Nation; Have We Lost Our Mind?* (an in-your-face call to Christian commitment); *The Good, The Bad, The Ugly and the Hilarious*, featuring stories from his ministry experiences; and *The Believer, The Bible and the Bottle*, a common-sense look at alcohol consumption and Christians. He has also edited and/or contributed to several other works. Additionally, as a freelance writer, Dr. Martin has authored articles that have appeared in *Charisma, Ministries Today*, and a number of other publications.

Dr. Martin is a graduate of several institutes of higher education and holds a doctorate in ministry from Austin Presbyterian Theological Seminary in Austin, Texas. He and Lynda Morehead Goetz were married on July 3, 2016, both having lost their spouses in 2014. Larry has two children, Matthew Martin and Summer Jo Martin; Lynda also has two children, Lindsey Goetz and Ryan Goetz (Rachel). The couple has four wonderful grandchildren, Matthew Martin Jr., Isaac, Anna, and Louisa Goetz.

www.ingramcontent.com/pod-product-compliance
Lightning Source LLC
Chambersburg PA
CBHW071423090426
42737CB00011B/1553